EXORCISING BLACKNESS

EXORCISING BLACKNESS

Historical and Literary Lynching and Burning Rituals

TRUDIER HARRIS

INDIANA UNIVERSITY PRESS

BLOOMINGTON

Library of Congress Cataloging in Publication Data
Harris, Trudier.
Exorcising blackness.
Bibliography: p.
Includes index.
1. American fiction—Afro-American authors—History
and criticism.   2. Lynching in literature.   3. Afro-
American men in literature.   4. Castration in literature.
5. Race relations in literature.   6. Violence in
literature.   7. Afro-Americans—Crimes against.
8. Lynching—History.   9. Afro-Americans—History.
I. Title.
PS153.N5H28   1984   813'.009'896073   83-49284
ISBN 0-253-31995-1
1   2   3   4   5   88   87   86   85   84

For Frank,
who may yet escape the legal lynchers

CONTENTS

Chapter 4

Chapter 5

Chapter 6

Chapter 7

PREFACE

If black people in this country are to really know who they are, then they must, as Ralph Ellison, Jean Toomer, Richard Wright, and other black writers have asserted, understand black American history. This is especially true of black writers; they can begin to appreciate the sources and influences which shape their literary works only by knowing black history. Whether they openly admitted their debt to specific historical occurrences or simply assumed from their treatments of them that the sources were clear, black writers throughout their generations of creativity in America have shown a closeness to their history which sometimes overshadowed their art, frequently enhanced it, and always made it richer in texture. Clearly the history of slavery in this country, and the permanent psychological stamp it has made upon all of us, is one explanation for the persistence of black writers in keeping history alive in their works. When slavery in fact evolved into slavery in the form of sharecropping, that system, too, made its indelible impressions upon black people and upon black writers. And the brutality which white Americans used to keep both systems in place has provided "fictions" as engaging as those which could be concocted by the most imaginative minds.

The intensity of the historical experiences under which black people have lived in America, then, has understandably so penetrated their literature that there are times when the two cannot be easily separated. Recognition of this fact has led to special conference sessions on black American literature and history and to special issues of journals devoted to discussion of the influences upon and the uses of history within black American literature. One such special session, "The Uses and Meaning of History in Modern Black American Literature," was held at the 1977 Modern Language Association meeting. The papers from that special session became the special issue of *Black American Literature Forum* for Winter 1977.

Violence against black Americans is one recurring historical phenomenon to which every generation of black writers in this country has been drawn in its attempt to depict the shaping of black lives. Especially compelling has been violence that takes the form of lynching. Black writers in fictions ranging from the realistic to the surrealistic, and from the symbolic to the impressionistic, have portrayed scenes of lynching. Some of these scenes are so specific in the atrocities depicted that exact historical parallels can be found for them. I explore those connections in this study. I am interested in documented historical lynchings that were commonplace enough to become as stylized or ritualized, after numerous repetitions, as are those portrayed in black American literature. I examine some of those parallels to illustrate how closely black writers are sometimes tied to their history, and to emphasize what a powerful impact certain elements of their history have had upon them. Black writers begin with the realistic depictions of violence in their history, then move to a political level where such depictions become statements of the oppression of a people.

Lynchings were carefully designed to convey to black persons in this country that they had no power and nothing else whites were obligated to respect. Black people were made to feel that their lives were their own only as long as whites were not in a whimsical mood to take them. Black males were especially made to feel that they had no right to take care of their families to any degree beyond that of bare subsistence, and no right to assume any other claims to manhood as traditionally expressed in this country. Lynchings became, then, the final part of an emasculation that was carried out every day in word and deed. Black men were things, not men, and if they dared to claim any privileges of manhood, whether sexual, economic, or political, they risked execution. Especially was that true if a black man dared to show the ugliest (from the white male's point of view) part of his manhood by accosting white women, for such accusations became the most emotional incentive to white men to carry out lynchings against black men. Though black men and women were lynched in the ritual manner for other offenses, such as daring to look at or speak to a white person, wearing fancy clothes, having too much education, slapping a white person, or killing a white person, the intensity of emotional retaliation for presumed sex crimes by black men was poignant in its destructive vindictiveness.

The antagonistic relationship between Blacks and whites initially inspired the ritual and, through the years, kept it going through many refinements. Blacks had been intruders upon culture, from the point of view of the whites, from their very entry into the United States. When these intruders violated the code of sufferance by which they were allowed in the society, the community responded as a group to punish them. Ritualized violence resulted when Blacks were accused of committing a specific offense, that is, stepping out of place, which is what any of the accusations or "crimes" would amount to. Accusation was equated with guilt (the law was irrelevant) and punishment ensued to restore the "threatened" white society to its former status of superiority. The punishments, according to black writers, become a way in which whites consolidate themselves against all possible encroachments upon their territory by Blacks, whether the encroachments—physical, psychological, or otherwise—are committed wittingly or not.

What is especially interesting about these portrayals of lynchings and burnings in black literature, however, is that the manner of portrayal, like that which is being portrayed, has become traditional. The ingredients of the ritual and the tradition can be summed up in the following description. A crowd of whites, attributing to themselves the sanction over life and death and viewing themselves as good and right, are reduced to the level of savages in their pursuit and apprehending of a presumed black criminal; they usually exhibit a festive atmosphere by singing, donning their Sunday finery, and bringing food to the place of death. Women and children join the men—women performing their wifely duties and children becoming initiated into the roles they will play in adulthood. The time is frequently the Fourth of July, or that date will be referred to for ironic contrast. An innocent black man or woman is victim. In works with pre–Emancipation settings, Blacks are forced to watch the spectacle; in works with postslavery settings, a black community slinks into various shanties as preparations are made for the inevitable death. A castration or some other mutilation usually accompanies the killing in addition to a gathering of trophies from the charred body. Sometimes the crowd lingers to have its picture taken with the victim. Burial of the remains by the recently emerged black community takes place several hours later (sometimes referred to, but usually not dramatized in the work); before Emancipation, the body was left as a warning to other slaves. Values, status quo, and perpetuity are identified with the whites, while insignificance and expendability are identified with the Blacks.[1]

Black writers from Charles Waddell Chesnutt to Sutton Griggs, from Paul Laurence Dunbar to James Weldon Johnson, from Richard Wright to James Baldwin, and from Langston Hughes to Ralph Ellison have all presented the tragic consequences, usually death by lynching and burning, which frequently awaited black men who found themselves accidentally or voluntarily in "questionable" circumstances with white women. This particular accusation and form of punishment points to another tradition within the literature—that which suggests that black people, by their very existence in American society, were emasculated because they were stripped of economic and political power, and of any kind of social status. This tradition of presenting black male characters as powerless and emasculated is a counterpart to the works in which black characters are actually deprived of the very power of living and literally emasculated by the specific act of physical castration during lynchings and burnings.

The tradition of presenting black characters as symbolically emasculated is prevalent in black American literature between 1853 and the mid-twentieth century; it parallels the tradition of presenting characters who are literally emasculated by lynching and burning, depictions which appeared repeatedly between 1853 and 1968. Almost all of the deaths have as their causes the improper interactions of black males and white females. But what happened in depictions after 1968? Are black writers now beginning to suggest that black males and white females can interact with each other without some fatal violence occurring? Sometimes, in very recent works, the consequences for such interactions are as minimal as hateful stares, or interracial couples are simply ignored.

In an effort to trace this history—both in and out of fiction—I review the tradition of actual ritualistic lynchings, proceed from there to discuss in detail the literature of emasculation and the literature of ritualistic lynchings and burnings, then move on to explore the literature I identify as going beyond ritualistic lynchings and burnings. In each of the works I discuss in this penultimate section, the circumstances under which a black man and a white woman encounter each other are such that a traditional, ritualistic murder could result. However, the authors have chosen to develop their novels in a different way. That is partly a function of time period and the decrease of lynching in the United States as well as a function of the lessening need in black writers to be aggressively and single-mindedly nationalistic.

The very fact of their masculinity has led more black male writers to be concerned with ritualized violence. For this vein of black American literary expression, there seems to be an aggressive attempt by black male writers not only to reflect the historical realities which have influenced them, but to identify personally with their representations of that reality. Black women writers, less directly significant historically in the quadruple equation involving white males and females, and black males and themselves, seem to be equally less concerned with graphic depictions of the violence inherent in lynching and burning rituals. In raw numbers, far fewer

women writers show lynchings, and they do not use the sexual motivation as the primary cause. Black male writers, on the other
hand, seem to be more conscious of the history of implied sexual
competition between themselves and white males, and particularly of the role white women have played in that competition.
Therefore, they are much more likely to draw upon that history
and oral tradition as the motivation for the lynchings they depict.

Historically, in their ritualistic lynchings of black people, white
Americans were carrying out rites of exorcism in which they seemed
determined to eradicate the black "beast" from their midsts, except when he existed in the most servile, accommodationist, and
helpful of positions. Black individuals who could not be subsumed
into the category of "good niggers" could be eliminated. From one
perspective, this study is a historical survey of rites of exorcism
and of how those rites have been portrayed by one group of writers.
What becomes clear rather quickly, though, is that whites may
have been able to eradicate thousands of black bodies from their
communities by lynching, burning, and otherwise killing them,
but they could never eradicate from their own minds the stereotypical conceptions they had of an entire race, especially as far as
the men of that race were concerned.

For black writers who portray such lynchings and burnings in
their works, they, too, seem to be acting out a communal role. The
last section of this study asks why the black writer has persisted in
presenting such graphically brutal lynching and burning scenes
over such a long period in the history of Afro-American literature—
how much is voluntary, how much is determined; how much is political, how much is the true substance of art; how much is racial
memory, how much is personal fear; how much is confrontation,
how much is its own form of exorcism.

ACKNOWLEDGMENTS

I began research for this book in 1975 and continued the work through an NEH Fellowship-in-Residence for College Teachers during 1977–78. At Brown University, in a seminar entitled "The Black American Experience: Insiders and Outsiders," I had the opportunity to discuss my work with Harold Pfautz and Rhett S. Jones, the seminar directors, and to get suggestions and comments from the seminar participants. I am grateful to all of them for the reading done and the suggestions made.

I am also indebted to the National Research Council and the Ford Foundation for providing the fellowship during 1982–83 that enabled me to complete this project. Residence at The Mary Ingraham Bunting Institute at Radcliffe College and at the W. E. B. DuBois Institute for Afro-American Research at Harvard University provided me with the office space and the access to libraries necessary to get this work done.

Thanks to the many people who have listened to me talk about this work over the years and to those who read portions or all of the manuscript for me. I am especially indebted to Karen E. Fields of Brandeis University, to Martha Chew of the Massachusetts College of Pharmacy and Allied Health Sciences, and to Joyce Flynn of Harvard University for their careful readings, comments, and insistence upon excellence. I am also grateful to Deborah E. McDowell for allowing me to borrow key sources from her library and for providing invaluable suggestions.

As usual, a cadre of friends and colleagues around the country has been unfailingly supportive. I thank them all.

I am also grateful to be able to quote from the following works:

James Baldwin, *Going to Meet the Man*, © 1948, 1951, 1957, 1958, 1960, 1965 by James Baldwin, and *Another Country*, © 1960, 1962 by James Baldwin. By permission of Doubleday and Company, Inc., and Edward J. Acton, Inc.

David Bradley, *The Chaneysville Incident*, © 1981 by Harper and Row. By permission of Harper and Row, Publishers, Inc.

Sutton Griggs, *The Hindered Hand*, © 1969 by Mnemosyne Publishing Company. By permission of the publisher.

Chester Himes, *If He Hollers Let Him Go*, © 1945 by The Chatham Booksellers. By permission of Roslyn Targ Literary Agency.

James Weldon Johnson, "Brothers—American Drama," from *St. Peter Relates an Incident*, © 1935 by James Weldon Johnson. Copyright renewed © 1963 by Grace Nail Johnson. By permission of Viking Penguin Inc.

Claude McKay, "The Lynching," from *Selected Poems of Claude McKay*, © 1981 by Twayne Publishers. By permission of Twayne Publishers, a division of G. K. Hall and Company, Boston.

Toni Morrison, *Tar Baby*, © 1981 by Alfred A. Knopf, Inc. By permission of the publisher.

Walter F. White, *The Fire in the Flint*, © 1924 by Alfred A. Knopf, Inc. By permission of the publisher.

John Wideman, *The Lynchers*, © 1973 by John Edgar Wideman. By permission of Harcourt Brace Jovanovich, Inc., and John Wideman.

Richard Wright, "Between the World and Me," from *Partisan Review*, Vol. 2, July–August 1935; reprinted in *The Long Dream*, © 1958 by Richard Wright. By permission of Partisan Review and Doubleday and Company, Inc.

EXORCISING
BLACKNESS

CHAPTER 1

Ritual and Ritual Violence
in American Life and Culture

Ritual as an American Way of Life; Lynching as a
Peculiarly American Ritual

 Anyone reading Sutton Griggs's *The Hindered Hand* in 1905 would have had a shockingly stomach-turning response to the following graphic passage in the novel. It describes the deaths of Bud and Foresta Harper, a young black couple who dare to defend their home against a white intruder. They break taboo by killing the white man, Sidney Fletcher, who has come to kill Bud, and they must pay the penalty:

> The mob decided to torture their victims before killing them and began on Foresta first. A man with a pair of scissors stepped up and cut off her hair and threw it into the crowd. There was a great scramble for bits of hair for souvenirs of the occasion. One by one her fingers were cut off and tossed into the crowd to be scrambled for. A man with a cork screw came forward, ripped Foresta's clothing to her waist, bored into her breast with the corkscrew and pulled forth the live quivering flesh. Poor Bud her helpless husband closed his eyes and turned away his head to avoid the terrible sight. Men gathered about him and forced his eyelids open so that he could see all.
>
> When it was thought that Foresta had been tortured sufficiently, attention was turned to Bud. His fingers were cut off one by one and the corkscrew was bored into his legs and arms. A man with a club struck him over the head, crushing his skull and forcing an eyeball to hang down from the socket by a thread. A rush was made toward Bud and a man who was a little ahead of his competitors snatched the eyeball as a souvenir.
>
> After three full hours had been spent in torturing the two, the spokesman announced that they were now ready for the final act. The brother of Sidney Fletcher was called for and was given a match. He stood near his mutilated victims until the photographer present could take a picture of the scene. This being over, the match was applied and the flames leaped up eagerly and encircled the writhing forms of Bud and Foresta.

1

> When the flames had done their work and had subsided, a mad
> rush was made for the trees which were soon denuded of bark,
> each member of the mob being desirous, it seemed, of carrying
> away something that might testify to his proximity to so great a
> happening.
> Little Melville Brant found a piece of the charred flesh in the
> ashes and bore it home.[1]

This passage contains most of the ingredients I have identified as
being characteristic of the ritualized violence whites used to lynch
and burn black people; an offense has been committed to which
the group responds in community spirit with burning, mutilation,
gathering trophies, and initiating children. Yet, this literary portrayal parallels almost exactly a historical account of an execution,
and vividly illustrates how history and literature are tied together
in this phenomenon. The incident was reported in the Vicksburg,
Mississippi, *Evening Post* and is so comparable in its descriptions
of the mutilations and in its phrasing that it is almost certain Griggs
had seen the item before writing his novel:

> When the two Negroes were captured, they were tied to trees and
> while the funeral pyres were being prepared they were forced to
> suffer the most fiendish tortures. The blacks were forced to hold out
> their hands while one finger at a time was chopped off. The fingers
> were distributed as souvenirs. The ears of the murderers were cut
> off. Holbert was beaten severely, his skull was fractured, and one
> of his eyes, knocked out with a stick, hung by a shred from the
> socket. . . . The most excruciating form of punishment consisted in
> the use of a large corkscrew in the hands of some of the mob. This
> instrument was bored into the flesh of the man and woman, in the
> arms, legs and body, and then pulled out, the spirals tearing out big
> pieces of raw, quivering flesh every time it was withdrawn.[2]

The intertwining of history and literature as exemplified by these
two quotations provides the focus for this study. How did punishment of Blacks become so ritualized when lynching or burning was
involved? What prompted these kinds of rituals? How do we explain them?

One explanation is to consider the history of interactions between Blacks and whites in this country as a possible cause for
such stylized violence. Another is to consider the specific punishments that were consistently applied to Blacks who were thought
to have broken a law, violated a taboo, or simply stepped out of the
place assigned to them. Increasingly, these punishments became

identified with the efforts of white males to keep white females out of the reach of black males, or to use that excuse as a reason for the general suppression of black people. The history of interpersonal relationships between these characters, then, set the stage for black writers' portrayals of rituals that began in history, were amplified in oral history and in folklore, and became the inspiration for political, personal, and artistic commentaries.

In many ways, the history of black people in the United States is a history of deception that has performance as its basis. Certain performances, such as fooling ole master about the location of a recently cooked pig, or swearing that a plow really did break of its own accord, became so commonplace during slavery that they can be said to have become ritualized; the frequency of repetitions made each player know, from his social position and political standing (or lack thereof), precisely what his predetermined role was. Such knowledge encouraged each player or performer in the ritual to act out his communal role; individuality was submerged to what each side believed was the good of the group. The slave believed he should try to salvage some dignity in spite of his dehumanizing existence—if he could do so without punishment. The master, no matter how much he professed that slaves liked their condition, knew that they had not volunteered for servitude; consequently, his role was to keep them subservient, to be ever watchful for potential rebellion from them, and to maintain his superiority under all circumstances. A typical exchange might have been as seemingly innocuous as the following:

> White man (meeting a slave along the road): Howdy, boy, what's your name?
> Slave: John, suh.
> White man: What you doing out here?
> Slave: Mars Williams, suh, he sunt me to git a piece of rope from Mars Jim.
> White man: So you belong to Frank Williams, eh?
> Slave: Yassuh, Massa.
> White man: I know Frank Williams, but you look kind of scrawny to me. Is he a good master? How he treat you?
> Slave (who has received three whippings this week): Oh, fine, Massa, fine (enthusiastically). He the bess massa in the whole wurl.
> White man: You don't look it. You sure he give you enough to eat?
> Slave: Oh, yassuh, Massa. Massa Williams is a upstandin' Christian gentulman. Plenty to eat, suh, plenty.
> White man: Well, go long wid you, you lying devil.

His role defined by the desire for self-protection, and by lack of knowledge about his questioner, the slave will never reveal the truth of his existence. For all he knows this stranger could be Master Williams's lawyer, or doctor, or visitor from out of town. He dares not risk any more information than that which will evoke a favorable report to his master; otherwise, he might find himself with additional lashes or sold onto some plantation "down the river" which will be much harsher than his present condition. So he plays his role, executes the ritualistic behavior that thousands of slaves like him would execute under similar circumstances. So too with the role of the master; he is forever testing those in bondage to gauge their satisfaction or dissatisfaction with their existence. Even when he suspects, indeed knows, that he is being lied to, he has not been given anything concrete to use against the slave.

And the master really did not wish to be relieved of his illusions. It was important to his peace of mind to believe that slaves were indeed content. That freed him, at least superficially, to sleep more easily at night and to hope that slaves would not rise up, in rebellion, and cut his throat in his sleep. If he could convince himself that slaves were content, that also soothed any potentially troublesome doubts he may have had about holding other human beings in bondage. His role was paralleled in many forms throughout slavery and Reconstruction, and into the twentieth century. Whites loved the images of Blacks in minstrel shows because such images similarly soothed. The white mistress was very happy when mammy cooed over her babies because that meant all was right with the world. By lying to herself, she joined her husband in contributing to the stereotype of the contented darky; their security and peace of mind rested upon such delusion. Their actions and performance helped in the creation of the only kind of black person they could accept, and this self-delusion explains, in part, why they were so harsh in their retaliations when this fiction jumped out of their heads to attack them.

It is not surprising, therefore, to discover that some of the slaves' strategies for survival, through extensive and customary use, took on the character of formulaic occurrences, especially in a community that was given to ceremony in other ways, such as in the elaborate balls the masters would host and in the slaves' equal love for dress-up, dance affairs. Nor should we find it surprising that the white masters, who expected much work of their slaves but who also knew that the slaves were not really in love with working for nothing, similarly developed ritualistic behavior for dealing with the Blacks whom they considered intractable and untrustworthy.

Something as simple as calling forth field hands to testify to North-
erners about the enviable quality of the life of the slave occurred
often enough to make that practice in itself ritualistic. The roles
whites and Blacks so clearly played out during slavery continued
after the Civil War in the actions designed to keep Blacks "in their
place" and in those in which Blacks tried, as much as possible, to
break out of their constraints.

If slaveowners and slaves defined their day-to-day patterns of existence by ceremony and performances, it is not surprising that
more unusual events would also be executed according to for-
mulae. Punishment for crimes was one such unusual occurrence,
and one particular punishment, lynching, became especially ritualized for Americans. The history of that phenomenon as it defined
relationships between Blacks and whites is one which has influenced the literary output of every generation of black writers in
this country. To understand what those writers found so repulsively appealing about ritualized lynching, it is prudent to review
that tradition of punishment as it developed within a country
which had already shown a propensity for ceremony, and to suppression of one group and domination by the other.

It is necessary in any society to have forms of punishment for individuals who break the laws of that society. If the group is to survive, individual members must respect the laws which have been
established for the good of the whole. How Blacks were eventually
punished under lynch law represented the "refinement" of a tradition which had begun in frontier America. In the newly founded
America, which, even in the 1800s, was still very much wilderness
and frontier, it is understandable—though not acceptable—that legally constituted authorities inflicted punishments that bordered
upon the barbaric. In territories where people literally took the law
into their own hands, punishments were often summarily administered, frequently without substantial evidence of guilt. For slaves,
who were not considered members of the society but as the property of those who did belong, punishments for violations of laws
were particularly swift and repressive.

After the Civil War, lynching became the special punishment for
black offenders. And the one "crime" for which lynching became
the only punishment for black men was sexual indiscretion with
white women. Castration quickly became a part of the summary
hanging prescribed for black males accused of sexual offenses. This
element in particular would capture the imaginations of many
generations of black writers who, in their works, made the elements surrounding the lynching of black men a ritual which would

be repeated in literary works for more than a hundred years. In history as in literature, the crowds would gather to punish the black offender in a mood which bordered upon hysteria. White men, women, and children would hang or burn (frequently both), shoot, and castrate the offender, then divide the body into trophies.[3] The white participants in the mobs would frequently bring food and drink to the place of execution and would make a holiday of the occasion. To insure that an audience was available for really special lynchings, announcements of time and place were sometimes advertised in newspapers.[4]

The history of lynching had not always contained all these elements. Summary justice in the frontier and border states did not always end in death. It usually consisted of whipping, or tarring and feathering, or being ridden out of town on a rail. To be lynched, or to be a victim of Lynch's law, meant, at that time, that punishment for a crime had been meted out without a court hearing, or by a self-constituted court.[5] To be "severely lynched" could mean an individual had received one hundred lashes. Or that he had been whipped, then tarred and feathered. A man could be lynched, then hanged. Or lynched, then run out of town. James E. Cutler, in his study of lynching in the United States, comments:

> Leaving out of consideration the Carolina Regulation and the summary practices which were incident to the Revolutionary War, there existed almost exclusively down to 1830 what may be called the frontier type of lynch-law pure and simple. This form of lynch-law procedure has always been justified on the ground of necessity, and has been condemned only because of its liability to abuse.[6]

Shortly after 1830, according to Cutler, a change took place. Anti-slavery agitation brought summary punishment back into well-established communities in an effort to put down abolitionism. A man might be whipped for saying that Blacks, in the abstract, had a right to freedom, or for subscribing to the *Liberator*. As the breech between North and South widened, more deaths resulted from Lynch's law.

> Previous to 1840 the verb lynch was occasionally used to include capital punishment, but the common and general use was to indicate a personal castigation of some sort. "To lynch" had not then undergone a change in meaning and acquired the sense of "to put to death." . . . It was not until a time subsequent to the Civil War that the verb lynch came to carry the idea of putting to death.[7]

Blacks, who, because of their value as slaves, had not been wide-spread targets—though certainly they could be lynched—quickly became new game for lynchers. With the increase in punishment directed at this group, the term "lynching" became common parlance after 1860. Blacks began to be lynched more frequently because of the increase in economic competition, in retaliation for crimes committed by a small element in celebration of new-found freedom, as a form of reprisal on the part of Southern whites for Northern interference, and as one of the "sporting" activities of the Ku Klux Klan. Cutler comments that "the negro had ceased to be valuable as property and was looked upon as a dangerous political factor in the community; to take his life was thought to be the easiest and quickest way to dispose of him."[8]

Between 1882 and 1927, an estimated 4,951 persons were lynched in the United States. Of that number, 3513 were black and 76 of those were black women.[9] Murder, rape, and "minor offenses" were the major causes of lynchings and burnings. In his seminal study of lynching in the United States, Cutler points out that of the 2060 Blacks lynched for "various causes" between 1882 and 1903, 783 were lynched for murder, 707 for rape (". . . either attempted, alleged, or actually committed") and 208 for "minor offenses"; many were also burned or "roasted alive."[10] The number of black men lynched or burned for rape between 1882 and 1903 comprises only 34 percent of the total (and guilt, in many instances, was not certain). This percentage is significant because the primary motivation for the ritualistic lynchings depicted by black writers centers upon crimes allegedly committed by black men against the persons of white women. Protecting white womanhood became *the* emotional stimulus to a mob.

Lynching became, as Walter White put it, "an almost integral part of our national folkways." As the crime of lynching Blacks increased, the barbarity with which such executions were carried out also increased:

> The nature as well as the quantity of the lynching of Southern Negroes was horrifying, for they came to be regularly subjected to fiendish tortures that had seldom been inflicted on the white victims of lynch law. The lynching of Southern Negroes came to be accompanied routinely by the emasculation of males and the burning of both sexes.[11]

And again from Cutler: ". . . as the practice of lynching continues the punishments inflicted tend to increase in severity and the victims are tortured more and more before death comes to their relief."[12]

Both Richard Maxwell Brown in his study of vigilantism and Cutler in his study of lynching recognize the move toward ritualistic executions of Blacks, but Brown specifically notes some of the elements that black writers have observed as being traditional. Brown associates the taking of trophies from bodies with frontier vigilantism, a practice which continued into the 1890s. A particularly desperate criminal was treated as follows:

> The next day Dr. Osborne "skinned 'Big Nose' George and cut away the top of the skull, in order to remove the brain. The skin was tanned and made into a medical instrument bag, razor strops, a pair of lady's shoes, and a tobacco pouch. The shoes were displayed in the Rawlins National Bank for years."[13]

Nat Turner, according to Cutler, met a similar fate when his body "was delivered to the doctors, who skinned it and made grease of the flesh."[14] Sometimes the excessive bullet-riddling of the bodies of lynched victims made any semblance of skin and flesh unrecognizable.

A historical parallel of the ritual as presented by black writers appeared in *The New York Times* for December 7, 1899. A mob of thousands gathered for the execution, women included, thus making the execution a community, family affair. The desperate need to maintain the status quo is clear in the excessive number of individuals needed to punish one man. There is mutilation and torture of the burned man, relic or trophy hunters, and the initiation of children. Richard Coleman, black "confessed murderer of Mrs. James Lashbrook," is the victim of the mob's revenge. The incident occurred in Maysville, Kentucky.

> At the Court House a mob of over 2,000 men, headed by James Lashbrook, the husband, had been hastily formed. A demand for the prisoner was made, accompanied by threats from the leaders. There was a brief struggle in which weapons were hastily drawn by the officers, and then the Sheriff and his assistants were overcome by force of numbers, and the prisoner was pulled from among them. Up through the centre portion of the town the mob marched, the prisoner being held by the vanguard and dragged along with the aid of ropes loosely attached to his body. He was the target of hundreds of missiles, and several times he sank half conscious to the ground while the crowd pressed forward, striking at him with clubs, sticks, and whips until his head and body were scarcely rec-

ognizable. More dead than alive, he was dragged along and forced to his feet. Scores of women joined the men. High above the noise, the wretch could be heard pleading for his life. This spectacle continued until the grounds were reached where the final work of the mob, was accomplished. . . .

The place of execution had been selected weeks ago, in accordance with all the other arranged details of the programme mapped out by the leaders of the mob. The prisoner was dragged to the sapling and strapped against the tree, facing the husband of the victim. Large quantities of dry brush and larger bits of wood were piled around him while he was praying for speedy death. James Lashbrook, the husband of the victim, applied the first match to the brushwood. A brother of the victim struck the second match. Someone with a knife was slashing at the prisoner's chest. By a sort of cruel concurrence of action on the part of the mob not a single shot was fired. The purpose seemed to be to give the wretch the greatest possible amount and duration of torture. As the flames arose Coleman's horror increased and he made vain efforts to withdraw his limbs from the encroaching fire. The ropes securing him to the tree were burned and his body finally fell forward on the burning pile. Even then, although it was not certain whether he was living or dead, the vengeful purpose of the crowd led them to use rails and long poles to push his body back into the flames. It is not certain how long life lasted. . . .

During the process, while his voice could be heard, he begged for a drink of water. At the end of three hours the body was practically cremated. During all that time members of the family of Mrs. Lashbrook had remained to keep up the fire and keep the body in a position where it would continue to burn. It is said that on the march through the city the prisoner's eyes had been burned out by acid thrown in an eggshell. In all the thousands who constituted the mob there was not a single effort made to disguise or conceal identity. No man wore a mask. All the leaders of the mob are well known and there are hundreds of witnesses who can testify to their participation in the tragedy. They are leading citizens in all lines of business and many are members of churches. . . .

The coroner held an inquest on the charred remains of Richard Coleman and rendered the simple verdict, "Death at the hands of a mob." The body was left lying there. Relic hunters took away teeth and bones and flesh and every fragment of the body that they could lay hands on. All the afternoon children, some of them not more than six years old, kept up the fire around the blackened body by throwing grass, brush, bits of boards, and everything combustible that they could get together. This they kept up until dark. . . .[15]

Space is given to this detailed account to emphasize that black writers do not exaggerate, indeed do not have to rely overly much

upon their imaginations, in their presentation of mob violence and
its ritualistic aspects.

A similar historical account from the 1940s is related by one of
the participants in the mob; although he does not give the specific
year of the execution, the account nonetheless serves to illustrate
that the ritualized nature of historical lynchings and burnings continued into the twentieth century, parallel to the continued presentation of such acts in works created by black writers.[16] The motivation for this lynching is a threat to Southern white womanhood.
A startled young white woman reports that Shine Wilson (whose
nickname is surely significant in terms of racial stereotypes) has
"tried to git holt of her in the woods and rape her." For his try—if
indeed that is the truth of the matter—Shine is executed. Communal spirit defines the lynching and burning. As the mob, led by the
girl's father, pursues Shine, the father stops to take stock of lynching equipment:

> "I'm astin' some of you to go back to town and git some kerosene.
> Looks like we come off without no rope and I'll thank you to see
> that we git that too. Reckon we got guns and we got plenty of
> knives. Don't want to overlook nothin' in a takin' care of this here
> nigger that forced my daughter Minnie."[17]

Torture is also a part of the ceremony:

> "I ain't tellin' nobody just what we done to that nigger but we used
> a broken bottle just where it'd do the most damage, and any time
> you want to see a nigger ear all you gotta do is go to see old man
> Smith and ast him for a peep at one. . . . Yes, ma'am, we done
> things I never knowed could be done and things I certainly ain't
> mentionin' to no lady."

Kerosene is poured over Shine, his hands and feet are tied, and he
is set to burn "over a bunch of twigs." The participant remembers:

> "Funniest thing I ever smelled was him a burnin', and the way his
> flesh cooked it sizzled same as if we was a cookin' a pig or a cow,
> and then the groanin' got lower and lower and finely it was just
> little gasps and then it wasn't nothin' a tall. Skinny Slaton said
> they wasn't no sense in a lettin' him burn up all the way. So he
> pulled Shine offn the fire and put a rope around his neck and him
> and one or two others tied him up against a tree. Well, said Skinny
> Slaton, shore as I'm born I'm gonna borrer me a kodak tomorrer
> and I'm a comin' back here and I'm gonna take me some pitchers of
> that. Don't look human, does it? Seen a few niggers lynched in my
> life but this beats it all, Skinny says."

Understandably, the black community is out of sight during Shine's gruesome death. However, it has a role to play in history, as in literature. True to the tradition,

> "in the cool of the evenin' his [Shine's] maw and his little brothers and sisters come a sneakin' up and cut him down. . . . Ralph [a white observer] said he never seen nothin' like the look on Maggie Wilson's face when she looked right clost at her oldest boy a hangin' on that tree. Ralph said he looked for her to die of heart failure then and there and she kep tellin' the young chillun to go on back home or to hide their eyes and not look at their brother, but they didn't pay no mind to what she told them, just come on up and stood there a lookin' as if they was little old men and wimmen instid of little chillun."

The New York Times's account presents the facts, but the participant's account provides insight into the social and psychological forces so essential to the carrying out of the ritual. White superiority must be maintained even when no crime has been committed; black male sexuality must be destroyed (obviously the object of the broken bottle); and black people must realize thoroughly their helplessness and powerlessness. The black children envision their fate in terms of possible victimization, just as the white children earlier envision theirs in terms of power. The ingrained nature of both behaviors and the history informing each response provide the ingredients for exploring lynching and burning rituals against the backdrop of rites of exorcism in ancient societies.

Ritual: A Larger Context for Understanding Exorcism

I have defined ritual initially as a ceremony, one which by countless repetitions has made it traditional among a given group of people or within a given community. Such repetitions are homage to certain *beliefs* that are vital to the community. For example, the rite or ceremony of baptism reflects a belief in God and the need for immersion. Marriage ceremonies reflect a belief in the family as essential to the survival of various societies. By extension, lynching and burning rituals reflect a belief, on the part of whites, in their racial superiority. Simultaneously, such rituals reflect a belief in the inferiority of Blacks as well as a belief in the denial of anything white, especially white women, or representative of "whiteness" (education, clothes, social status) to Blacks.[18] To violate the inviolable, as any Black would who touched a white woman or became mayor of a town, is taboo. It upsets the white world view or conception of the universe. Therefore, in order to exorcise the evil and restore the topsy-turvy world to its rightful position, the violator must be symbolically punished. If the guilty party is not found, a substitute, or scapegoat, will do. Symbolic punishment becomes communal because the entire society has been threatened; thus the entire society must act to put down the violator of taboo.

Acts of ritualized violence require group participation in order that the individuals involved may avoid feelings of guilt. The procedure can be compared to that used in firing squads where all squadsmen must fire at the victim and thereby be blamed and blameless, guilty and guiltless. The concept of law and order destroyed the offender, not the men pulling the triggers. In like manner, various concepts, not individuals, destroy black victims. Usually punished for disregarding some traditional taboo, the black men and women serve in their deaths to establish these practices as inviolable. As Jacquelyn Hall suggests, lynching became a "communal ritual that articulated and thus helped to maintain a set of entrenched cultural preoccupations."[19]

The great anthropologist, Sir James George Frazer, has studied ritual and taboo extensively in undeveloped societies.[20] His analysis of ritual provides interesting contrasts to its nineteenth- and twentieth-century American counterparts. Frazer maintains that human scapegoats, who took upon themselves the sins of the group and the disfavor of the gods, were sacrificed only when the survival of the society was in question, in cases of drought, famine, or pestilence. The person sacrificed may have been diseased, or of great muscular strength, or a volunteer. His or her death was deemed necessary for the health or re-fertilization of the world and for the lives of the people. White mobs could make these claims, but only in a perversion of the original rituals. Their claims to executions for the sake of survival of their society were fixed in a mental perception of themselves as superior to other human beings, not in a belief in the physical annihilation of their culture from natural forces. There were no droughts, pestilences, or famines to support lynching in America, and the alleged threats of survival to the society were not grounded in the immediate context of life and death as were those in earlier societies. The expulsion of evil for American whites had none of the cosmic consequences it had for the ancient societies Frazer studied, but it was equally destructive. Also, many of the victims of early scapegoat rituals were allowed as long as a year to prepare for their inevitable deaths; dying was not as immediate and certainly not as purposeless as lynchings and burnings; in fact, there were implications that the victims shared their executioners' purpose. The sacrificed victims in early societies were considered parts of their communities; an additional reason for expelling Blacks was the refusal to recognize them as part of the community and a preventive to those Blacks who might hope to belong to the community.

In applying ancient concepts of ritual to summary punishment as presented in William Faulkner's "Dry September," John Vickery makes a comment relevant to all similar actions in literature and American history:

> Originally the choice of the victim was based on all the religious, social, and scientific knowledge possessed by man; a catastrophe affecting existence itself—such as drought or blight—demanded immediate and drastic remedies. The contemporary crisis, on the other hand, involves only society's mores, not its struggle for physical survival. And not only is the occasion intrinsically less significant, but there is even the likelihood that it has not actually taken place. In short, unlike primitive man, who could actually see the disaster he was seeking to remove, "none of them gathered in the barbershop [where the decision to kill the black man is made] . . . knew exactly what had happened."[21]

The crowd acts out the ritual of the expulsion of evil without understanding its significance, Vickery adds. He refers to Faulkner's story as an "ironic rendering of the primitive scapegoat ritual." The crowd destroys without fully understanding why, and there is no release for any at the end—no rain falls, no bountiful harvest is forthcoming.

Peoples of cultures of classical antiquity and still earlier saw the scapegoat ritual, the expulsion of evil, as a periodic part of their lives. They had holidays, and they had sacrifices. For white Americans, there was no regular ritual cycle. There might be one execution in a year, or two hundred. Whenever the crowd was convinced a violation had occurred, a sin had been committed, the group could be encouraged to act in the expurgation of that sin.

The intensity of mob action has led some social critics to speculate on the theory of a "collective mind" operating at the moment of violent mob destruction, that the participants are no longer themselves and are acting foreign to their experiences and beliefs. I contend that such mob action serves to reinforce belief; two researchers who share this position have tried to disprove the consideration of a collective mind. "Human nature in the crowd," writes Doris Lorden, "is the same as human nature among dispersed persons."[22] Norman Meier, G. H. Mennenga, and H. J. Stoltz agree:

"... in the crowd the individual does not ... become a creature of irrational hate, capable of any excesses, including the taking of human life; but rather acts in accordance with the dictates of past habit and attitude formation, only, ... possibly to a greater degree."[23] There is not a change in the basic structure of beliefs which mobilize the crowd into action; rather, there is a period of strain during which those beliefs manifest themselves in collective behavior. A group identifies an "evil" with a particular "agent," such as communists, Jews, or Blacks, exaggerates it to evoke the already hostile beliefs about that "agent," and thus mobilizes itself to take aggressive action.[24] The already generalized belief that Blacks are a threat is heightened when there are rumors of rioting or rumors of whites being attacked or raped; during this period of strain, a leader comes forward and draws the diffuse aggression into a unified force for revenge. Therefore, the actions of white lynch mobs and the ritualistic nature of their behavior cannot be attributed to some strange and foreign beast being released at the time of cruelty. The individuals are socialized into the roles they play amid the intense agitation of the mob. What is at stake is clear to each participant, no matter how great his emotional excitement.[25]

Each member of a mob knows that public sentiment is in his favor. Therefore, as Cutler points out, he has nothing to fear in the way of consequences for his actions. "Crowd behavior," Lorden adds by extension, "is not at all possible except on an emotional or sentimental level."[26] The community agrees that the ritual should take place, and it does.

Once the crowd gathers at the scene of execution, mutilation and beating of the victim are sure to occur. In ancient Greece, scapegoat victims were likewise beaten, but the purpose the beating served was obviously different from that administered by white Americans to their black victims:

> When a city suffered from plague, famine, or other public calamity, an ugly or deformed person was chosen to take upon himself all the evils which afflicted the community. . . . Then he was beaten seven times upon his genital organs with squills and branches of the wild fig and other wild trees, while the flutes played a particular tune. Afterwards he was burned on a pyre built of the wood of forest trees; and his ashes were cast into the sea.[27]

In explanation of these acts, Frazer comments:

> . . . the ancients attributed to squills a magical power of averting evil influences, and that accordingly they hung them up at the doors of their houses and made use of them in purificatory rites.

. . . the object of beating the human scapegoat on the genital organs with squills and so on, must have been to release his reproductive energies from any restraint or spell under which they might be laid by demoniacal or other malignant agency, . . . we must recognize in him a representative of the creative and fertilising god of vegetation.[28]

Actions of the crowd were linked specifically to eliminating the calamity by sympathetic magic. Again, in a violent perversion of the traditional form of the ritual, white American males castrated black men presumably in an effort to eliminate the threat of black sexuality to white women, and, as will be developed later, perhaps in an effort to transfer some of that sexuality to themselves. The connection for the ritual action is made (sexuality/genitals), but cosmic significance is again absent and, within the rationale of the traditional ritual, renders the action a perversion of a previously justifiable concept. The intent of the beating and castration for white Americans was as much to inflict painful punishment on the victim as to expel evil.

As the most emotional cause of lynching, the violation of sexual taboo deserves special consideration. To the white male psyche, rape defines any intimate or assumed intimate alliance between black man and white woman, whether voluntary or not. Naturally the white woman was "forced," because no white man could conceive of any white woman voluntarily pursuing or accepting a black man. Rape, as here defined, is not cosmic, but it is the most offensive evil (more Blacks were lynched for murder, but rape seems to have led more easily to the ritual) that can be committed against white society by black men.[29] Therefore, even the rumor of rape must be avenged; a taboo violated, even in the abstract, cannot go unpunished.

A reporter investigating a lynching in a Southern community got a clear insight into how supposed attacks on white women could be used to account for lynchings for other reasons. A black man accused of attacking a white woman was burned at the stake. The reporter asked one of the men who had observed the burning several questions, including whether or not the presumed crime had taken place and if the victim had had anything to do with it.

No, I was told; that was really irrelevant. No particular crime was being avenged. The Negro population was being warned never to forget that the coloured man in the South is still a slave, that between him and the white man there can be no law, no claim to justice.[30]

The answer contains the essence of the prevailing attitude: violators, either real or imagined, must be squelched when the society
views itself as being threatened. The gods must be appeased at any
cost. A violator, any violator (but he is usually "big, black, and
burly"), must be sacrificed. The purity of Southern white women
must remain on its pedestal.

The myth of the purity of Southern white womanhood became
the strongest belief in whose defense the ritual or ceremony of
lynching and burning could be carried out. Psychosexual forces at
work are indeed complicated, as history and black literature reveal. White men, who had coupled with black women in a leisurely
manner during slavery, could not tolerate the possibility of similar relations existing between their women and black men. Ida B.
Wells, black newspaperwoman and antilynching crusader at the
turn of the century, tried to explain the problem this way. She
maintained that the "alleged propensity of black men for raping
white women was a myth created to protect the sexual pride of
white men." She elaborated:

> You see, the white man has never allowed his women to hold the
> sentiment "black but comely," on which he has so freely acted him-
> self. Libertinism apart, white men constantly express an open pref-
> erence for the society of black women. But it is a sacred convention
> that white women can never feel passion of any sort, high or low,
> for a black man. Unfortunately facts don't always square with the
> convention; and then, if the guilty pair are found out, the thing is
> christened an outrage at once and the woman is practically forced
> to join in hounding down the partner of her shame.[31]

Winthrop Jordan offers a similar comment:

> No matter how firmly based in fact . . . the image of the sexually
> aggressive Negro was rooted even more firmly in deep strata of ir-
> rationality. For it is apparent that white men projected their own
> desires onto Negroes: their own passion for Negro women was not
> fully acceptable to society or the self and hence not readily ad-
> missible. Sexual desires could be effectively denied and the accom-
> panying anxiety and guilt in some measure assuaged, however, by
> imputing them to others. It is not we, but others, who are guilty. It
> is not we who lust, but they.[32]

Jordan does not root his discussion in traditional ritual, but the
transfer of guilt is an essential part of the scapegoat ritual as defined by Frazer. The scapegoat takes upon himself the sins of the
society. He becomes guilty and the people are in turn cleansed, or

purged of their sins. In many ancient instances, the crowd would each in turn touch the victim for an actual physical transfer of sin and guilt. For American whites, the transfer is more psychological. Gordon W. Allport discusses this phenomenon in his seminal work, *The Nature of Prejudice*. He, too, emphasizes the cleansing process groups undergo when they can project their basest fears and desires onto other groups, including sexual fears and repressions. Allport's comments on scapegoating as a theory of prejudice are also revealing; if one group can blame another for a variety of wrongs, and can become aggressive against that group, then it engages in another form of elevating itself above the despised group and separates itself from those it considers guilty of societal or behavioral sins.[33] James P. Comer, a black psychiatrist who has studied race relations extensively, supports this notion that the lynchings were psychologically informed by the need to transfer undesirable characteristics to Blacks:

> The conduct of the whites who participated in murdering and lynching blacks suggests that these grisly events served as a catharsis by purging the evil the whites feared in themselves and "projected" onto the blacks. Black victims were castrated, tortured, burned and mutilated by white men, women and children in drunken, orgy-like atmospheres. The throwing of the Christians to the lions might well have been more humane.[34]

Ralph Ellison illustrates the transfer of sin and guilt from immoral white men to innocent black boys in the battle royal scene of *Invisible Man*. James Baldwin, in a climactic presentation of the ritual, vividly portrays the psychological and sexual dimensions of such transfers in "Going to Meet the Man." In each literary work, white women are taboo; the pedestal of their purity must not be violated; the myth must be kept intact.

Two psychologists likewise recognize that the transference of guilt and sin from white men to Blacks helps form white attitudes toward potential sexual encounters between black men and white women.

> There is little question that the Negro female was attractive to the white male for mating purposes. The universality of laws prohibiting marriage of whites and Negroes is an eloquent testimonial to this fact. These two features, the sexual usefulness of the female and her role as a mammy, could only have the effect of increasing the white man's fear of the Negro male, her rightful mate and legitimate possessor. This could not help but lead to the fantastic exaggeration in the white man's mind of the Negro's sexual prowess.

And this, in turn, would necessitate more repressive measures against the Negro male—all caused by the white man's guilt and anxiety. The necessity to "protect" the white female against this fancied prowess of the male Negro thus became a fixed constellation in the ethos of the South.[35]

This comment, in addition to Wells's and Jordan's, vividly illustrates the psychology of myth-making.

Unfortunately, some myths, once established, acquire the power to destroy. In an effort to diminish the potency of the white-woman-pedestal myth, Southern white women, members of the very class which was often assumed to be the justification for lynching, founded "The Association of Southern Women for the Prevention of Lynching" shortly after November, 1930. They gathered signatures of prominent people who were opposed to lynching, wrote to governors and sheriffs, met with black organizations which were also fighting lynching, confronted mobs, and gathered evidence to show that lynchings were carried out for reasons other than protecting their honor. They did a great deal to educate the public about the true causes of lynching, but they were a little late to prevent the majority of lynchings in this country. The peak years were 1892 and 1893, just before several states began passing anti-lynching legislation. Nevertheless, the history of the Association's efforts are an interesting commentary on myth-making and the need to sustain that myth with ritual.[36]

Black sexual crimes provoked immediate and violent responses and the accusation of such crimes became the battlecry any time a black man put himself in the way of whites. Lynchings for alleged sex crimes became cover-ups for other suppressions whites wanted to effect, whether they admitted that or not. A black man who wore an expensive suit and tipped his hat to a white woman could be killed for stepping out of place. His alleged crime would be that of being uppity with a white woman, but his real crime would be success, a success evaluated on the basis of his attire, which the whites believed was appropriate only for whites. Such a reaction is illustrated in Walter White's *The Fire in the Flint* (1924), in which a black man becomes a doctor, and in Langston Hughes's "Home" (1933), in which the protagonist is a prominent musician. Whites could also use lynchings for alleged sex crimes to gain economic control, along with the obvious control of sexual activities between black men and white women.

Ultimately, lynching and burning rituals functioned to sustain a belief in racial, economic, psychological, and moral superiority in whites and to reinforce a clearly designed concept of place for Blacks. Deviation meant death. Ritual served a need for whites. As Clude Kluckhohn explains, "ritual is an obsessive repetitive activity—often a symbolic dramatization of the fundamental 'needs' of the society, whether 'economic,' 'biological,' 'social,' or 'sexual.' Mythology is the rationalization of these same needs, whether they are all expressed in overt ceremonial or not."[37] Whites, feeling a need to believe themselves morally and culturally superior, used lynching rituals, and when these were no longer historically possible, more subtle rituals, against Blacks to support those beliefs. Examination of the roles of the two principal players in the drama of ritual violence will make clear the values whites tried to maintain as well as provide insight into the psychosexual backdrop of one strain of black American literature.

White Men as Performers in the Lynching Ritual

The history of lynchings and burnings in this country is the history of racial control by a specific form of violence. Its effects were as psychologically pervasive as were the methods of intimidation which Gladys-Marie Fry discusses in *Nightriders in Black Folk History*.[38] Fry explores how, under the cover of sheets and darkness, white men in the South used forms of intimidation ranging from beatings to lynchings in order to keep Blacks contained politically and socially during the years of Reconstruction. Mysterious and ghostly in their appearances before their victims, these white men conveyed to Blacks that there was always someone watching over their shoulders ready to punish them for the slightest offense or the least deviation from acceptable lines of action. Certain patterns of behavior, made into rituals by habit and custom, were outlined to black people by whites, and when one black individual dared to violate the restrictions, he or she was used as an example to reiterate to the entire race that the group would continually be held responsible for the actions of the individual. Thus an accusation of rape could lead not only to the accused black man being lynched and burned, but to the burning of black homes and the whipping or lynching of other black individuals as well.

The white male's function, ostensibly, was to protect his home and especially the white woman who was the center of it. That immediate reason for punishing black men when they came into questionable contact with white women had as its basis the larger reason informing almost all black and white relationships in this

country: the white man's craving for power and mastery as indications of his ultimate superiority not only in assigning a place to his
women, but especially in keeping black people, particularly black
men, in the place he had assigned for them. The notion that the
white man was really trying to prevent "mongrelization" of the
white race is just that—a notion. No such concern for racial purity
defined his actions with black women; consequently, his objections
to miscegenation were designed to control the behavior of black
males and white females without interfering with his own sexual
preferences.[39] No one stopped to consider that, during the years of
the Civil War, when white men left their wives, daughters, and
homes in the hands of black men, not a single instance of rape was
reported. The issue, then, really boils down to one between white
men and black men and the mythic conception the former have of
the latter.

James Baldwin has long argued that the prevailing metaphor for
understanding the white man's need to suppress the black man is
that attached to sexual prowess. White men have originated and
passed along to their women the myth of the black man's unusual
ability in sexual intercourse. So long has the myth been a part of
his culture and his psyche that the white man can no longer separate reality from the larger-than-life beliefs that his ancestors created. In his modern manifestation, then, the white man becomes a
victim of his culture's imagination. Unlike any other victim of beliefs, however, he is the one in the American context who has most
power to respond to his beliefs, whether they are real or not. When
he acts to save his woman from the mad, rampaging, overly endowed black man, at one level he believes he is acting in the best
interest of all. He sees himself as savior, father, keeper of the purity
of his race. In this capacity, he must show his women that there is
nothing to fear by capturing the source of that fear, then torturing
and killing it. Thus, the white man attains kingly status by determining what is wrong with his society, ferreting it out, and reestab-
lishing the order which was the norm before the disturbance.

At a deeper level, he is acting out his fear of sexual competition
from the black man. By maintaining that sexual contact between
black males and white females is taboo, he eliminates that mythic
phallic symbol, which he himself has created, from competition
with himself; for there is always the realistic possibility that if
black men are so favorably endowed, white women may prefer
them as sexual partners. To prevent that, the white man tells his
women that coupling with a black man is tantamount to coupling
with an ape or some other subhuman species. Despite the insis-

tence on black subhumanity, however, the myth of black sexual superiority represents a potential competition that, in the folk imagination, is always detrimental to the white man. The stereotype about black male sexuality has proved so powerful that it has found its way into many black folktales where, instead of being denied, it is turned into a positive trait at the expense of the white male characters who appear in such folk narratives. Consider, for example, the following black folktale in which the length of the sexual organ is the key to freedom:

> Three men were sent to court: a white, a Negro and a Mexican. They got to court and the judge said, "If you have fifteen inches of length between you, I'll let you go." The judge called for the bailiff to measure the penises. So he measured the Negro's and it was seven and one-half inches long. Then he measured the Mexican's and it was five and one-half inches long. Next he measured the white man's and it was two inches long. That was fifteen inches. Therefore they were set free. When they got outside the court, they all started laughing and bragging. The Negro said, "You'd better be glad mine was seven and a half inches." The Mexican said, "You'd better be glad mine was five and a half inches." The white man looked at them and said, "Both of you better be glad that I was on hard."[40]

The folk imagination turns the stereotype of the over-endowed black male into a positive thing and makes the white man's under-endowment the butt of the joke. The exaggeration in the tale, which makes the white man the biggest braggart, serves to underscore how pathetically he has been slighted by nature. Through their humor, black folk have been able to use the stereotype of the black man's sexuality to their own advantage and to show that, as far as black men and white men are concerned, there will always be some kind of sexual measurement going on. By understanding how he is viewed in that larger white world, the black man is better prepared to deal with it. Thus the tale not only illustrates the necessity within the black folk community for understanding more about the oppressor than the oppressor understands about Blacks, but it also shows that that bestial quality so often attached to black male sexuality is made into a valuable asset for the white man as well as for the other characters in the tale.

As long as the potential sexual competition between black males and white males was suppressed historically, there was no need for any open jealousy on the part of the white man. The nature of the hunt and the kill, however, suggests that there was still a major

factor of jealousy operative in the (sexual) power relationship between black males and white males. In simultaneously perpetuating and attempting to destroy the myth of black male sexuality, the
white men involved in the lynchings and burnings spent an inordinate amount of time examining the genitals of the black men
whom they were about to kill. Even as they castrated the black
men, there was a suggestion of fondling, of envious caress. The
many emotions involved at that moment perhaps led the white
men to slash even more violently at what could not be theirs, but
which, at some level, they very much desired (without the apish
connotations, of course).

Many scholars have recognized that the inclusion of castration in
the atrocities committed against black men by white men sprang
from envy and sexual competition between them. Daryl Dance is
one cultural analyst who refers to the "ritualistic castration" of
black men for "familiarity" with white women, and who asserts
that "the very nature of the lynch mob's punishment of Blacks—
the sexual mutilation of the victim—suggests the white man's
efforts to wrest from the Black man that symbol of manhood (that
testament of superiority) which he so fears."[41]

A desire to harness the finest qualities in one's enemies has long
been recognized as a trait in man. For some warriors, eating the
hearts of their most challenging enemies became a literal way of
trying to transfer some of the opponent's courage to themselves.
For white males involved in the lynchings and burnings of black
males, there is a symbolic transfer of sexual power at the point of
the executions. The black man is stripped of his prowess, but the
very act of stripping brings symbolic power to the white man. His
actions suggest that, subconsciously, he craves the very thing he is
forced to destroy. Yet he destroys it as an indication of the political
(sexual) power he has and takes it unto himself in the form of souvenirs as an indication of the kind of power he would like. In some
historical accounts, the lynchers were reputed to have divided
pieces of the black man's genitals among themselves. Again, James
Baldwin is especially good in illustrating how sexual and political
power are linked in lynchings.[42]

The details involved in the process of stripping the black male of
his sexuality suggest that the group of whites who usually attended
such gatherings engaged in a communal orgiastic climax which
made the sexual nature of the ritual explicit. There was initially
tension involved in the pursuit of the assumed sexual offender;
often the homes of other Blacks were rifled and general destruction
preceded the capture of the black man.[43] Tension increased in get-

ting the offender from the place of capture to the place of execution, a process which might involve finding a suitable tree for the lynching or a territory large enough to accommodate all those wishing to view the lynching. Tension continued to mount as various members of the crowd gathered the implements necessary to carry out the ritualized punishment—rope, wood, tar and feathers if desired. The height of the tension was reached when the rope was actually around the offender's neck, and when the fire had been started. The climactic release began with the crackling of fire against flesh, with the gathering of souvenirs, and with the cries of the victim; it concluded in the yells of the crowd when they knew the victim was dead, yells which gave way to the silence of complete (sexual) purgation, the ultimate release from all tension.

From one perspective, then, there is an ironic reversal in that there is a communal rape of the black man by the crowd which executes him. They violate him by exposing the most private parts of his body and by forcing him, finally, into ultimate submission to them. Comparable to sexual snuff films, in which the victims participate against their wills, or without knowing what the end of the film will be, and provide pleasure without intending to do so, the lynched black man becomes a source of sexual pleasure to those who kill him. As Lillian Smith, a Southern white woman writing about the social and sexual mores of the South points out, "the lynched Negro becomes *not an object that must die* but a receptacle for every man's dammed-up hate, and a receptacle for every man's forbidden sex feelings."[44] Killing the black man, therefore, provides a peculiar kind of satisfaction.

His death also enables white males to act out a fear of castration even as they are in the process of castrating the black man. Perhaps the worst fear any man can have is the fear that someone will cut off his penis; the white man, heir to that fear just as the black man is, designs as the peculiar punishment for black men that which all males fear most. His action simultaneously shows his kinship to the black man and denies the connection. He does to the black man what, in his worst nightmares, he perhaps imagines other adversaries doing to him; before he becomes victim, he victimizes.

Keep in mind, too, that it is the white man's tradition to call the black man "boy." If the black man is indeed a boy, then he can be easily controlled in everyday affairs. Calling him a boy suggests, as well, the strange lens through which the white man must view the black man sexually. "Boy," an effort at controlling language and thereby controlling the reality the language is designed to reflect, wipes out the symbolic, sexual implications of the black man as

Man. So when the "boys" step out of their place by accosting white
women or being accused of accosting them, the "men" must punish
them accordingly.

The Ultimate Taboo: White Women as Initiators of the Lynching Ritual

In an Afro-American folk rhyme, a black man, looking at an attractive white woman, muses to himself: "Oh, Lord, will I ever
. . . ?" and a white man, overhearing the implied wish, responds,
"No, nigger, never." Undaunted, but momentarily subdued, the
black man rejoins: "As long as there's life, there's hope," and the
summary conclusion belongs to the white man: "And as long as
there's trees, there's rope."[45] Like Dudley Randall's W.E.B. in the
poetic exchange of philosophies between DuBois and Booker T.
Washington, the individual who appears in the final position carries emphasis. So, too, in the little folk exchange above; the power
to punish, to carry the last word, is given to the white man as pro-
tector of the most forbidden taboo for black men: white women.

This rhyme, circulated within the black oral tradition, capsulizes the history of the relationship between black men and white
women, and the role white men have played in maintaining the
status quo. The black man recognizes that he cannot respond to a
white woman simply as a man responds to a woman; custom and
tradition have transcended any potential healthy involvement between black men and white women.[46] If the black man dares to approach the white woman, so the wisdom of black folk ages conveys,
he must contend with the white man. The black man does not question why the situation is the way it is; that is merely the sequence
of historical occurrences to which he finds himself heir. To touch
the forbidden fruit is to risk life and limb.

Black folk tradition is permeated with tales that portray those
risks to life and limb. A famous tale depicts the ignorance of a slave
who, in trying to imitate what a fellow slave claims *he* has done,
puts his hand under old mistress's dress; he is beaten nearly to
death and should consider himself lucky that he is not killed. What
the first slave neglected to tell his too-eager friend was that the
mistress's dress was hanging on a clothes line drying when he put
his hand under it. This tale is perhaps as innocent and as humorous as tales of encounters between black men and white women
can be. The second slave risks sticking his hand up old mistress's
dress precisely because he is so attracted to the possibility of free-

dom of action that his friend's story elicits. At the base of his reaction is the assumption of a sexual connotation in what has been described, and the first slave, thoroughly aware of that misconception, nevertheless allows his friend to proceed with the act which almost causes his death. Blacks generally laugh at the tale because they do not believe the first man is being vicious; instead, they credit the second man with being stupid, for surely any black male during slavery—and those for many generations after that—must have known the consequences of putting himself into any situation with a white woman which could remotely be construed as sexual.

In her collection of folklore, Daryl Dance devotes a section to the white woman and the black man.[47] One of the tales she includes captures another version of that threat to life and limb which surrounded the interactions of black males and white women, and it identifies that threat with the South:

> This black guy say, [excitedly] "I'm gon get me a *white* woman, a *white* Cadillac, and a *white* suit, and ride down the roads o'Georgia in dat car!"
>
> The guy say, "Well, you go right ahead—you know what I'm gon do. I'm gon get a *black* woman, a *black* Cadillac, a *black* suit, and ride down them same roads o'Georgia—and see your black ass hanging."[48]

The bragging tone indicates, initially, that the first speaker is aware that his assertion is unusual, that it goes against the grain of expected behavior. His emphasis on the whiteness illustrates that it is the color which attracts him, not something of intrinsic beauty in either the woman, the car, or the suit. As long as they are all white, they will signal to all observers that this black man has not been confined by the unwritten rules of society. On the other hand, the realistic view provided by the second speaker indicates how illusory it is for the first man to think he can escape his cage; his vision is a fantasy which will not end in celebration.

Again the humor of the tale revolves around a realistic insider's knowledge as opposed to the dreamer's. The realistic voice reiterates that contrast and makes the listeners mediate between the hope expressed in the first voice and the negation expressed in the second; it fits into the mold of many tales in black folk culture in which the tradition bearers tend to laugh at the most repressive forces which could affect them and to make light of features in themselves which others have judged to be unattractive or at least antithetical to those they see in the larger culture.

These tales show that, in the black folk imagination, as in historical reality, the white woman is taboo to the black man. She is
beauty; he is beast. She is to be protected; he is what she needs
protection from. Her existence must be continued; he is expendable. She is the bearer of the best of her race's traditions; he bears
nothing worthy of respect. She inspires confidence; he inspires
fear. She is pedestalized; he is trampled beneath the feet of those
who have created her pedestal. She can control his life by mere
whim; he has little control over his life as far as she is concerned.
She is innocence; he is guilt.

The myth of the Southern white female's innocence has caused
the deaths of many black men in history and in literature. The fragile, sweet-faced white girl or woman is pictured as the essence of
victimization. The burly black brute who pursues her to her death,
as the lecherous Gus does in *Birth of a Nation*, represents all the
repressed evil and all the hidden, chimeric threats that white imaginations can conceive. For what can be worse for a white female, so
the logic goes, than to be violated by her worst nightmare? Especially when that nightmare wants to rape her, to take what has
been represented to her as the source of her whiteness, what is essential for perpetuation of the white race.

Male keepers of the popular white imagination perpetuated the
myth of the innocent Southern white woman as victim, and frequently influenced the assumed white female victims to continue
that perpetuation.[49] Often indoctrinated to accept their own almost goddesslike chosen status, these sometimes insecure women
screamed rape at the mere sight of a black man in a setting in
which they were not accustomed to seeing him. And these women,
like the white woman in Richard Wright's "Big Boy Leaves Home,"
were victims—of their own heritages and of their own racially
heightened imaginations.

For another portion of that white female population, however,
the theory of victimization does not apply. Some used the hysteria
attached to the myths about interracial sexual encounters to their
own advantage for the purpose of sexually exploiting black men.[50]
These Southern white women were intelligent enough to know that
they had the mob at their beck and call, and they were crass enough
to use it if their sexual advances to black men were rejected or
warded off. *Mandingo* (1975), the film in which Ken Norton plays
the role of a prize fighting slave who is summoned to his mistress's
bedroom, is not solely a creation of the movies. Norton's character
was without recourse in his bid to reject his mistress, and she
placed him in a precarious position by threatening to tell his be-

loved master that the slave had forcibly seduced her if he did not willfully consent to do so. The resulting birth of a black child— summarily killed by the attending white doctor—is only matched by the master boiling his prize fighter in oil.[51] The scheming white mistress's sexual exploitation of the slave fighter thereby turns him into a victim and also makes a victim of her child and herself. The master's ultimate anger, however, turns in the direction to which tradition has pointed it: toward the burly black man who, though slave and confined, is still considered responsible for the sexual violation.[52]

Any white woman who wishes to initiate sexual contact with a black man knows that accusation usually goes in only one direction if she and her partner are discovered. White womanhood must be defended against all claims to innocence by the black man. Even white prostitutes, historical accounts have shown, were defended against black men who had sexual contact with them.[53] For the sake of the myth and the white race, no amount of compartmentalization (at least not public) is allowed to exist where white women are concerned. Individual indiscretions must be overlooked in the face of the larger racial "good." White women who were brave enough to capitalize upon that abstract notion of who they were could enjoy sexual favors from black men who were coerced into submission, or from those who genuinely enjoyed their excursions into those fenced-in, forbidden orchards. Not all of those innocents existed in reality. But all acquired innocence in the white male imagination.

Few historians recounted the documented instances of respectable white women having affairs with black men, of white women who married black men, and of those less than respectable white women who were aggressive in pursuing black males for sexual purposes during and after slavery. Such material was not usually recorded because not recording it upheld the myths about the white women. The historian was usually heir to that tradition. What white woman in her right mind, his thoughts probably ran, would desire to sleep with a black beast—*if* such a thought even surfaced in his mind. The iconoclasts among historians and other cultural analysts and social observers are few: Ida B. Wells-Barnett and Winthrop Jordan have recognized inconsistencies in what whites practiced as opposed to what they believed, and Wells uncovered instances of black males having liaisons with respectable white women. More recently, Catherine Clinton has also touched on this phenomenon.[54] Two white women, one at mid-century and one more recently, who have been willing to examine their roles

against the grain of popular stereotyping and pedestalization are
Lillian Smith and Adrienne Rich. Smith discusses the racist views
which she was forced to adopt in her Christian middle-class Georgia
home, and Rich, in a different vein, explores the effect upon black
men and women of the traditional white ways of viewing them.[55]

How white women were viewed has shaped literary creations by
both black male and female writers. As a prelude to her study of
black women novelists, Barbara Christian traces the historical
images of white women during the latter third of the nineteenth
century and the corresponding devaluing of black women.[56] If that
element was important to the kinds of literature black women created, it was even more important to that black men, who felt so
strongly the oppressive shadow of white women upon their lives,
were able to create. The sense of smallness black males were made
to feel in relation to white women reflected the smallness they
were made to feel in relation to white males and the society they
controlled. White women joined white men in taking power away
from the black man, and both inspired a "literature of emasculation," which would parallel the portrayals of lynchings and burnings in black American literature. The literature shows the path by
which black men came to be devalued, and it shows the connections between those portrayals and ones of ritualized violence.

CHAPTER 2

Fear of Castration:
A Literary History

Emasculation: Psychological, Political, and Social

Sterling Brown has surveyed the early images in which Blacks were cast in the American literary imagination. One favorite image is that of the powerless old darky who hobbles through the pages of the works in which he appears seeking favors from his master or praising his goodness.[1] This character, along with others, represents the powerlessness of Blacks in relation to the larger white population. Such figures form the background of political impotence against which literal castrations would be carried out in the lynching and burning rituals. Many Blacks managed to salvage a bit of dignity by playing the role of Uncle Tom and Aunt Thomasina; such roles allowed them to improve their own situations as much as was possible under the constraints peculiar to their existence. It was very early conveyed to all Blacks, and especially to black men, that full humanity was not to be granted to them. This lesson was taught in everyday incidents, reinforced by invoking the Bible, and solidified in images depicted through the popular and literary imaginations. The black man became the harmless eunuch who could be tolerated if he accepted that role, or the raging beast who could be killed without conscience if he did not. The black woman became the lascivious slut when her sexual favors were desired and the matronly mammy when whites needed someone to care for their children.

Most central to this discussion is the emasculation of the black man. The image of the harmless darky came to epitomize the black man who was socially and psychologically emasculated. Hand-me-down hat in hand, baggy pants slightly torn at the knee, stooped shoulders, head bowed, without sexual consciousness or ability, eyes forever on the tip of the master's shoe, a "yessuh" forever on the tip of his tongue, this character soothed white consciences and justified their claims to superiority. Another side of this emasculation was manifested in the stereotype of the black male who, though as immaculately dressed as his slave existence would allow,

29

nonetheless gave up his manhood by identification with the whites, or in return for the little goods whites allowed. This character would continue into twentieth century literature in the form of various black "leaders" who traded their community's best interests for the material goods they were allowed to own within the black communities. Whether dressed in baggy pants or encased in dignity, this eunuch lived on white sufferance. His symbolic castration became symptomatic of the condition of all Blacks in the United States. Without social status, or political or economic power, he was virtually emasculated in his dealings with whites during slavery and in the aftermath of slavery. Grier and Cobbs comment upon this historic pattern for black males:

> Under slavery, the black man was a psychologically emasculated and totally dependent human being. Times and conditions have changed, but black men continue to exhibit the inhibitions and psychopathology that had their genesis in the slave experience. . . . The black man . . . is regarded as socially, economically, and politically castrated, and he is gravely handicapped in performing every other masculine role.[2]

Black males who found themselves so emasculated conformed to rules, or ritualistic patterns of behavior, as strict as those Richard Wright identifies in "The Ethics of Living Jim Crow." In that essay, Wright describes the unwritten rules that governed the interaction of black people with whites in the South. A black man was expected to laugh, for example, when he witnessed the white owner of a store and his son dragging and kicking a black woman who was unable to pay a furniture bill, and he was to consider it "lucky" that "they didn't lay her when they got through" with the bloody beating. A black man was also supposed to smile and say "Yes, sir" when he was struck in the face with a whiskey bottle, or when a white man fondled the black woman he happened to be escorting home.[3] In other words, the "ethics" demanded from the black man happy acquiescence in his own emasculation. A black man in Mississippi knew, at the turn of the century and for many years thereafter, that he could not look a white man in the face and call him a liar. He knew that he was expected to be quiet when the white man spoke, and he knew that he was always to efface himself if the white man desired the space he stood on or anything he might have possessed. Wright's actions in "The Ethics of Living Jim Crow" are a series of initiations, frequently painful, into the limitations on his person. Those physical, psychological, and social limitations caused Wright, on Southern soil, to be just as emasculated as his less-educated and less-perceptive black brothers. Although Ralph Ellison was born in frontier Oklahoma with all the frontiersman's opportunities for shaping his own destiny available to him, he recognized, with Wright, that there was "much misery in Negro life." Though he celebrated the positive effects of American life on the black experience, there was still a point in his writing career at which he reacted to the negative sociological conditions of black people in the United States. In the lynching story, "The Birthmark" (1940), for example, his vision of black life is comparable to that Wright witnessed and recorded, and he shows, in this stage of his development, that Blacks as a group in the United States were essentially emasculated. "Ellison portrays black Americans," writes Robert O'Meally of the early Ellison short stories, "as the hapless, angry victims of social abuse, trapped in the cul-de-sacs of their environment; their birthmark, like Willie's [a character in "The Birthmark"], is a scar of castration."[4]

Ellison and Wright join other black writers, who, equally influenced by their history, have portrayed such emasculated black males in their works for more than a hundred years. The figure of the older black man, in his emasculated role, became, for these writers, the antithesis of all protest and discontent. Seldom, if ever, was such a character merely wearing a mask to hide more rebellious feelings; when he was wearing one, it did not differ substantially from his real personality. These characters range from Sam in William Wells Brown's *Clotel; Or, The President's Daughter* (1853), to Gabriel Grimes in James Baldwin's *Go Tell It On the Mountain* (1953), and beyond. Openly wanting peace with the whites in power, and frequently imitating them in dress and manner, this character during the second half of the nineteenth century could be easily identified in literature by his polysyllabic pronouncements and by his shuffling attempts to efface all traits of his personality except those which were acceptable to his white master or employer. In the presence of other Blacks, he took on the role of guardian of manners and tastes which would define those "siddity" Blacks who formed the blue-vein societies at the turn of the century. Closely identified with the white master at times, like his mammy counterpart, this male could frequently be considered just as "feminine" as she. Consider, for example, the voice of the speaker in Paul Laurence Dunbar's "When Malindy Sings." The voice which commands Miss Lucy to "go way and quit dat noise" and to "put dat music book erway" because her training can never approach Malindy's natural talent is not clearly male or female in its blackness.[5] Rather, it is a voice ever subservient to the whites around it except in allowable limits; what is clear is that it is a powerless voice which executes polite dissent from the white mistress only because it is permitted to do so. Like mammy praising her white charges, or Uncle Tom asking for whiskey for his cold, the voice identifies a safe tone of reaction, a way of life in which it can co-exist with the white world in which it has been formed.

That voice has its beginnings in black American literature, however, in the creations of William Wells Brown. Sam, who is a slave on the plantation in Natchez to which Currer, Clotel's mother, is sold, is one of the leaders among the house slaves. Though he considers his very black color to be "a great misfortune,"[6] he tries his best to make up for it by imitating his master's manners so precisely among the slaves that they envy him nonetheless. The fact that he is a "single gentleman" adds to his attractiveness among the predominantly female population of house servants. He spends an hour and a half a day brushing up his "hare," greasing it and his face with butter, managing thereby to "cut a big figure" with the servants. With his ruffles standing "five or six inches" from his breast, he succeeds in being a fair imitation of his parson master: "The parson in his own drawingroom did not make a more imposing appearance than did his servant" (p. 99). By similarly imitating his previous master in his medical profession, Sam has earned a reputation as the "Black Doctor." That status gives him "a high position amongst the servants" and provides him with the little bit of dignity which separates him somewhat from the rest of the black population.

Unfortunately, Sam is a buffoon. In the prelude to the tale, Brown relates his own adventures as a preparer of slaves for the market, and one of the responsibilities he had was shining the faces of the slaves so they would look younger and perhaps happier than they were in reality. Sam uses the same technique by assuming a self-image that unintentionally perpetuates the slaveholders' world. His self-image comes from doing the very best under the dehumanizing conditions in which he finds himself. Certainly, his job in the "big house" may be an easy one in comparison to that of other slaves, but it is still one in which he cannot claim himself as a man. He cannot choose, without his master's permission, the woman who will end his single status. He can only cut such a fine figure at the dinner table among the servants because his master has passed along to him the hand-me-down shirts and suits he no longer needs. Sam can play rooster among the hens in a barnyard which has been reduced to the size of his master's kitchen and must still be attentive to the sounds of the weasels just beyond its doors.

While it is Sam who will later lead a song in celebration of the master's death, it is done in the woods a long way from the house and in a dialect Brown has obviously superimposed upon the usual one in which Sam speaks. Sam progresses from making comments like "Pass dem pancakes and molasses up dis way, . . . and none of your insinawaysion here" (p. 100) to singing of his master's death in these words: "Come, all my brethren, let us take a rest, / While the moon shines so brightly and clear; / Old master is dead, and left us at last, / And has gone at the Bar to appear" (p. 118). In a novel which is pieced together from much historical information and without careful attention to chronology, it is not surprising that Brown would not retain consistency when he needed someone to lead a song after the master's death. And since Sam has been respected among the other slaves as a leader of sorts, that duty naturally falls to him. The point is that whether or not Sam slips in one scene in response to the master, he can never be his own master. Even his single status, which has sexuality and the possibility for courtship underlying it, does not undo his emasculation. For certain, many of the emasculated men of black American literature had families and children. Many times, it was because of their families that their emasculation had to continue. They knew they had to bow and scrape before the white masters and employers if they wanted anything for their families.

Sam, like his descendants, is emasculated because he cannot control his destiny to the extent that those in power above him can, and he can never claim property, a house, or the kind of job which should accrue to him by virtue of his masculinity—if standards for the rights of masculinity were uniformly applied across races and cultures in the United States. He must reign over the kitchen, not the parlor. His condition is defined by his slavery, but it is a condition which similarly defined the lifestyle of many free black men who followed Sam. Charles W. Chesnutt's works near the turn of the century are peopled with characters who exhibit various degrees of kinship to their formerly enslaved black brethren. The character of Sandy in *The Marrow of Tradition* (1901) is a more polished version of Sam in Brown's *Clotel*.[7] He wears the hand-me-downs from his former master with the stiffness of a maitre d'. He is more exacting in his claims to honor than are his former masters, but he is ultimately no more able after slavery than before to claim anything at all. When he is wrongly accused of a crime, he is not looked upon as an individual who has judged himself by certain standards and who has served his "white folks" faithfully. He is instead identified with the masses of Blacks.

Peter, another of Chesnutt's faithful servants of the Sandy variety, appears in *The Colonel's Dream* (1905).[8] Peter also continues to play a slave's role after the fact, and he finds his reason for being in caring for the young white boy who is placed in his charge. When he is killed in an attempt to rescue the child from an oncoming train, his years of effacing himself may be remembered, but they have not granted him the right to be buried in the white cemetery along with the body of the child. The white family's grateful burial of him there backfires in an unexpectedly graphic way: his body is dug up and the coffin deposited on Colonel French's porch. Defiled even in death, Peter serves to illustrate how far from being considered equal as humans are those Blacks who, to some extent, deny their own humanity. Perhaps that is precisely Chesnutt's point. When black males wield the knife against their own masculinity, is not their fate already sealed? Particularly if such knife-wielding occurs after slavery? Peter exists in a world which, from Chesnutt's point of view, offered Blacks the opportunity to move forward in terms of education and self-definition. That Peter continues to play voluntarily the role that he was forced to play in slavery makes him pathetic, but beyond much consideration past initial sympathy.

More pointedly didactic than Chesnutt, Richard Wright would portray these powerless black males with pencil-sharp vividness in the stories he wrote during the entrenchment of the sharecropping system. In the 1930s, sharecropping was as much a system of slavery as that state which had existed for Blacks in this country prior to 1860. Invisible chains of debt took the place of rope and shackles, but the mental state which existed during slavery did not change much. Blacks were still locked into circumstances from which few acceptable escapes existed. Men who may have been brave enough to steal away during the night could just as easily find themselves hanging from trees the next morning as to find themselves on new plantations which were really no better than the ones from which they escaped. Heir to a Mississippi in which race relations existed much as they had eight or ten decades before, Wright took his patrimony as his subject. His stories in *Uncle Tom's Children* (1938) carry the tone and mood of emasculation as surely as they exemplify the powerlessness of Wright's black male characters. Forced to depend for their very survival upon the whims of plantation owners, these men barely rise above the level of animals in the deterministic environment in which they find themselves. Ever subject to violence, they repeatedly discover that self-assertion means death. Death frequently waits in their paths whether or not they become assertive. Certainly that is the case with Mann, in "Down by the

Riverside."[9] His only concern in the story is with getting his pregnant wife to a hospital during a flood; the resulting chain of events
suggests that he would have been better off if he had simply let his
wife die at home. His ability to care for his family can never be severed from what he owes the whites and how he should react when
he is in their presence. He is not expected to feel for his family in
the same way that whites care for theirs, and when he does, they
quickly convey to him that he should have retained the animal
classification to which they had assigned him—beast of burden,
sexually active without emotional involvement, accepting the
death of a wife and child as if they were equivalent to the loss of
toenails.

The world Wright defines for black males is one in which they
are to be constantly on guard against the loss of manhood or to live
so self-effacingly with the whites that their masculinity has as little
attention called to it as possible. Non-threatening black men in
Wright's world can just as easily find themselves literally and figuratively emasculated as can assertive black males. The kinship they
share is one which resides in the heads of the whites with whom
they come into contact, and they can do little or nothing to keep
those chimeric images from bursting forth into white consciousness and leading to physical violence. Before any physical violence
occurs, they resemble in some ways the acquiescent characters created by Chesnutt.

The tradition of symbolic castration which can be seen in Brown,
Chesnutt, and Wright continues into the mid-twentieth century
with the character of Gabriel Grimes in *Go Tell It On the Mountain*
(1953) and with Grange Copeland and his son Brownfield in Alice
Walker's *The Third Life of Grange Copeland* (1970). Gabriel Grimes,
as the character of the harmless preacher, fits into one of the categories whites have been more willing, to some extent, to tolerate.
The notion of preachers being sexually harmless continues the idea
of emasculation, and the notion of preachers as holding back the
reins of black discontent suggests the kind of compromise which
will be treated in the following section with Bledsoe in Ralph
Ellison's *Invisible Man* (1952) and with Tyree Tucker in Richard
Wright's *The Long Dream* (1958). We all remember Gabriel as a
hellraiser within the black community in which he lives, and he
will grow to be a tyrant within his own family; however, to the
whites who reside near him, he is a "safe nigger" who can be counted
upon to do what is right during a period of racial unrest. When a
black soldier is killed in his community, Gabriel can go out to get
medicine for his wife in spite of the tension in the area. He passes

several groups of white men who look as if they are "itching" to kill
him, but who resist because they know he is a preacher. When
someone spits upon the sidewalk as he passes, he "heard it re-
provingly whispered behind him that he was a good nigger, surely
up to no trouble."[10] Though preachers as a group have certainly
played important roles in the political development of Blacks in
this country, it is no less true that the stereotyped image of the
chicken-eating preacher who goes humbly to the whites to seek
favors is another version of the hat-in-hand eunuch whom Sterling
Brown identified in his study so many years ago. The accuracy of
that evaluation is attested to by the way in which Gabriel chooses
to deal with whites on his job; he takes out whatever difficulty they
cause him in stern-handed displeasure toward his own family.
Logically, he may on occasion have to bow and scrape to keep his
job, but the fiery person he is shown to be in his home and community would suggest that it is simplistic to locate his actions with
whites solely in his desire for security. Perhaps partly out of his
own fears, he has given up a portion of his manhood; he regains
that which has been lost by lording it over his family and over the
poor sinners who dare to come before the throne of grace.

Grange Copeland and his son Brownfield fit into this category
of those who have been psychologically, socially, and politically
emasculated because of the sharecropping system under which
they initially live and work. It is a system that drains the life energy from men who must see reflected in the eyes of those for
whom they work the evaluation that they are less than human.
That evaluation combines with their own knowledge that they
can do very little to improve their situations and turns them, especially Brownfield, into self-destructive, brutalizing beasts. Richard
Wright's black sharecroppers seldom turn their frustrations toward
their own family members; but the men in *The Third Life of Grange
Copeland* find that one of the most satisfying releases available to
them. Grange makes his family suffer mentally, and Brownfield
makes his suffer physically. Witnessing his wife Margaret trying to
make a home out of a shack in a pasture, watching his son grow up
without the amenities of childhood, realizing that he is hopeless to
keep the plantation owner from taking Margaret to bed, Grange
deserts his family in that sharecropping first life and goes to New
York. His departure is a culmination of many things, for he has not
particularly cared that Margaret has taken to sleeping around (he
has been doing it for years); his leaving is the official recognition
that all his hopes for family life and security have dissolved. Before
his departure, however, he has been the victim as well as the vic-

timizer in what has happened to him. He has tried to escape his
mulish existence by drinking and by taking a lover in a town near
the plantation; it is in part because of both of these things that
Margaret shows so little resistance to the white man's sexual advances and to bearing an albino child by him. Powerless to change
the situation under which he must work and constantly feeling
himself being "screwed," Grange takes the one option he believes is
left to him: he leaves. In later years, he will realize that it was an
unmanly thing to do, that his not caring for his family and his very
leaving were indications of how severely he had allowed himself to
be dehumanized and emasculated. He says after he has returned
to Georgia many years later:

> "The crackers could make me run away from my wife, but where
> was the *man* in me that let me sneak off, never telling her nothing
> about where I was going, never telling her I forgave her, never tell-
> ing her how wrong I was myself? . . . And the white folks could
> have forced me to believe fucking a hundred strumpets was a sign
> of my manhood, . . . but where was the *man* in me that let me take
> Josie [the woman who had been his lover and to whom he is now
> married] here for such a cheap and low-down ride, when I didn't
> never care whether she lived or died, long as she did what I told her
> and I got me my farm!" [11]

Grange has allowed himself to be reduced to the level of bestiality
identified with engaging in sexual intercourse without caring for
the partner; through this reduction, he has stripped himself of
manhood by engaging in the very acts by which others had defined him.

On another level, Walker develops a different notion of sexuality
in the character of Grange. By allowing Grange to grow and become aware of what has happened to him, Walker approaches one
of James Baldwin's thematic concerns in suggesting that racial
power is equal to sexual power. If a man's ability to take care of his
family has been taken away, and if his very bed has been invaded
by the force which has refused him decent work, then he is truly
emasculated, and, by extension, literally without sexual power.
Grange may pursue Josie and make love to her, but that does not
change the fact that he has no control over his own bedroom and
over his own wife.

Through Grange's character, though, Walker also shows the ability of the black male to transcend those forces which have stripped
away so much of value to him. Grange holds a small portion of
himself free from that stripping long enough to find a base from

which to grow into manhood again. Unlike Grange, Brownfield, his son, never manages to rise above the evaluation of beast. He fails to see that he is in his situation as emasculated sharecropper in part because of his own inertia and in part because of the gripping reach of that system. However, he initially had a choice. Left alone at fifteen after Grange's departure and Margaret's poisoning of herself and the baby, Brownfield had found his way to another town and was given work. He could have kept going on to other things; instead, he started to enjoy being stud to Josie and her daughter Lorene. His fate was sealed when, in order to marry Mem, Josie's adopted school-teacher daughter, he went out and committed himself to sharecrop. What he thought would be a short period of time extended into years, during which he constantly blamed everyone except himself for the mess he had made of his life.

In Brownfield, Walker shows what can happen to the black male who thoroughly adopts someone else's definition of himself. Brownfield does the beastly things Captain Davis, Mr. J. L., and his other employers expect of him. When he finds he cannot escape poverty, degradation, and debt, "his crushed pride" and "battered ego" make him force Mem to leave her job as a teacher. He sets out to destroy her by being "her Pygmalion in reverse" (p. 55). He turns from accepting her corrections of his speech to insisting that she "talk like the *rest* of us poor niggers" (p. 56). He frightens his children into speechlessness and beats his wife unmercifully. On one Christmas Eve, when he has no money to buy presents for the children, he gets drunk and beats Mem senseless when she insists that the children are afraid of him. He knocks out one of her teeth and loosens "one or two more" (p. 58). Through extensive similar treatment, Mem becomes skinny and shockingly unattractive. Having transformed his wife into someone he despises, Brownfield will have no reluctance from this point on to beating her at will and to abusing her in whatever ways appeal to him. His bestial behavior also manifests itself in other ways. Walker reports that, for the fun of it, "he poured oil into streams to kill the fish and tickled his vanity by drowning cats" (p. 59). He literally becomes a monster who can sing "yessuhs" in chorus to the plantation owners for whom he works, but who beats his wife into ugliness, drives one of his daughters insane and another to prostitution. Brownfield voluntarily gives up all semblance of caring and all semblance of manhood. In a significant scene, Mem points out the precariousness of his gender role. After many years, she decides that she is going to move her daughters into town, and she explains to Brownfield her reasons for doing so:

"I have just about let you play man long enough to find out you ain't one." [P. 91]

"And just think of how many times I done got my head beat by you just so you could feel a little bit like a man, Brownfield Copeland." [P. 94]

"If you ever lays a hand on me again I'm going to blow your goddamn brains out—after I shoots off your balls, which is all the manhood you act like you *sure* you got." [P. 96]

Mem's one big outburst, her one solid instance of determination, is quickly pushed into the background as Brownfield pretends to do what she wants, gets her pregnant and weak, refuses to pay the rent or the heat in the new house, and drags her back to another ugly shack in the middle of somebody's cotton field. He cannot allow improvement in his status when it comes through Mem's efforts, so he reduces her to a condition which makes even him wince. His actions are frequently defined by childishness on the one hand, such as when he becomes jealous of his children when Grange brings them fruit and food, and bestiality on the other, such as when he kicks Mem across the floor during one of his frequent beatings of her. His final beastly act is to kill Mem with a shotgun blast in the face.

Brownfield's actions, frequently in the vein of the "bad nigger" who attempts to show others what a "man" he is, illustrate what can happen to the black man who equates his manhood with his humanity. When one is taken away, he gives up the other. From Walker's point of view, such a response is not acceptable. As long as black people live in America, they will be subjected to various pressures and crises; to give up caring for other Blacks simply because one cannot protest, go out and shoot an oppressor, or buy what one wants, is a sad illustration of the oppressor's triumph over black minds and hearts. Indeed, Walker suggests that Brownfield makes the whites into gods because of the power he assigns to them to control his every action. His brutal execution of power over his own family in a desperate effort to regain what he senses has been taken away from him makes him just as emasculated as a Sam, or a Peter, or a Sandy. He does to his own family what emasculated black men in other literary portraits do to the communities in which they live.

Trading Masculinity for Power

We may also view symbolic castration in more complex terms. By bowing and scraping to the right white men, some black men have been able to attain a measure of status and financial security within their own communities. They have traded outward signs of masculinity in dealing with the white world for the power that ac- crues to them in keeping the black community in line for the local whites. These are the men to whom the whites will come when there are signs of unrest; they are the ones the whites trust to know what black people are thinking and what it will take to keep them reasonably in their places. In exchange for being the big fly who swats the little flies, these performers must constantly walk a tight- rope to save face before both Blacks and whites, though certainly the opinions of the whites are infinitely more important to them. They may hate the way in which the whites with whom they deal call them "nigger" and "boy," or, derisively, "doctor" or "professor," but they will destroy any black individual who dares to stand in the way of the little bit of perverted power they do hold.

Psychological descendants of Booker T. Washington, these liter- ary paper tigers can be seen in Ralph Ellison's Bledsoe in *Invisible Man* (1952) and in Richard Wright's Tyree Tucker in *The Long Dream* (1958). By contrast, Dan Taylor, in Wright's "Fire and Cloud," is an example of one of the tightrope-walking power holders who decides to get off the tightrope by harnessing support from the community over which he is allowed to exert control. Before his change, how- ever, he had been comparable to the other men in being "allowed" to exert a certain amount of influence, including saving a young black man from a lynch mob.[12]

Dr. Bledsoe, president of the Tuskegee-like school in Ellison's novel, is a man who runs his college like an army camp. He must keep all his soldiers orderly and have them ready for inspection whenever any of his inquisitive benefactors should arrive from the North. He holds his position at the largesse of the whites who will support the school, but who have no interest in actually being on campus and running it. Therefore, they hire a "nigger driver," one who is loyal to their notions of what the school should accomplish in its academic programs and one who is personally ambitious enough not to endanger his own career by refusing to carry out their wishes. He must be so good in carrying them out, in fact, that he should anticipate what they want even before they articulate it. Bledsoe performs the role admirably. He does so, however, at the expense of a certain amount of inner dignity and at the expense of intrinsic respect for his own people. He comes to view them as the children who need herding and molding, and he does that without any particular love for them. In fact, he will chastize them even more severely than those for whom he works, for any blot they are allowed to place upon the school's record ultimately reflects upon him. He must keep his little bit of pasture clean, green, and impressive, and he carries out his obligations with a vengeance.

As the epitome of the emasculated man allowed to operate in his little space, Bledsoe, as seen by the students, faculty, and community, is someone to be envied. It is in part this envy which gives him a certain amount of power over his charges. They see before them a black man who has "made it," one who has pulled himself up from all the unfavorable connotations of his blackness and who has made a respectable place for himself in the world. He becomes a model for the students and a symbol of pride for his faculty, for they see him in the role of president, seldom in his hat-in-hand postures before the school's white benefactors. He demands and inspires awe and fear in the black people around him, and he operates with such an unassailable degree of self-contained dignity that he is almost a parody of himself.

For the invisible man, then, Bledsoe becomes one of those successful men whom he would like to emulate. His fear that he has put that possibility in jeopardy by driving Mr. Norton, a white trustee, to the cabin where the black Trueblood has told the story of incestuously impregnating his wife and daughter makes him anxious about Bledsoe's response. It simultaneously brings Bledsoe before him as the symbol of what he may have threatened by making the mistake with Norton. He visualizes Bledsoe as "the example of everything" he hopes to be:

> Influential with wealthy [white] men all over the country; consulted in matters concerning the race; a leader of his people; the possessor of not one, but *two* Cadillacs, a good salary and a soft, good-looking and creamy-complexioned wife. What was more, while black and bald and everything white folks poked fun at, he had achieved power and authority; had, while black and wrinkle-headed, made himself of more importance in the world than most Southern white men. They could laugh at him but they couldn't ignore him . . .[13]

And indeed they do not wish to ignore him. They wish to be in touch with him so that he can keep other Blacks in place for them. As is usual with the invisible man, he sees but he does not fully comprehend. Certainly the show-and-tell symbols of power are what Bledsoe would like everyone to reflect upon and appreciate; they suggest, as is implied in the invisible man's observation, that Bledsoe has escaped the pitfalls of his blackness. He has money and his two Cadillacs, but he also has what every black man should

want—a creamy-complexioned wife. Since white women are taboo, the next best thing is preferred.

The protagonist sees the indications of Bledsoe's way of thinking
and the source of his power, but, typically, he refuses to analyze beyond its surface meaning. Certainly the letters from the superin-
tendent have been significant in Bledsoe's treatment of the invisible man, for they have allowed him additional opportunity to do a
favor for white men he considers to have power and influence. Ap-
preciation of Bledsoe's power in the abstract is part of the unin-
formed portion of the invisible man's education; he will shortly see
another side of that power.

What the protagonist sees is the facade of the emasculated holder
of power. It is only after the fiasco at the Golden Day, the bar/
whorehouse to which he has taken Norton to recover from his encounter with Trueblood, that he will see the true Bledsoe, the man
who is willing to crush anyone into insignificance who dares to upset his hold on his school and the minds of the white men who support it. Bledsoe, like the "nigger driver," must punish the black individual who gets out of line so that he can retain his position as
"driver"; consequently, in that syndrome which has its basis in history, he becomes more exacting in his desire for punishment than
perhaps the offended white person would have been. Bledsoe believes that the invisible man should not simply be punished; he
should be broken completely and forever placed beyond the reach
of the school. If his association with the school is not dissolved, the
invisible man may return in the form of a nightmare threat to
Bledsoe's power, or Bledsoe may envision his white benefactors
keeping a scorecard of offenses against him, one which they will
pull out someday in the future and use to emasculate him a second
time by removing all of his bases of power. So he destroys others
before they have the opportunity to destroy him.

One side of Bledsoe is revealed in the scene in which he goes with
the invisible man to soothe Mr. Norton after their return to the
school, and the other is revealed when he later confronts the invisible man alone. With Norton, Bledsoe is the deferential eunuch,
overly solicitous, willing to do anything to please the white man
and to be forgiven for the offense which falls upon his head as
president of the school. His ability to assume the role necessary
is reflected in the change he undergoes before entering Norton's
room. From angry accusations and commands to the invisible
man, he transforms into an experienced mask-wearer, pausing and
composing "his angry face like a sculptor, making it a bland mask,
leaving only the sparkle of his eyes to betray the emotion" (p. 79)

the invisible man has seen so recently. Once in Norton's room, Bledsoe "rushes" forward with "a strange grandmotherly concern in his voice" (p. 80), and he proceeds to execute a masterful act:

> "Mr. Norton, *Mister Norton!* I'm so sorry," he crooned. "I thought I had sent you a boy who was careful, a sensible young man! Why we've never had an accident before. Never, not in seventy-five years. I assure you, sir, that he shall be disciplined, severely disciplined!" [P. 80]

"Grandmotherly" Bledsoe approaches the mammy figure in the extent of his concern for the white person who is in his care. His primary goal is to soothe Norton as the precious "child" whose welfare rests in his hands. To comfort the child, the grandmother must show him that the danger which threatened him is no longer real because grandmother has control over the boogieman. In Norton's presence, Bledsoe thus presents the invisible man as a villain who deserves no less than the severest of punishments. By so doing, he overshadows Norton's desire to forgive with his own evaluation that the offense is too great to leave unpunished. He is no longer the grandmother but is now the implacably stern father.

Alone with the invisible man later, Bledsoe is a combination of the authoritarian and the white oppressor. He greets the invisible man with derision for having "carried Mr. Norton out to the Quarters" and introducing him "to the quality" (p. 106). Bledsoe's sarcasm is a mere prelude to his wrath. He finds it difficult to believe that the invisible man could be so naive about dealing with whites, that he would respond so straightforwardly to "orders" and to a desire to "please" the white man. Bledsoe's education about one of his favored juniors, however, is matched only by what the invisible man learns about his president. Bledsoe calls him a "nigger" when he insists that no one has "told" him to drive Norton to Trueblood's shack and demands that he tell the truth. Shocked out of a verbal response, the invisible man can only think: *"That . . . He called me that"* (p. 107). He begins to see that Bledsoe has no respect for black people. In the ensuing conversation, when Bledsoe learns of the discussion with the vet at the Golden Day, he concludes: "A Negro like that should be under lock and key" (p. 108). He executes his belief, for that same vet is on the bus going north with the invisible man, a testament to Bledsoe's power over Blacks.

Reacting to Bledsoe's conclusion that he must be "disciplined"—in spite of the promise to the contrary made to Norton—the invisible man's education about Bledsoe continues as he threatens to "fight" and to "tell everybody" of Bledsoe's duplicity. Bledsoe calls him a "fool" and mocks his ignorance about "how things are done down here" (p. 109). Whites, he tells the invisible man, may support the school, but he controls it by being subservient when necessary and by being confident in his power. His final declaration about his position is most revealing: "I'll have every Negro in the country hanging on tree limbs by morning if it means staying where I am" (p. 110). Part of what Bledsoe says is true, and part of it is meant to threaten the still impressionable invisible man. Certainly Bledsoe has power, but he is not independently powerful. Then, too, in spite of his claims to the contrary, he does not want the invisible man spouting off accusations to anyone. The extent to which he wants to get rid of him is revealed later in the destructive letters he writes to the invisible man's prospective employers. Perhaps the truest thing he says is the comment about hanging; he will indeed sacrifice anyone who stands in his way in order to retain the position he has, no matter that it has stripped him of much human dignity and that it has made him uncaring about other black people.

Viewed as an insignificant fly which needs to be swatted out of the way, the invisible man is only a little test for Bledsoe's power. Mindful of protecting his flank, yet recognizing that the invisible man is not a formidable opponent, Bledsoe defeats him with a maliciousness born of a touch of humor. He joins the many others in the invisible man's life who determine to "keep this nigger boy running." Bledsoe sends him to New York and gives him hope as distant as the horizon that he may one day be able to return to school. Unaccustomed to witnessing such power, the invisible man will go through many days of rejection in New York before he finally begins to see the light. Just as with many other incidents in his episodic life, the protagonist may learn something from his experience with Bledsoe, but he has not in any way affected the latter's hold on his little black empire.

His rather extreme reaction to the invisible man's encounter with Mr. Norton underscores the precariousness of the power Bledsoe wields. At any moment, through any unexpected whim, Bledsoe may find himself no longer in control of what he values most. That insecurity, even when it hides behind the face of security, reveals even further the extent of Bledsoe's emasculation. Even as he shapes lives and plans futures, he can never be in control of himself or of his environment. Someone else will continue to shape the reality he will adopt as his own. Someone else will continue to pull his puppet strings and make him dance upon request. His is the house of illusion which he can operate only because the master illusionist prefers not to be bothered with petty details.

We see a lot more of Tyree Tucker in the world he has created for himself in Richard Wright's *The Long Dream* (1958) than we see of Bledsoe.[14] Tyree Tucker is distinguished, for a "nigger" and a "boy," on the basis of his funeral parlor and other investments, and he is the black individual to whom whites come to gauge sentiments of other Blacks. First of all, Tyree has chosen a "permissible" profession: undertaking has long been recognized as a business which does not cross racial lines. Somebody has to bury Blacks, he concludes at one point, and whites are not going to touch dead Blacks: "They wouldn't touch a black man's dead body even to make money, so they let me bury 'em" (p. 65). Therefore, his business is "right" for not bringing possible offense to the whites—preachers and undertakers almost always fall into the same category of exclusion, but they can slip from that category if they push their achieved status too far.

Like Bledsoe, Tyree likes being at the top of the black community, likes having the house, car, and money to which other Blacks point with envy. He recognizes more clearly, however—and is willing to admit—that he is where he is because of white sufferance and not solely out of his own enterprise. When a young man in his community is discovered with a white woman, Tyree is as anxious to get his own son home to safety as is any father in the black community. With him, the surrender of manhood for power is much more clearly revealed than it is with Bledsoe. We see Tyree's awareness of his susceptibility even as he plays the dangerous game of one-upmanship with the local whites. He understands, too, that if his son ever gets into trouble because of a white woman, there is little he will be able to do to help him:

> "Son," he said slowly, "soon sap's going to rise in your bones and you going to be looking at women. . . . Look, son, BUT DON'T LOOK WHITE! YOU HEAR?" [P. 64]

His surprisingly understanding, almost forgiving attitude once the black offender has been killed by mob action reflects his perception of the world in which he is forced to live:

> "They killed 'im . . . And I'm *glad!*"
> "Don't say that," Emma reproved him.
> "Papa!" Fishbelly sang out his astonishment.
> "Yeah. I know. You think I'm hard to say anything like that. . . . But I know what I'm saying. It's a good thing he's dead. . . . Lissen: when them white folks git all roused, when they start thinking of us like black devils, when they start being scared of their own shadows, and when they git all mixed up in their minds about their

women—when that happens they want *blood*! And won't nothing on this earth satisfy 'em but some *blood*! And there can't be no peace in this town 'less they git their *blood*! When white folks feel like that, *somebody*'s got to die! Emma, it was either you, me, or Fish—. . . or *some*body! . . . We can live only if we give a little of our lives to the white folks. That's all and it's the truth." [P. 70]

Perhaps we gasp in horror and reject Tyree's philosophy, especially since this is early in the story and we have not yet seen anything of him which would merit our respect. We will discover, though, that that evaluation comes from over twenty years of being the "chosen black spokesman" for his community and from dealing behind the scenes with the police and the mayor. His brutal honesty indicates his determination to survive in the jungle he has inherited. Like Bledsoe, he did not make the world, and he is not overly concerned with the loss of dignity and altruism it has exacted from him.

Too young to fully understand the workings of the world into which he is born, Fishbelly, Tyree's son, will judge his father to be "castrated" long before he sees him cowering before whites. There are many scenes in which we are given opportunities to see Tyree lording his commanding presence over Blacks and, conversely, groveling before the whites when it is necessary for him to do so. It is necessary because he operates, with the permission of the chief of police, a string of whorehouses, the profits from which are shared with the chief. He is also allowed to operate a dance hall and bar, in spite of its violations of fire regulations, with the nod of the chief and the fire department. His work with the "syndicate" in his area enables him to retain the position of power and respect which makes him so enviable to other Blacks. His ultimate loyalties, in terms of material acquisitions, are to himself and to his family; he is almost overly attentive in trying to educate his son in the ways of the white world. Fish accuses his father of being "scared" of whites and considers his father's life "hopeless" until he is given the opportunity to see the inside of Tyree's relationship with some of the town's most powerful whites, especially the chief of police. He comes to understand that his father is a master at deception, a master at cajoling, pleading and crying when necessary to try to get what he wants. The difference between the Tyree who performs with these folks and the Tyree who runs the funeral parlor is the difference between a worm and a butterfly.

In an extensively drawn-out scene (pp. 237–51) in which Tyree pleads with the chief of police to save him from prosecution after his dance hall has burned down and killed forty-two people, the role Tyree plays with the whites is made repulsively vivid. Tyree moves from offering the chief a drink, to melodramatic histrionics, to crying, begging, pleading, and finally to falling to the floor, grabbing the chief's pant leg, and crawlingly exhorting his assistance. The culmination of his act is so powerful that even Fish is moved beyond his usual attitude toward his father. Tyree springs "tigerishly forward, sliding to the floor and grabbing hold of the chief's legs" (p. 250). He declares that he is "lost" unless the chief helps him. Prostrating himself without restraint, and begging without shame, Tyree succeeds in fascinating everyone in the room. Fish observes "two Tyrees: one was a Tyree resolved unto death to save himself and yet daring not to act out his resolve; the other was a make-believe Tyree, begging, weeping—a Tyree who was a weapon in the hands of the determined Tyree" (p. 251). He watches the chief being drawn into Tyree's act and observes that the "terrible stare" in his eyes is "evenly divided between hate and pity" and that "the chief could just have easily drawn his gun and shot Tyree as he could have embraced him" (p. 251). Tyree's performance is so effective that the chief actually resigns himself to trying to stack a jury in Tyree's favor; after all, Tyree and Dr. Bruce are to be tried; the chief will never be implicated publicly.

At once powerful and revolting, the scene reveals several things about the man who has traded masculinity for power. First of all, no matter how artful his performance, he is forced to grovel, forced to present himself as less than a man before an individual who has the power of life and death over him. Surely he has done what the chief wanted by running the dance hall and giving the chief his share, but he has done that with the knowledge that he was the weaker and the expendable partner. His compromise has given him status within the black community, but he has nothing which will help him beyond that community; the chief's initial advice to Tyree is that he sell all his property and prepare to fight his case in court (the mayor will later give him the same advice). He concludes from this that the whites have changed the rules of the game. When he is no longer of use to them, they plan not only to send him to jail, but to take his property in the process. Twenty years of cooperation have not erased the essential instability of the relationship or the possibility that it could be dissolved on a moment's whim by any of the white men. Thus Tyree finds himself another tightrope walker in a world where the skill required to perform that feat may not ultimately save one.

The analogy to master and slave is appropriate here, for Tyree, like John in the many tales told about his encounters with old master, must recognize the limits of his ability to push for his own security. A dangerous game, the one he plays must be timed perfectly, and even that perfection is no guarantee of winning. As Addison Gayle recognizes, however, there is no greater master of role-playing than Tyree; consequently, if he fails, what can be the fate of other black men who dare to play similar roles? Wright, Gayle asserts,

> sees Tyree as an artist, one who has perfected the art of survival, who has discovered the key to dealing with white folks: "Obey em! . . . Don't dispute em! Don't talk back to em. Don't give em no excuse for nothing. . . . Say 'yessir' and 'nawsir' to em. And when they talking, keep your mouth shut." In this universe, life depends upon man's talent at mimicry, his ability to perform roles perfectly, to be continuously creative, to lie to white people who want and expect the lie: survival means that one must act in such a manner that one's performance becomes flawless, while being able at all times to distinguish between the role and one's own identity.
>
> Tyree is the master mimic, and the talents he exercises so well, he wishes to pass down to his son, in much the same way that one leaves a rich inheritance.[15]

We have seen Tyree in his greatest performance; unfortunately, it begins the series of events which will lead to his death, not to peace with the chief. Finally, Tyree understands that his act has not worked well enough for him to trust his life to the chief, so he decides to turn over to a local prosecutor the canceled checks with which he has paid bribes to the chief. That act brings about his shooting death and reiterates the point that the black man who trades an outward show of masculinity for power from the whites can never become complacent in the relationship he has with them.

Gayle's comment about distinguishing role from identity is not as clear-cut with Tyree as he suggests. Certainly Tyree knows where he is in relationship to the chief, but his son and his wife do not for most of the novel. Fishbelly's youth is a possible motive for his being kept ignorant, but that does not explain why Tyree keeps all his affairs hidden from his wife. Instead of trusting her, he views her as a pathetic, church-going buffoon who is more a burden than a wife; the origins of his contempt are not made clear. Tyree begins the process of transferring what he knows and how he operates to his son, but he is killed before that process is complete. The point is, then, that if role and identity must somehow be meshed even within the black community, where does one leave off and the other begin?

Life for the emasculated, powerful black man becomes, to a large extent, one of isolation. He is forever thinking, planning, calculating his next move against or with the whites; little of his time is available for family activities or simply for relaxation. He is as forever on guard as were the slaves who followed Harriet Tubman out of Maryland. It is never clear where Tyree finds comfort, for even his satisfaction with the respect his neighbors pay him must be tinged with the bittersweet memories of the unstable base on which it rests. Though Tyree seems secure and unassailable from the outside, he is just as vulnerable to symbolic castration as is Bledsoe, and he is just as willing to sacrifice other Blacks to keep his position.

When the men are looking for someone to take the blame for the fire at the Grove dance hall, Fish, desperate to help his father, casually suggests that they claim that Fats, the manager, received the fire violation notices and ignored them because he cannot read; Fats also has a jail record. Tyree accepts the suggestion with glee and leaps "monkeylike" across the room, grabbing the phone and encouraging the chief to inquire from the hospital about Fats's condition. Keenly disappointed that Fats died a short time before, Tyree will shortly launch into his final performance for the chief. Neverthless, his willingness to put the blame on Fats and to pay him for going to jail in his stead ties him to Bledsoe's willingness to sacrifice the invisible man's education in order to maintain the status quo. Tyree is perhaps a bit more tolerable than is Bledsoe, but they are cut from the same cloth.

Both men are afraid of being toppled from their little thrones of power within the black community. No matter what their activity, they are ultimately passive in relation to the whites who have control over them. They can be acted upon; their ability to act upon those to whom they owe their power can be acceptable if it is benign and negated if it is not. When Tyree becomes a potential threat to the police, he is summarily executed; whatever he could do to them will never be matched by the finality of his death. Both he and Bledsoe, though they play their games under slightly different circumstances, are finally reduced to an ugly kinship. Bledsoe's control of his genteel, middle-class college is finally no more respectable or secure than is Tyree's control over his whorehouses; the games each man must play to stay where he is are tied together by history: both have given their balls to white men and should not be surprised if they are handed back on something less than a silver platter.

"O Lord, Will I Ever?"

If black men can be made into eunuchs through the general conditions under which they are forced to live with their own people,
they immediately fear castration when they find themselves accidentally in the presence of white women. Those who are voluntarily in their presence are no less susceptible to some vague notion of
having trod upon territory which is not permitted to them without
consequences. Richard Wright's story, "The Man Who Killed A
Shadow," vividly illustrates the simultaneous uneasiness and degradation black males frequently feel in the presence of white females. Saul, like so many Wright characters and several other literary figures, and like so many black men historically, is acutely
uncomfortable in the job he has cleaning a library in the National
Cathedral in which the only other person usually present is the
white female librarian. Working class and basically inarticulate,
Saul feels the history which weighs down upon him as a black
man. He knows that white men believe he is inferior to them, and
he knows that fear is his dominant emotion, yet it is more generalized than specific. He is numbed into seeing himself on one side
of the sharp division between black and white; consequently, it is
not immediately relevant to him when he gets warning of how that
vast "white shadow-world" could affect him individually:

> Even when he was told about the hard lives that all Negroes lived,
> it did not worry him, for he would take a drink and not feel too
> badly. It did not even bother him when he heard that if you were
> alone with a white woman and she screamed, it was as good as
> hearing your death sentence, for, though you had done nothing, you
> would be killed.[16]

Numbed into further silence because he can do nothing to prevent
police cars from screaming into the Black Belt, Saul develops an
additional detachment that removes him almost as far from his
own emotional life as Wright's narration removes him from us.
Saul's life is related with sketchy inevitability, with declarative, in-
formational sentences sealing his fate almost as surely as the deterministic mode which pervades the story. To be black and male is to
be fenced in, chained inside of emotional responses and eternally
frustrated by the ever-present fear those outside can evoke in one.
   As long as Saul can drown his sorrows in whiskey and move list-
lessly from job to job, his life plods on, and he has no reason to
single himself out as being any different from the mass of his buddies with whom he drinks and tries to forget his very existence.

When the white librarian forces him to notice her, however, his troubles begin. Like two stylized actors upon a stage which has history and custom as its backdrops, the black man and the white woman are instantly in conflict with each other. The white woman, still a virgin at forty, perhaps believes she can induce the black man to remove that stigma from her. She complains that he does not clean under her desk, an action which brings a reprimand from his employer and forces Saul to pay attention when she asks that he perform that job. The white woman relies upon her stereotypical notion of the black man's sexual prowess in an effort to force him to acquiesce in seducing her. When he is confused, fearful, and hesitant, she must push the issue because she has gone beyond the role usually assigned to her and cannot return to her sanctuary without feeling as if she has exposed or compromised herself. Her initial exposure—the baring of flesh—will become psychological and racial, and that is something she cannot tolerate. On the other hand, what Saul sees in the initial exposure begins for him the process of moving from generality to individuality. The woman sits "with her knees sprawled apart and her dress was drawn halfway up her legs" (p. 163). Her "pink panties" are visible, but her face is "beet red," and she sits "very still, rigid, as though she was being impelled into an act which she did not want to perform but was being driven to perform" (p. 163). Her posture shocks Saul into immobility.

Having demanded that Saul "clean" under her desk, and having exposed herself so that the "cleaning" takes on sexual overtones, the woman is not prepared to tolerate Saul's hesitancy. Obviously an outsider in her own community, she nevertheless has the whiteness which she hopes will cow Saul into acquiescence. She may consider him beneath her socially and racially, and perhaps even less than human, but she needs him to assist in her progression to a level of humanity she has not known—that of sexual experience. To have made such a request of such a person has made her vulnerable beyond compromise; Saul must, from her point of view, do as she says, or pay the consequences. Therefore, when he insists that he has cleaned under her desk that morning and questions her "making trouble" for him, she is adamant about her suggestive request: "'Why don't you do your work?' she blazed at him. 'That's what you're being paid to do, you black nigger!' Her legs were still spread wide and she was sitting as though about to spring upon him and throw her naked thighs about his body" (p. 163).

Thus caught in a situation from which he cannot escape into the masses of Blacks, or seek advice from his drinking buddies, Saul is forced to deal with the state of affairs as an individual. Angered by the woman's insult, he slaps her, and she screams. That individual action and her response make him immediately aware of the history of chimeric responses he has evoked in the woman and in himself; his reaction conveys that history:

> She was backing away from him, toward an open window at the far end of the room, still screaming. Oh God! In her scream he heard the sirens of the police cars that hunted down black men in the Black Belts, and he heard the shrill whistles of white cops running after black men and he felt again in one rush of emotion all the wild and bitter tales he had heard of how whites always got the black who did a crime and this woman was screaming as though he had raped her. [P. 164]

The racial memory her screams evoke in Saul leads to the woman's murder. His inarticulateness makes him incapable of verbally calming her down, and perhaps his lack of words underscores how ineffective they would be. In order to prevent her from screaming, he beats her to death with a piece of firewood, telling himself that it is the signaling scream he wants to stop; he is almost oblivious to the fact that he is taking a life in the process.

Saul's fate is sealed in the same way is that of Bigger Thomas, simply by virtue of his having been in the presence of a white woman at the wrong time. That situation is as precarious as is the woman's change of mood from wanting Saul's sexual favors to being afraid of the very thing she has wanted. She has barely said anything to him during the entire time he has worked in the library, and it is a measure of her socialization that the only way in which she conceives of communicating with him is in sexual terms. Earle V. Bryant discusses the sexual dimensions of the interaction between Saul and the woman in a recently published article.[17] According to Bryant, Saul has no interest in the "shadow-woman"; it is her sexual stereotyping which causes the incident and her death. The question of sexual *interest*, however, is ultimately not a concern to the powers who can mete out punishment. What is important to them is that the black man violated their concept of his place by being near the white woman in a situation containing the *possibility* of sexual contact. That in itself seals his death warrant. Referring to the white woman as the "Great Taboo" for black men, Bryant capsulizes Saul's predicament with the white woman and the general predicament in which most black men in this country find themselves.

> In attempting to silence the shadow-woman, then, Saul is impelled
> by a keen awareness of the taboo white society has placed on black
> male-white female encounters that have even a hint of the sexual
> about them, and by an equally keen awareness of the consequences
> that await any black male brash enough to "step out of line" with a
> white woman.[18]

Not killed as summarily as some other Wright characters would
be, Saul is nevertheless destined for death. His fear in the presence
of the white woman underscores the plight all black men must suffer who, through circumstances or will, find themselves in this
uniquely tabooed trap of history and custom.

Many black male characters in other literary works echo the uneasiness Saul feels in the presence of the white woman. The invisible man, in Ellison's novel, has a hysterically humorous reaction
to the predicament. When he is forced to press his body against
that of a huge white woman on his first subway ride in New York,
he wants to scream out to the passengers around him that he is
touching the woman against his will. His Southern upbringing
tells him he is in a situation which violates everything he knows
should define his actions; therefore, he extricates himself from the
woman and the subway as quickly as possible.

The same situation—a Southern black man in the North on
public transportation with a white woman—occurs in Charles W.
Chesnutt's "Uncle Wellington's Wives," and elicits a similar response from the man. Wellington, having decided to leave his black
wife and go north in search of adventure and the possibility of getting a white wife, is initially no less afraid to sit next to a huge
white woman on a street-car. He overcomes his fear—and then
only slightly—when the car lurches and he is thrown into the lap
of the huge woman.[19] Wellington's and the invisible man's senses of
being out of place with the white women are no less matched by
Bigger Thomas's encounter with Mary Dalton, though certainly the
tone of fear and the possibility for violent reprisal is much more
acutely presented in Wright's than in Ellison's or Chesnutt's work.[20]
These men share their blackness, their maleness, and the taboos
which have defined both in the United States; whether their reactions to white women at any given moment are hilarious or serious, they know that the "second sight" they carry with them
about their place in the world serves them in good stead in more
instances than not.

In Chester Himes's *If He Hollers Let Him Go* (1945), Robert (Bob)
Jones, the protagonist, works not only to overcome his fear of the

white woman, but to destroy her in the process; both efforts become definitions of manhood and means of overcoming a fear of castration. In James Baldwin's *Another Country* (1962), Rufus Scott actually makes the step of mentally destroying the white woman with whom he has an affair. The fascinating point about his case is that, though there are technically no "legal lynchers" to punish him, he is so awed by his own violation of taboo and so warped by his tendency to violence that he kills himself. By so doing, he in effect takes over the function of the mob; during and after his affair with white Leona, he becomes so violent and obsessively self-destructive that it is impossible for him to live a peaceful and healthy life. Consequently, he punishes himself for accomplishing the very destruction—making Leona pay for loving a black man— he has set out as his objective.

Rufus and Bob Jones differ from most black male characters treated in this discussion in that they are initially confident in their masculinity and in their abilities to deal with the white women at the basic male/female level. As overtones of race and sexual stereotyping enter into their relationships, however, they find themselves heir to many of the emotions which have defined their literary relatives. Their confidence is undermined and they become just as vulnerable to the forces within and outside them as are the other characters. Bob must finally confront the legal system and be offered the choice of going into the Army or into prison as a result of being accused of raping a white woman; the war option "saves" him, because the judge and lawyers are in cahoots to send black men to the service as long as it will keep white men out. Rufus, who initially uses sexual mastery over Leona to prove to her what a man he is, is eventually bogged down in the insecurity and degradation he feels when he walks down the street with Leona in the Village; eyes of whites convey to him that, though he walks with the white woman, he is still a "nigger" and still barely a grade above the animals.[21]

Himes's hero exudes more confidence than one would perhaps expect in a black male character in a fictional world set in the early 1940s. Bob goes from Cleveland to California and finds work in a shipyard. His physique is one reason for his confidence:

> When I came out to Los Angeles in the fall of '41, I felt fine about everything. Taller than the average man, six feet two, broad-shouldered, and conceited, I hadn't a worry. I knew I'd get along. If it had come down to a point where I had to hit a paddy I've had hit him without any thought. I'd have busted him wide open because he was a paddy and needed busting.[22]

The physique which induces such pride in him will provide part of the evidence which will make his guilt so easy to assert in the rape case, for how could some poor defenseless white thing, no matter how large, protect herself against this hulking brute? He may no longer be in the wilds of Africa, or in the illiteracy of slavery, but he is still on the rampage against the virtue of white females. As his body becomes a case against him in the series of events which lead to the accusation of rape, Bob is caught between attempts to efface himself and a simmering rage that he should be so facilely intimidated on his job.

Prior to the incident with the white woman, however, the racist atmosphere at the shipyard has rather quickly changed Bob's consistent good feelings about himself to ones in which his actions are undercut by a foreboding fear. Each morning he wakes to it seeping into his skull and spine, spreading to his groin "with an almost sexual torture," and settling in his stomach "like butterfly wings" (p. 2). He lives "scared, walled in, locked up" (p. 4). Every day is a fight, even when he is tired of fighting; every day is filled with some tension-ridden encounter with a white person. No wonder, then, Bob has such a difficult time on his job. The tension increases when he is promoted to "leaderman" of a "coloured gang": many of the whites believe that no black man should have such a job. Consequently, the ones who must assist his gang are reluctant to do so, and those who are superior to him never stop viewing him as an oddity they are forced to tolerate. The ship thus provides an ideal setting for the white woman to act out her little play with Bob and to call the mob of white shipyard workers to her rescue.

Bob's story, related in the first person, captures his frustration with the world in which he must live and with himself for not being more readily able to adapt to that world. If he could be an Uncle Tom, or even a Sandy, he might be able to save himself. His fight, as Richard Yarborough points out in a recent article on the novel, is that of a black American who discovers that the American Dream does not apply to him.[23] Each time he tries to get a piece of that American pie, he finds that the rats have nibbled it down to a crust, or that it sits in a window, beckoning him with its beautiful flakiness, forever just out of his reach. Though he prides himself on being a man in America, where manly attributes are desirable in the abstract, Bob beats his head against a stone wall each time he tries to make those abstractions exist in his own world.

Wanting to assert his manhood, yet trapped by his history, Bob finds himself stymied when he would like to be assertive. His first sustained encounter with Madge, the white woman, shows that inactivity as well as a range of emotions informed by history and popular culture. Disgusted by her phoniness, aware of their joint stereotypes from history, angered that she is teasing him, Bob is nevertheless simultaneously attracted to the woman. His recognition that she is not the fairest of the flowers of her sex cannot abate that almost irresistible feeling, and it is perhaps only a small part of the disgust he feels with himself for having been so emotionally manipulated.[24] At least thirty, and a "peroxide blonde with a large-featured, overly made-up face" and blue babyish eyes "mascaraed like a burlesque queen's" (p. 19), the woman goes into "a frightened, wide-eyed look" when she sees Bob, as if she were a "naked virgin" and he were "King Kong." She repeats the act each time she sees Bob, but on one occasion it evokes a more complex and confusing response from him:

> But now it sent a blinding fury through my brain. Blood rushed to my head like gales of rain and I felt my face burn white-hot. It came up in my eyes and burned at her; she caught it and kept staring at me with that wide-eyed phoney look. Something about her mouth touched it off, a quirk made the curves change as if she got a sexual thrill, and her mascaraed eyelashes fluttered.
>
> Lust shook me like an electric shock; it came up in my mouth, filling it with tongue, and drained my whole stomach down into my groin. And it poured out of my eyes in a sticky rush and spurted over her from head to foot.
>
> The frightened look went out of her eyes and she blushed right down her face and out of sight beneath the collar of her leather jacket, and I could imagine it going down over her over-ripe breasts and spreading out over her milk-white stomach. When she turned out of my stare I went sick to the stomach and felt like vomiting. I had started toward the ladder going to the upper deck, but instead I turned past her, slowing down and brushing her. She didn't move. I kept on going, circling. [P. 19]

Known as a ladies' man among his buddies, one who can handle any woman with minimal effort, Bob shows here how easily his confidence can be undermined and what a mixture of emotions he can be made to feel about this white woman from Texas.

The two are set up as antagonists—by virtue of sex, color, and stereotypes. Their repeated encounters will be a series of little dramas, and both of them will be conscious of acting out the roles history has determined that they should play. Underneath the role-playing is an attraction that Bob recognizes and that the woman will later show is mutual. The fact of that attraction, however, pales in comparison to the attitudes they would have to exorcise from themselves and those they would have to change in the society around them before they could possibly have a chance of getting to know each other simply as two human beings. Unfortunately, such tasks are impossible for them, and they join Saul and the librarian in responding to each other as racial and sexual stereotypes.

Racial stereotyping is apparent when Bob needs a "tacker" for the mechanics in his gang and discovers that Madge is the only one available. After being coaxed out of her frightened act, she maintains that she "ain't gonna work with no nigger!" (p. 27). Responding impulsively, Bob retorts: "Screw you then, you cracker bitch," at which she asks the two white mechanics working with her: "You gonna let a nigger talk tuh me like that?" (p. 27). In this brief encounter, Bob's authority has been insultingly undercut, and he is further reduced to being placed in a confining, "niggerish" category from which, to the woman's mind, he deserves no consideration, let alone respect. Having been called to action by their history, the two elderly white mechanics near Madge only make a half-hearted attempt to support her before Bob departs. Her knowledge that they will attempt to respond, however, is what gives Madge the edge in her later encounter with Bob. If it comes down to a matter of black and white, with sexual dynamics thrown in, then the white woman will win every time. Bob may relieve his frustration by cursing her, but he is the one who is reprimanded for his action; nothing is said to Madge about her having failed to perform a job for a leaderman. And not only is Bob reprimanded; he is demoted to mechanic, and he gets no redress from his union when he complains of the injustice.

Very early in the novel, therefore, Madge becomes the backdrop against which many of Bob's actions are carried out. His rage at her makes him stalk a white man with whom he has had a fight. It also makes him difficult with his girlfriend Alice, and it intensifies that general foreboding fear he has felt so consistently since his arrival at the shipyard. Madge becomes for him a specific symbol of all that has been denied to him on his job because of race, as well as a general symbol of his condition as a black man in a country made for whites. "When I thought about Madge," Bob says, "that cold scare settled over me and I began to tremble. Just scared to think about her, about living in the same world with her. Almost like thinking about the electric chair. I knew if I kept sitting there thinking about her I'd get up and go out to the shipyard and kill her" (p. 71). Another assertion that comes to naught, it nevertheless illustrates the constant state of near neurosis which characterizes Bob.

His encounters with Madge perpetuate his uncertainty about how to deal with her. She goes from her initial pretended terror—an act usually put on for the benefit of white workers nearby—to having a "friendly" lunch on board ship with him. Bob attempts to dismiss her to his fellow workers and to assume a tone of masculine solidarity, but finds instead the white world united against him. In response to one of Madge's performances of simulated terror, Bob says, "get a load of this," to a coworker and finds the man "studying" him "with that sharp speculating curiosity of white men watching Negroes' reactions to white women" (p. 117). Adding fuel to the fire which will inflame the mob later on, Madge uses history to her advantage again and again. When Bob tries to confront her alone to get the matter straightened out between them, when he plans to use his masculinity to get the better of her ("let's stop all this jive and get together like we want"), he cannot execute his plan: "But when I got to her I lost my nerve. I couldn't say a word. I just couldn't do it, that was all. She was pure white Texas. And I was black. And a white man was standing there. I never knew before how good a job the white folks had done on me" (p. 124). Bob feels "absolutely subhuman" for being such a "coward," but he cannot bring himself to confront the woman, not even when she "sneers" with the knowledge that she is perfectly aware of his unexecuted intentions. She uses her whiteness, he surmises, like the flag before a bull:

> And that was what scared me. Luring me with her body and daring me with her colour. It ate into me, made me want her for her colour, not her body. In order to have her I'd have to challenge her colour; I couldn't take the dare. . . . So I went outboard and down the wooden gangway, roughing people out of the way. I felt castrated, snake-bellied, and cur-doggish, I felt like a nigger being horse-whipped in Georgia. Cheap, dirty, low. I wanted to grab some bastard and roll him down the stairs. My face felt tight. The taste of white folks was in my mouth and I couldn't get it out.
>   What I ought to do is rape her, I thought. That's what she wanted. [P. 126]

The almost tangible sign-posts Madge places around herself through her color serve as their own form of emasculation as far as Bob is concerned, thereby further diminishing his ability to deal with the woman. Her color combines with her teasing attitude a short while later when she eats her lunch on the deck, invites Bob to join her (pretending initially that she has not recognized him as the "boy" with whom she has had the fight earlier), and almost bares her breasts in front of him to arouse him sexually.

Thus thrown off guard once again about Madge's intentions, Bob decides to see her in her own territory, in the hotel room she has rented. He finally gets in, and in a long scene (pp. 144–48) in which they act out their aggressions and attractions toward each other, the perverted psychosexual dynamics of race relations are made clear. During a physical struggle, Madge "dares" Bob to force her sexually, maintaining that she will get him "lynched right here in California" (p. 146). She calls him a "cruel black bastard" and claims that all "niggers" do is "lie up and get drunk and dream of having white women." Though she asserts she is a "Christian woman," she opens her robe, exposes her nakedness, and taunts Bob with the "beautiful," "pure white" figure she maintains will get him "lynched in Texas." Repulsion, attraction, playfulness and danger underlie the "game" they play until, in another struggle, Madge says, "All right, rape me then, nigger!" (p. 147). Brought to his senses by the word "rape," and conscious of his increasing degradation, Bob escapes from the room only to have the woman follow and try to continue the "seduction" scene. His hasty drive away from her can only fire her anger, for now that she clearly wants him, he should be sensible enough, from her point of view, to follow through with the act.

Alone with Bob in her room, Madge can tease him and use her power over him in provocative ways. When they are alone in a cabin on the ship the next day, her power over him is cold, detached, traditionally in the vein of the threatened white woman who cries out for help against a rapist. Bob has come to the cabin and accidentally discovered Madge sleeping there. It is to her, and especially his, misfortune that she closes the door and tries to continue her seduction. When voices are heard in the hallway in an area where all doors should be open, attempted seduction on her part becomes attempted rape on his. She plays her role well, screaming out to the questioning voices beyond the door,

> *"Help! Help! My God, help me! Some white man, help me! I'm being raped!"* [P. 180]

Having set up the call and the color to defend honor, Madge makes the contrast complete as Bob, too stunned to respond, feels a "cold numbing terror" sweeping over him in paralyzing "waves":

> *"Stop, nigger! Don't, nigger! Nigger, don't! Oh, please don't kill me, nigger. . . ."* [P. 180]

Racial lines having been drawn, and the sexual dimension added, it is only a matter of time before Bob's fate will be sealed. He knows that, but he is powerless to fight the forces which are now madly torching through the locked door. He turns his anger upon Madge instead:

> Abruptly a raw wild panic exploded within me. The overwhelming fear of being caught with a white woman came out in me in a great white flame. I gave one great push, threw her off of me and half-way across the room, jumped to my feet, grabbed at the first thing I touched, and leaped at her to beat out her brains. She had landed off balance and when I hit at her she ducked, went sprawling on her back on the deck. I went to swing again, slipped, and my foot sailed in the air and I sat down on the end of my spine on the iron deck. Pain shot up my spine like a needle, shocked the fury out of me. I braced my hands on the deck, pushed to my feet. She lay there without moving and looked up at me. But there was no fear in her face. . . . There were only the two of us in pressing chaos. Looking at each other; our eyes locked together as in a death embrace; black and white in both our minds; not hating each other; just feeling extreme outrage. I felt buck-naked and powerless, stripped of my manhood and black against the whole white world. [PP. 180–81]

Far more articulate in verbalizing his plight than a Bigger Thomas ever could be, Bob is no less trapped. The last sentence capsulizes his predicament; a physically hulking black man, stereotypically an oversexed "buck," is stripped of all the sexual power he presumably has. "Buck-naked," a perfectly innocuous phrase from Afro-American verbal tradition used to intensify a condition of nakedness, summarizes the paradoxical position in which many black men find themselves. They are alone with their blackness—and their now contained sexuality—against the entire white world.

Once the process has been set in motion, it is only a short time to the meting out of "justice." Beaten during the "rescue" attempt and thereafter taken to the shipyard's hospital, Bob tries to escape when he is being transferred to the local jail. He actually reaches his car and succeeds in driving around a while before he is apprehended. In jail, he experiences a different kind of fear: "The whole structure of American thought was against me; American tradition had convicted me a hundred years before. And standing there in an American courtroom, through all the phoney formality of an American trial, having to take it, knowing that I was innocent and that I didn't have a chance" (p. 187). The only chance he has is to choose his manner of punishment: he can either go to jail or to the Army. Suspecting, but not having been confirmed in his suspicions, that "they'd grilled Madge and learned the truth, or learned enough to guess at the rest" (p. 201), is still not enough to make American justice work in Bob's favor. Considering himself "beat," he stoically accepts his induction into the Army.

The disaster which befalls Bob's encounters with Madge is made even more poignant by the relationship he has with Alice, his girl-friend. Blue-veined, upper black middle class Alice has adopted all the values of the society which is so oppressive to Bob. She is a "supervisor of case work in the city welfare department" and her father, a doctor, is a "pompous little guy" who is "one of the richest Negroes in the city if not on the whole West Coast" (p. 6). Intra-racially, then, Bob is involved with a family which could look down upon his two years of college and his job in a shipyard. Indeed, Alice has big plans for him to return to school, finish his degree, and, if she has her way, become a doctor or a lawyer. And the problem with Bob, whose actions frequently reveal more than he is willing to admit about himself, is that he is as attracted to what Alice represents as he is drawn to Madge. They represent two parts of the same vision of the world. Alice is as "white" as she can be and still claim kinship to Blacks. Bob's attraction to her points out how history influences him; the Talented Tenth, "better" class of Blacks are attractive to him no matter how derisive he is about their habits and about their values.

Bob's attraction to Alice is also a gauge for measuring his own inferiority complex. In spite of that looming physique of which he is so proud, he is malleable in Alice's hands. This offspring of a woman with "Caucasian features" (p. 49) insults Bob and refuses to stand by him in his initial confrontation with Madge. She admonishes Bob to apologize to Madge and ask for reinstatement after he is demoted. She also tells him that he is "darker" than she likes, that he is "boorish" and dresses "like a gangster," and that he is a "filthy Negro" (pp. 92, 93). Yet she tells herself that she loves him and later promises to marry him. These two play out a game almost as dangerous as the one Madge and Bob play. Alice is beauty and Bob is beast in an intraracial division which has also been shaped in part on the basis of color. Alice, to Bob's mind, represents the very best in womanhood the race can offer, and he is almost desperate to hang on to her. He goes to other women for the sexual release he knows Alice would consider "too niggerish," and he excuses insults from her that he would never take from anyone else. His degradation in their relationship underscores the difficulties

he has with the whites. What they want to do with him—strip him
of his manhood—Alice is doing.

The matter of manhood enters into the relationship with Alice in
another way. Alice frequently socializes with whites, and Bob discovers her going out on a date with a white man on the evening he
ends up in Madge's hotel room. Perhaps it is in part out of the helplessness he feels in reaction to a white man dating "his" girl that he
finagles his way into Madge's room. Alice is symbolically helping
the whites take Bob's manhood away from him. Even though she
promises to marry Bob, she refuses to assist him in his attempt to
escape after the accusation of rape. When he calls her, she insists
that he turn himself in and let justice prevail. After all, she maintains, they live in a civilized world where lawyers—and she knows
many of them—can fight the good fight in court, so Bob should
trust the system. When he refuses to follow her advice ("If you're
innocent you have nothing to fear"—p. 193), she refuses to offer
him financial assistance and the use of her car. Alice is safely within
the system, and she believes in its justice. She has never known
what it has meant not to have the very best the world could offer a
black person; she is not in love enough to jeopardize what her status means. Bob's hanging up on her, after having verbally freed her
from any commitment to him, is his severing of connection with
that "whiter than white" black world of which she is a part. He
knows that, from the point of view of the whites who are hunting
him down, he is a "nigger"; Alice will never believe that either
whites or Blacks will place her in such a category. With or without
the support of the woman in his life, a black man accused of raping
a white woman has no future, but that bleakness could be made
more palatable if the black woman did support her man. The fact
that Alice does not, and has not throughout the novel, ensures that
Bob's mental emasculation is almost as acute as the "justified" taking away of his freedom. His masculine value stripped from him or
perverted on too many fronts, he can only find himself "beaten."
"Systematic racism," Edward Margolies writes of Bob, "has awakened in him deep castration fears—has indeed psychologically
emasculated him, robbing him of his self-esteem since he is constantly being reminded of his 'place' in the scheme of things."[25]

Believing equally that his masculinity is perverted and used
against him, Rufus Scott in Baldwin's *Another Country* (1962) will
find himself not only psychologically beaten, but physically beaten
as well. Rufus Scott, confident and talented musician, casual lover
of women, friend to white males, idealized big brother to his
younger sister Ida, begins his relationship with white Leona by as-

serting his acceptance of stereotypical black male sexuality. It is initially not a burden, and he seduces Leona with all the fire of a young man giving what he knows he is capable of giving. What is not yet a burden, however, is nonetheless a consideration. Rufus believes Leona has come to him because she thinks black males are more sexually endowed than whites.

By beginning his relationship with Leona with such stereotypic notions informing it, Rufus can only go downhill. He will find it impossible to believe that Leona sees him as an individual male, not as a chimeric representation of all black males. His dealings with her will show that, in spite of his physical sexual prowess, Rufus is no less emasculated in his relationship with the white woman than are many literary characters who come before and after him. A victim of his own history and his own imagination, Rufus accepts all the notions of what he is as a representative black man and, among those many externally imposed ideas, he has difficulty knowing what he is in reality. As his relationship with Leona goes along, he will find himself acting out more and more the roles which history and custom have assigned to him. He commits suicide as much to escape from those as from the pain which his acceptance has caused.

Rufus seduces Leona in a symbolic rape. He wants to pay her back—as Eldridge Cleaver claimed he did in his discussion of rape—for all he has suffered as a black man at the hands of whites. During their trip from the jazz club where they have met to the party where he seduces her, Rufus remembers his training in boot camp in the South, how he had been beaten into the dirt by a white officer. Overtones of what the oppressive South means for all black people thus prevent Rufus from ever seeing Leona as an individual. Instead, she becomes one component of that white blob of power, and he sees his opportunity to exert his own power play by subduing her. Poor, timid, previously abused Leona is thus ripe for what Rufus wishes to heap upon her. On the balcony where they have sex, Rufus pulls Leona to him "as roughly as he could."[26] As she tries to pull away from him, he knocks the highball glass out of her hands and taunts her: "Go ahead, fight. I like it. Is this the way they do down home?" (p. 23). When she begins to cry, he adds: "Honey, you ain't got nothing to cry about yet" (p. 23). Though he is high on drugs and initially fumbling in his seduction, he is still aware enough not to let go of the stereotypical ideas he has about himself and about Leona. A part of him makes him feel a certain amount of tenderness for Leona even as he is making her cry, but that does not halt the torrent of passion which has been unleashed

in both of them. Enjoying the physical coupling in spite of his desire to abuse, or perhaps because of it, Rufus is victimized by his
history even at the height of passion:

> Her breath came with moaning short cries, with words he couldn't
> understand, and in spite of himself he began moving faster and
> thrusting deeper. He wanted her to remember him the longest
> day she lived. And, shortly, nothing could have stopped him, not
> the white God himself nor a lynch mob arriving on wings. Under
> his breath he cursed the milk-white bitch and groaned and rode his
> weapon between her thighs. She began to cry. *I told you*, he moaned,
> *I'd give you something to cry about*. [P. 24]

Their bodies brought together by mutually pathetic and desperate
needs, Rufus and Leona are willing to war with each other even as
they work to satisfy themselves and, in the process, each other.

Giving Leona "something to cry about" epitomizes the sexual
confidence Rufus has at this point and which will be undermined
very shortly when he must be seen with Leona in public, not in the
dark corners of a highrise balcony. Somewhere in the reaches of his
mind, the image of himself as a superstud combines with the white-
female taboo and makes him evoke the image of the lynch mob.
That evocation is a prelude to his loss of confidence, for it has as its
center the notion that he is trespassing upon territory forbidden to
him even as he tries to convince himself that he can conquer that
territory and use it for his own purposes. His cursing of the "milk-
white bitch" highlights both his attraction to Leona and the challenge she represents for him; he must not conquer her as mere
woman, but as *white* woman. His "thrusting," his thoughts of the
"lynch mob," and his use of his penis as a "weapon" are all images
tied to violence and destruction, not to making love. With this kind
of background for their physical coupling, it is questionable if
Leona and Rufus could ever make love with each other.

From the vengeful insistence that he will give Leona something
to cry about, Rufus moves to an insecurity manifested as early
as the next morning. His white friend Vivaldo arrives at Rufus's
apartment before he and Leona are dressed for the day. There are
awkward, "uncomfortable" moments, during which neither of
the men really knows what to expect of the other. Especially is this
true for Rufus, who begins to suspect that, because Leona is not the
prettiest woman in the world, Vivaldo will somehow be contemp-
tuous of him. He is unable to see that Vivaldo's concern may simply rest in the fact that he is anxious about the pace at which the
affair seems to be developing, and he knows what kind of environ-

ment Rufus and Leona will confront in the world beyond their doors.

That world begins to wear on Rufus very quickly. Curious and indignant looks from passersby as they walk through the park gnaw at Rufus's self-confidence. The eyes into which he looks reflect a dirtied, unacceptable blackness back to him. He finds it impossible to be objective about the implied condemnation.

> A young couple came toward them, carrying the Sunday papers. Rufus watched the eyes of the man as the man looked at Leona; and then both the man and the woman looked swiftly from Vivaldo to Rufus as though to decide which of the two was her lover. And, since this was the Village—the place of liberation—Rufus guessed, from the swift, nearly sheepish glance the man gave them as they passed, that he had decided that Rufus and Leona formed the couple. The face of his wife, however, simply closed tight, like a gate. [P. 29]

When Vivaldo leaves them alone for a few minutes, the eyes which rove over them become more critical in their evaluations:

> Without Vivaldo, there was a difference in the eyes which watched them. Villagers, both bound and free, looked upon them as though where they stood were an auction block or a stud farm. The pale spring sun seemed very hot on the back of his neck and on his forehead. Leona gleamed before him and seemed to be oblivious of everything and everyone but him. And if there had been any doubt concerning their relationship, her eyes were enough to dispel it. Then he thought, If she could take it so calmly, if she noticed nothing, what was the matter with him? Maybe he was making it all up, maybe nobody gave a damn. Then he raised his eyes and met the eyes of an Italian adolescent. The boy was splashed by the sun falling through the trees. The boy looked at him with hatred; his glance flicked over Leona as though she were a whore; he dropped his eyes slowly and swaggered on—having registered his protest, his backside seemed to snarl, having made his point. [PP. 30–31]

Studding is a private affair; acceptance is public. That was the contrast which defeated Bob Jones in *If He Hollers Let Him Go*, and the public reaction, combined with Rufus's own developing insecurity, will similarly defeat him. He will consistently be unable to believe that he is worth Leona's love, or that she cares for him as an individual. The society around him has taught him so thoroughly that he is not worthy of consideration that he cannot believe someone white actually takes the time not only to consider him, but to love

him. Believing that he is indeed black and ugly, he will become
uglier as his relationship with Leona progresses. Though he has not
been physically emasculated, he has been stripped of any psychologically comforting claims to masculine self-worth. His initial
pride in his studding power identifies him more with breeding animals than with loving men.

How Rufus devalues himself is apparent through several beatings
he heaps upon Leona and through one particularly poignant scene
in which Vivaldo rescues Leona from the apartment. Because Leona
dares to love Rufus, his warped self-image tells him she must have
also spent a great deal of time making love to other black men in
the South. He beats her for her presumed offenses and, in the process, is really beating himself for not being white and above being
rejected. Leona tells Vivaldo about Rufus's habits: "He's always
beating me, for nothing, for nothing! . . . He says I'm sleeping with
other colored boys behind his back and it's not true, God knows it's
not true!" (p. 51). Rufus surmises that Leona's husband has put her
out because she bordered on being a nymphomaniac. To him, only
a sexual explanation will account for Leona, because it is only the
sexual connection he sees in himself. In defense of his beating
Leona, Rufus says to Vivaldo:

> "It was her husband ruined this bitch. Your husband and all them
> funky niggers screwed you in the Georgia bushes. That's why your
> husband threw you out. Why don't you tell the truth? I wouldn't
> have to beat you if you'd tell the truth." He grinned at Vivaldo.
> "Man, this chick can't get enough—" and broke off, staring at
> Leona. [P. 53]

Humiliation, embarrassment, and total domination are what Rufus
accomplishes with Leona. She must be sexually loose, he concludes, because she is with ugly, black him. His obsession with her
telling him "the truth" is an obsession with achieving external confirmation of what he believes to be true about himself. In discuss-
ing with Vivaldo what he believes her case to be, Rufus leaves the
woman no room for privacy and little for human dignity. Her desperate love for Rufus makes her a pathetic creature, easily used
and thoroughly incapable of extricating herself from the situation.

Rufus, in abusing her, is really playing with fire. Vivaldo tries to
make it clear to him that he "could be killed for this" if Leona calls
a cop, that he would be put "*under* the jailhouse" (p. 52). Rufus takes
Vivaldo's comments and concern as indications that a white man is
once again trying to get the best of a black man, especially when
Vivaldo insists upon taking Leona away until Rufus has thought

through the matter. The conversation surrounding that scene reveals Rufus's essential problem; it is not that Leona is not good enough for him, but that, as she points out, Rufus does not believe he is good enough for her. He is therefore caught in a peculiar kind of irony. Once he has the opportunity to engage in an affair with a white woman, to prove, to his own mind, that he is just as capable as white men are, his history of viewing himself in a certain way will not allow him to accomplish his objective beyond the initial sexual triumph. Black men, he believes, are supposed to be better than white men sexually, but he has no model for how black men should *sustain* relationships with white women.

Although he might feel some attraction for Leona, he is unable to separate her affection for him from the general hatred he feels all whites hold toward Blacks, and he cannot separate any grain of affection in himself from the hatred he feels in turn toward the masses of whites. He tries to explain his feelings to Vivaldo once Leona has gone to Vivaldo's apartment:

> "How I hate them—all those white sons of bitches out there. They're trying to kill me, you think I don't know. They got the world on a string, man, the miserable white cock suckers, and they tying that string around my neck, they killing *me*. . . . You got to fight with the landlord because the landlord's *white*! You got to fight with the elevator boy because the motherfucker's *white*. Any bum on the Bowery can shit all over you because maybe he can't hear, can't see, can't walk, can't fuck—but he's *white*!" [P. 62]

To Vivaldo's comment that "not everybody's like that" and his assertion that Leona loves Rufus, Rufus responds:

> "She loves the colored folks so *much* . . . sometimes I just can't stand it. You know all that chick knows about me? The *only* thing she knows?" He put his hand on his sex, brutally, as though he would tear it out, and seemed pleased to see Vivaldo wince. He sat down on the bed again. "That's all." [P. 62]

His gesture an indication of his castration, Rufus finds himself aboard a rollercoaster to his own destruction. Unable to separate race from sexuality and stereotype from substance, Rufus is lost in a maze of confusion from which there is no exit. He mistreats Leona to the point of beating her into a nervous breakdown. Her removal to Bellevue and from there back to the South is what brings about Rufus's decision to commit suicide. On that night, when he is with Vivaldo and other of their friends for the first time in over a month—a month during which he has wandered aim-lessly and degenerated very quickly—the guilt he feels makes him want to disappear from the presence of those who are enjoying life. He feels "black, filthy, foolish" and thinks of Leona "in waves, like the pain of a toothache or a festering wound" (p. 70).

Rufus strips himself of much more than the whites ever could, for even if he were arrested for his treatment of Leona, a jail sentence would perhaps be his severest legal punishment; left alone, though, he punishes himself mentally and physically. He has tried repeatedly not to be emasculated by Leona, only to discover that he has emasculated himself. If he had allowed Leona to love him, just as a man, not as a superstud, that would have been a denial of the one portion of his identity he felt was intact; to be mere man meant to him to be sexually weak, therefore emasculated. Since his strongest identification as a black man is with his sexuality, he cannot dissociate himself from it—even when it means reducing himself as a human being. A man at war with himself, Rufus cannot afford to be gentle and loving. His refusal to do so indicates that the whites have controlled his mind to such an extent that his entire existence becomes one sustained reaction to them. He cannot exist outside the cage which has been defined for him. Nor does he really believe he has the right to exist outside that cage.

Rufus is therefore as psychologically constrained as are some of the earlier characters we examined, and he is no more able to begin to define manhood for himself. Externally imposed restrictions have become internal controls, and in spite of the opportunities for change implied by the liberalism of the Village, he is unable to evade the old definitions, to rise above the traditional stimulus and response. To himself, Rufus is a black man without value, one who may be immersed in the musical traditions of his culture, but who does not find sustaining strength in them, who may be aware of the games whites play with him, but who has not the moral strength to establish new games with new sets of rules. Rufus is finally as powerless as those black eunuchs who approached whites with their hats in their hands and as insecure as those black paper tigers who connived to hold on to the empires they had constructed from rice paper.[27]

CHAPTER 3

Literary Lynchings
and Burnings

William Wells Brown depicts a scene in *Clotel* in which a group of slavers pursues, captures, and later burns a slave to death for being "impudent" to his master. Four thousand slaves are brought in from neighboring plantations to witness the spectacle and to assimilate thoroughly what the consequences would be if they should dare to be similarly impudent. Brown's novel is the first in a long line of works in which black American writers show black people being summarily executed for some "offense" against whites. In particular, Brown's novel illustrates how politically powerless Blacks were in slavery. They could be lynched for any reason; however, accusations of rape would very shortly thereafter become the excuse to cover lynchings of Blacks who were progressing too fast economically or who were otherwise rising above the status the white community believed they should hold. Other writers joined Brown in depicting the unnamed excuses for lynching as well as the named ones. Such depictions came to show how politically conscious black writers were, as well as how they merged the literal history of suppression of Blacks with their symbolic statements of suppression in literature.

The tradition Brown began is a fascinating one to which each author adds his individual voice in addition to sharing in the collective portrayal of lynchings and burnings. As each author adapts and alters the scene to suit his or her purpose, it is sometimes not immediately relevant to the thematic or structural development of the work in which it appears. Indeed, lynching and burning scenes sometimes become accessory devices, embellishments to suggest the innate character of white society, its destructive nature and brutality. Persistence in the inclusion of the scene suggests, nonetheless, that it has reasons for being, reasons that are central to the history of Blacks in America as well as to the individual black writers and how they view themselves as writers.

Outside of literary purposes, the scenes fulfill a tradition within black American literature. The ritual becomes an "expected" way in which the black writer can show white attitudes towards Blacks from historical and cultural points of view and one of the easiest ways in which readers, particularly black readers, can be urged to identify with what those attitudes have meant in terms of destruction for Blacks. As rituals for whites reinforced their solidarity against Blacks, so too in a way do black writers' portrayals of such rituals consolidate for their black readers the threats that could originate in the white community. On a simplistic level, the scenes characterize whites as inherently violent and brutal. But this must be balanced against the function they serve for the black writer in relation to his black readers. The black writer becomes a kind of ritual priest in ever keeping before his black audience the essence of one of the forces that have shaped their lives. Jewish writers portray or allude to the Holocaust for the sake of racial memory; in like manner do black writers portray slavery, lynching, and burning.

Study of these scenes of ritualized violence is not intended to suggest that black writers have been unusually preoccupied with them or that they are the only kinds of violence presented in black literature. Either would be a gross exaggeration. The prevailing concern here is with the *persistency* with which lynching scenes appear across genres and through many generations of black writers.

Neither is this study intended to suggest that white American writers do not deal with lynchings and/or burnings.[1] It is clear, however, that the threat of lynchings and burnings has not menaced the survival of the white race in this country to the extent it has the black. Thus the white writers surveyed, even when they treat such subjects, are not inclined to portray gruesome details. Black writers show the ugly details and make history live again, if only for a brief moment, in the works they create.

Treatment of the lynching and burning scenes by black writers seems to parallel the rise of historical lynchings. Prior to 1860, Blacks were not lynched so regularly in the ritualistic manner described. And black American literature, in its early stage of development, focused more on slavery—the larger issue at that time—than upon lynching; lynchings and burnings were given only passing attention. Thus the treatment of lynching in Brown's *Clotel* in 1853 is rather mild in comparison to Baldwin's "Going to Meet the Man" in 1968. Although Brown's lynching reflects violence sanctioned by a group and contains some of the elements of the ritual defined here, it does not dwell upon the gruesome details to the extent later works do. After slavery, the increase in the ritualistic lynching of Blacks was paralleled by the increase in the depictions of lynchings in the literature. It is in the works with post–slavery settings that such treatment reaches the level of the full-blown ritual, obtaining ceremonial proportions where certain roles have been in-grained and are expected to be carried out whenever necessary; it is also in these works that the scenes become more central to the development of the works as literature.

Obviously the freed Blacks posed a greater threat to traditional white values than did slaves, thus forcing whites to go to greater lengths in reaffirming and protecting those values. Beginning with Reconstruction and going into the twentieth century, these cruel-ties increased, and, correspondingly, the depth of treatment by black writers also increased. As lynchings decreased—in a general way, though there were periodic rises—in the twenties, thirties, and forties, and as black writers searched for a distinct tradition and symbolism of their own, lynching and burning scenes reflect stylistic experimentation, symbolic language, and multiple levels of interpretation. Propaganda diminishes and art emerges; this pattern is clear from William Wells Brown and Sutton Griggs to James Baldwin and John Wideman. As successive generations of writers present the ritual, its dimensions grow, from the economic and the political to the sexual and the psychological; from punish-ment for minor offenses (either defined or undefined) to punish-ment for murder and taboo sex acts.

The Ritual as It Results from Minor Offenses

The earliest instances where elements of the ritual occur as a result of defined or undefined minor offenses by Blacks are in those works written during slavery or which have slavery as their cen-tral concerns. Minor here is interpreted to mean that no death or personal violation—rape—results from the "crime"; in many in-stances, if whites believed Blacks were merely *thinking* of criminal activity, that was enough to warrant the death penalty.

A vital part of the ritual or ceremony is not only that black vic-tims realize the power in the white world, but even more so that surviving Blacks realize this. Blacks living near the scene of a lynching or burning were often forced to witness the spectacle. A notable example is Brown's *Clotel*. In Brown's novel, Currer, Clotel's mother, is sold down the river to Natchez. On one occasion she and the other slaves on the plantation, along with those from surrounding plantations, are gathered to witness the execution by burning of a black man who ran away and, during his capture, "had the impudence to raise his hand against a white man."[2] Taboo has been violated, and order must be restored. Currer and the

other slaves have no choice but to view the burning. An unspoken
catechism develops which may be verbalized as follows:

> Master: "Why is this slave being punished?"
> Slaves: "Because he tried to run away."
> Master: "Why else is he being punished?"
> Slaves: "Because he raised his hand against his master."
> Master: "And what will happen if you run away or strike your
>   masters?"
> Slaves: "We will be punished likewise."

Through the burning of a single black man, the concept of place for
all Blacks is reinforced. Slaves—accept your lots, do not attempt
to escape, rebellion is futile. Order has been threatened, and order
must be restored through the ritual burning.

   Three works set in the twentieth century, and in which Blacks are
punished for minor offenses, contain more elements of the ritual.
These works are by James Weldon Johnson and Claude McKay. The
decision the narrator makes about passing for white in Johnson's
The Autobiography of An Ex-Coloured Man (1912) hinges on his witnessing of mob violence against a black man. Women and children
gather in a crowd at dawn when word goes out that some "terrible
crime" has been committed and that white men are pursuing the
offender. The narrator, passing for white, waits with the crowd.
A black man is dragged in and preparations made for hanging him,
but even as the rope is placed around his neck, someone calls out
"Burn him!" and the crowd proceeds to do so. The people are transformed into "savage beasts" in carrying out their violent act.[3]

> A railroad tie was sunk into the ground, the rope was removed, and
> a chain brought and securely coiled round the victim and the stake.
> There he stood, a man only in form and stature, every sign of de-
> generacy stamped upon his countenance. His eyes were dull and
> vacant, indicating not a single ray of thought. Evidently the real-
> ization of his fearful fate had robbed him of whatever reasoning
> power he had ever possessed. He was too stunned and stupefied
> even to tremble. Fuel was brought from everywhere, oil, the torch;
> the flames crouched for an instant as though to gather strength,
> then leaped up as high as their victim's head. He squirmed, he
> writhed, strained at his chains, then gave out cries and groans that
> I shall always hear. The cries and groans were choked off by the fire
> and smoke; but his eyes, bulging from their sockets, rolled from
> side to side, appealing in vain for help. Some of the crowd yelled
> and cheered, others seemed appalled at what they had done, and
> there were those who turned away sickened at the sight. I was fixed

to the spot where I stood, powerless to take my eyes from what I
did not want to see. [PP. 186–87]

The exact offense the burned man has committed against the society of whites is never revealed, but he is obviously thought to
have stepped out of his place and threatened the white power
structure. It is interesting here how the description of the victim
by the narrator reveals his separation from the victim, his racial
ambivalence, and, it can be inferred from that, his sympathy with
the whites (notice how careful he is to present them as less than a
unified group). He will, in a few pages, decide to identify perma-
nently with the power of the whites. Obviously his problem is more
complex, but the burning ritual has served to make permanent his
decision to pass for white.

Johnson makes the role of the crowd even more explicit in a
verse-drama he published in 1935, entitled "Brothers—American
Drama." "Mob" and "Victim" are the "characters" in the drama,
which is a stylized presentation of punishment meted out for an
unnamed offense. The scene opens in the woods where "Victim" is
to be punished. "The Mob Speaks," calling upon his companions to
observe this beast, this brute masquerading as man. Asked to explain who or what he is, "Victim" responds with an analysis of the
forces which have shaped his existence in America. Bored with the
depth, as well as the length and objective nature of the explanation, "Mob" concludes:

> Enough, the brute must die!
> Quick! Chain him to that oak! It will resist
> The fire much longer than this slender pine.
> Now bring the fuel! Pile it round him! Wait!
> Pile not so fast or high! or we shall lose
> The agony and terror in his face.
> And now the torch! Good fuel that! the flames
> Already leap head-high. Ha! hear that shriek!
> And there's another! wilder than the first.
> Fetch water! Water! Pour a little on
> The fire, lest it should burn too fast. Hold so!
> Now let it slowly blaze again. See there!
> He squirms! He groans! His eyes bulge wildly out,
> Searching around in vain appeal for help!
> Another shriek, the last! Watch how the flesh
> Grows crisp and hangs till, turned to ash, it sifts
> Down through the coils of chain that hold erect
> The ghastly frame against the bark-scorched tree.

Stop! to each man no more than one man's share.
You take that bone, and you this tooth; the chain,
Let us divide its links; this skull, of course,
In fair division, to the leader comes.

And now his fiendish crime has been avenged;
Let us back to our wives and children—say,
What did he mean by those last muttered words,
"Brothers in spirit, brothers in deed are we?" [4]

Acting as the voice of the mob, the speaker serves as a communal
director who choreographs the responses of the individuals who
have gathered in the group. He controls their actions and reactions
just as he controls what material appears where in the poem. In
fact, his voice becomes one of split-second counterpoint to the ago-
nies of the man being burned and to what the crowd witnesses; by
serving to announce and register what all the participants already
know, he underscores the brutality of the execution. His admonish-
ments to the crowd,—"hear that shriek!"—are, of course, superfluous for the actual participants in the drama; however, for us as
readers, it elicits regular, punctuated responses which heighten
what is being revealed to us.

Acting as a camera eye for the reader, as well as an emotional
bow-stringer, the speaker is both participant and observer. He is
objective reporter and involved murderer, and his constant commands show both roles; the simultaneity of his commentary and
his participation indicates that he is not reluctant to play either
role. He is not less guilty than the mobsters because he stands back
and directs them, and they accept him as leader as willingly as
they follow his directions. They are all defined by their purpose in
punishing the "fiendish crime," whatever that crime may have been.

Lack of subtlety in Johnson's forcibly stylized presentation suggests that it was concocted purely for the message it conveys.
White Americans are equally "fiendish" in the crimes they commit
to punish alleged crimes committed by Blacks. As the whites burn
the black man for some "violence" they believe he has committed,
their crime is shown to be even more savage than his. Judgments
whites project onto Blacks are in turn re-directed towards the
whites; in this case, a beast kills a man who is in turn presumed to
be a brute. But what could be more beastly than the cruel prolonga-
tion of pain, the *glee* at watching a man burn, the mad scramble
for souvenirs? The crowd protects its group values (its "we-ness"
against the "they-ness" of Blacks), but, ironically, it ultimately
turns the charge of bestiality back upon itself.

Johnson's presentation of the lynching/burning differs from most black writers' presentations in that the speaker chosen is one of the white participants in the mob. That may be the reason the poem becomes so stilted stylistically; perhaps it is difficult for Johnson imaginatively to get inside the head of one of the mobsters. In his earlier work, he had used a black character's reaction to the burning of a black man. Now, when he tries to use a white man, one of the upholders of the tradition, to show another kind of reaction, he is unable to move above the level of superficial characterization, and perhaps that is not his purpose. Maybe he simply wanted to expose the glee with which black human life can be taken by whites; that in itself eliminates the element of complexity because, as far as whites are concerned, all Blacks can be dispensed with easily—thus their reaction is one-dimensional. There are no extenuating circumstances or complications; therefore, the white character is simplistically drawn with the single dimension of hatred.

It is somewhat surprising, then, that the leader actually registers the comment he records in the last line of the poem. His actions suggest that he would be totally deaf to any mention of brotherhood, let alone to questioning what the now-dead black man had in mind when he uttered it. Therefore the words are not his as participant in the mob, but his as the reporter who has been manipulated throughout the poem to aim his comments to an audience beyond that in his immediate presence. The poem, then, becomes more a cry for attention as social commentary than as created art. Yet, the fact that Johnson wrote it underscores the importance black writers have placed upon a particular kind of violence perpetrated against their communities.

Claude McKay's poem, "The Lynching," also candidly portrays the group role in the ritualized execution of a black man for an undefined offense. The text of the poem is as follows:

> His Spirit in smoke ascended to high heaven.
> His father, by the cruelest way of pain,
> Had bidden him to his bosom once again;
> The awful sin remained still unforgiven.
> All night a bright and solitary star
> (Perchance the one that ever guided him,
> Yet gave him up at last to Fate's wild whim)
> Hung pitifully o'er the swinging char.
> Day dawned, and soon the mixed crowds came to view
> The ghastly body swaying in the sun.
> The women thronged to look but never a one
> Showed sorrow in her eyes of steely blue.

And little lads, lynchers that were to be,
Danced round the dreadful thing in fiendish glee.[5]

McKay depends upon historical associations for the racial connections to be made in the poem. Never once does he identify the victim as a black man, yet the celebratory antagonism the women and
children exhibit toward the lynched man in the last few lines of the
poem suggest that he could only have been black. The women, with
their "steely blue" eyes, have an ingrained lack of sympathy with
the hanged/burned man. Their role is to view the destruction and
take satisfaction in the punishment. Their sons undergo an initiation ritual, a rite of passage, that establishes their superior roles as
adults in the society, in the same way that the black boys in Ellison's battle royal scene in *Invisible Man* are forced to undergo an
initiation in the establishment of their inferior roles. Traditionally,
in such rites, the women can only passively condone the actions of
their men. The boys in the poem are being taught what their future
positions in relation to Blacks will be; to them, the black man can
be reduced to an inhuman "thing." He may be a threat to them, but
they have the power to make that threat inconsequential. The lads,
"lynchers that were to be," will become violent rulers of their society as a result of these violent practices from which they were not
shielded. Walter White recounts that after five Blacks were burned
to death in Florida, a white girl of nine or ten asked if he were
going to see the spot. When he answers affirmatively, she tells him
of "the fun we had burning the niggers."[6] "In the unconscious of
these immature minds," White continues, "are thus sown the seeds
of lynching as a panacea which will correct all ills and especially
those emanating from Negro sources."[7] Ritualistic action by their
parents signals to the youngsters that such action is good and
right. And they can dance as McKay's lads do.[8]

If the "awful sin" in the poem refers to what the black man has
been accused of doing against whiteness, it appears as if a minor
offense has been elevated to cosmic significance. If it refers to the
violence done the black man by the whites, it enhances the Biblical
comparison between the person lynched and Christ. Such a comparison emphasizes the absurdity of the crime against the black
man and points to the ridiculous nature of the values whites try
to uphold. In its comparison of the black man to Christ, McKay's
poem evokes Johnson's "Brothers—American Drama" and Gwendolyn Brooks's "The Chicago Defender Sends a Man to Little Rock."
Brooks asserts that the mob violence against the young black
schoolchildren is perhaps provoked by notions as "righteous" as

those with which His enemies executed Christ; what is happening to the children should not be so unexpected, for "the loveliest lynchee was our Lord."[9]

Ralph Ellison also illustrates in a short story, "The Birthmark," how the group acts to put down unnamed offenses and thereby convey the power and solidarity it possesses. Cutler, Richard M. Brown, and Walter White all discuss the problems of figures in authority, especially sheriffs, being overcome by mobs or literally giving up their charges to mobs.[10] In "The Birthmark," a highway patrolman and a coroner combine their authorities in "influencing" a hapless brother and sister to accept a verdict of "hit and run" when their brother has obviously been lynched. Although the actual lynching of the victim is not dramatized in the work, evidence of ritualistic execution is apparent from Matt's observation of his brother's body. There is evidence of lynching—Matt "saw the jaw hanging limply against the shoulder, the mouth gaping"; throat cutting—"A blood-creased cut started under the ear and disappeared beneath the chin"; beating—"The flesh was hacked and pounded as though it had been beaten with hammers"; and castration—"When Matt lowered his eyes he noticed the ribs had been caved in. The flesh was bruised and torn. It [the birthmark] was just below the navel, he thought. Then he gave a start: where it should have been was only a bloody mound of torn flesh and hair. Matt went weak. He felt as though he had been castrated himself."[11]

Clara, the dead man's sister, also sees the truth instantly. She screams: "He was lynched, Lynched! I'm gonna tell everybody, HE WAS LYNCHED!" (p. 17). In response to this outburst, the highway patrolman beats Matt and tells him to "shut this bitch up!" (p. 17). "'Goddammit, I said a car hit him!' the white man snapped. 'We don't have no lynchings in this state no more!'" (p. 17). Matt and Clara can save their own lives only by accepting this judgment; the verdict is as absurd as a story Grange Copeland tells. "I once seed a woman . . . had been strung up, slit open and burned just about up. . . . They said she was one of them people *bent* on suicide. Kill herself three ways. . . . they writ it up in the paper just that way. Said she was *one* nigger with determination!"[12] Public sentiment, here manifested in the newspaper account, sanctions the brutality in the same way the highway patrolman and the coroner sanction it in "The Birthmark." The crime, if any, committed in both cases and the resulting deaths serve to perpetuate group solidarity. Even when an offense is only believed to have been committed, designated "violators" must be punished.

The Ritual as It Results from Killing Whites

From days of slavery black men were taught not to raise their hands against whites. The concept of place required submission to cruelty without redress or retaliation. In a social structure of this nature, talking back to whites becomes a whipping offense, and raising a black hand to a white a hanging offense. If a black man or woman actually kills a white man (in self-defense or otherwise), a taboo considered to be inviolable has been broken, and order can be restored and values reinstated only through the death of the offender. Cutler records that "so long as the blacks were valuable as slaves *and accepted their inferior position without protest*, no one wanted to get rid of them" (my emphasis), but in cases of insurrections and the commission of barbarous crimes and, it may be added, insubordination, slaves "were killed without mercy, sometimes they were tortured and their bodies mutilated while still alive, and occasionally they were burned to death."[13] After any occurrence or hint of uprisings, examples had to be made so as to present established order as inviolable. After Nat Turner's rebellion, innocent as well as guilty slaves were "shot on sight" and "their heads were left for weeks stuck up on poles as a warning to all who should undertake a similar plot."[14] A parallel to this historical head-severing is that portrayed fictionally by Paule Marshall in *The Chosen Place, The Timeless People*; Cuffee Ned, the leader of a very successful slave revolt on the mythical Bourne Island, is eventually caught and killed. As an example to the other slaves, his head is severed from his body, placed on a pole near a heavily traveled road, and left for weeks as a warning. Frederick Olmsted reported, on one of his travels through the South, that a slave who had killed his master "was roasted, at a slow fire, on the spot of the murder, in the presence of many thousand slaves, driven to the ground from all the adjoining counties."[15] The restoration of order through example is again central. The white prerequisites for conduct by Blacks do not allow for any expression of black humanity or assertion of black rights; when these appear, they must be suppressed. The lesson was as important in real life as it is for the unfortunate slave who was burned to death in Brown's *Clotel*.

A similar incident occurs in Margaret Walker's *Jubilee*.[16] Two black women have been accused of murdering three people in their masters' families by poisoning their food.[17] They are executed by hanging, and "every able-bodied slave in the county was, by order of his master, forced to attend the hanging." Plans for the executions are set for the Fourth of July, "a day for political speeches and all kinds of festive celebrations" (p. 98). A picnicking atmosphere prevails. "Most of the white people seemed to be enjoying themselves in the holiday atmosphere and were in high, laughing spirits. . . . the Negroes were for the most part silent" (p. 99). The implied catechism of *Clotel* is made explicit in *Jubilee*. A white preacher reviews the "Servants, obey in all things your masters" text for two-and-a-half pages before the two women are killed to illustrate the consequences of not obeying masters. Again the concept of place is vividly presented.

Taking place on the Fourth of July, the hangings ironically illustrate the lack of freedom for Blacks. These women dared to put themselves in a position to be accused and they must pay the price of accusation. The system of slavery and the nation whose birth is being celebrated must be protected. In this scene, whites view themselves as authoritarian figures who are divinely endowed with racial superiority; hence, they are similarly divinely endowed to assume a paternalistic, if destructive, attitude toward another race.

Sutton Griggs's *The Hindered Hand* (1905) provides a gruesome illustration of the ritualistic execution of a black person known to have killed a white person.[18] Bud and Foresta Harper are tortured in a scene depicting the communal release of a tension brought on by the violation of a taboo. Griggs focuses especially on the initiation of children in that scene. Little Melville Brant has complained to his mother that one of his friends has been to several lynchings and he is, as yet, uninitiated. "Every time I tell anything big he jumps in and tells what he's seen, and that knocks me out. He has seen a whole lots of lynchings" (p. 129). Although confined to his room, Melville devises an escape and collects his "piece of charred flesh." He crows after the scene: "Ben Stringer ain't got anything on me now," and Griggs deprecatingly hails him: "The future ruler of the land!" In this comment and in Melville's action, it is clear that an initiation ritual is operating in addition to the other motives for the lynching and burning. Melville is given insight into his future role in his society in the same way that McKay's "little lynchers" are given insight into theirs. Melville can never return to the innocence of his pre-lynching days.[19] And the atmosphere in which he has been reared is not one which suggests that such a return would be desirable. One of Melville's adult models comments to a white man who has come looking for Bud and Foresta and who has asked about the cause of the deaths: "We lynch niggers down here for anything. We lynch them for being sassy and sometimes lynch them on general principles. The truth of the matter is the real 'one crime' that paves the way for a lynching whenever we have the notion, is the crime of being black" (p. 136). With such role-models, Melville can only learn his lesson well.

Griggs's presentation of the burning scene is additionally interesting because the guilty parties are actually brought to trial. Needless to say, they are found innocent. The unusual trial scene nevertheless reflects Griggs's hopes for justice in America. He allows radical and conservative factions of Blacks in the novel to be swayed by the more conservative, reflecting a belief in working within instead of outside the law. His presentations of historical material, especially the burnings, are specifically designed to convince his audience of the need for better laws and equal justice. Lest his readers accuse him of exaggeration, Griggs includes in a section of notes an eye-witness account to the burning tragedy on which Bud's and Foresta's is based.[20]

In "Blood-Burning Moon," Jean Toomer also presents an instance of ritualized violence occurring as a result of a black person killing a white person.[21] Tom Burwell, black, kills Bob Stone, white, in self-defense (again, matters of justice and legality are insignificant). The death of someone white at the hands of someone black is a step in undermining tradition, and the mob gathers. Tom is subsequently staked and burned: "A stake was sunk into the ground. Rotting floor boards piled around it. Kerosene poured on the rotting floor boards. Tom bound to the stake. . . . Torches were flung onto the pile. A great flare muffled in black smoke shot upward. The mob yelled" (p. 66). This black human being, who thought he was man enough to claim a black woman away from the arms of her sometimes white lover, is reduced to ashes for defending himself in the fight which resulted from that sexual competition.

Tom, like Bud and Foresta, is aware of the taboo he has defied in spite of its apparent justification. Realizing that Bob Stone is dead, Tom leans against the woodwork of a well and seems "rooted there." Normally a "bad nigger," he is too stupefied by his own defiance to act in a positive manner to save himself, and the mob wins. The mention of a name has been enough to set it in motion. With his throat slit, Bob Stone had managed to struggle to the white side of town. Collapsing into the arms of his kindred, he had simply said, "Tom Burwell. . . ." This bit of information is enough to set the keepers of taboo in motion. "White men like ants upon a forage rushed about. Except for the taut hum of their moving, all was silent. Shotguns, revolvers, rope, kerosene, torches. Two high-powered cars with glaring search-lights. *They came together*" (emphasis mine—p. 65). The group has been threatened, and the group

responds; the evil must be expelled immediately. In the words of
Sterling Brown, *"They don't come by ones / They don't come by twos /
But they come by tens."* [22]

Bob is descended from a race of Southern white males who took
what they wanted, including the bodies of black females. It is his
heritage to be conqueror, and he wants Louisa, the black woman
over whom he and Tom fight. But as the conflict ensues, the black
woman becomes less a physical entity than a symbol for the privilege of the powerful class, a privilege Tom dares to thwart. Having
the "Blood of th old uns in his veins," Bob would like to preserve
that privilege, and even though he is killed, the white community
makes its point as far as power is concerned.

Both Toomer's and Griggs's characters have acted in self-defense.
The black character who kills two white men in Walter White's *The
Fire in the Flint* (1924) does so for revenge. White, who investigated
so many lynchings for the NAACP, was undoubtedly inspired to
write his novel as a direct result of those activities. The novel focuses upon Kenneth Harper, a young black physician who has been
educated in the North and in France, and who returns to Central
City in southern Georgia shortly after World War I. Kenneth is confident that his talent will be recognized, and he is determined
to follow his father's policy of getting along with the whites, for
only "bad Negroes" get lynched, those who get out of their place.
Kenneth's brother Bob, on the other hand, has lived with the injustices in the South and has no high-faluting notions of peaceful
coexistence with the whites. Kenneth is forced to abandon his
stance and become involved politically. When he starts a cooperative society through which sharecroppers can buy supplies and
thereby reduce their dependency upon the landlords, he is marked
by the Klan. Bob, already known as an uppity "nigger," is watched
but not marked for execution until he kills the two white men who
have raped his sister Mamie.

White is certainly conscious of the ironies involved in reversing
the notions of defending womanhood. To the whites, who believe
that the black women exist for their pleasure, it is absurd to think
of Blacks reacting if one of the women is actually raped. Yet, Bob
takes a gun, shoots down the two offenders even as they are gathered in front of the local store to harass other black women, and
begins the run which he knows can only lead to his death. He seals
himself in a barn and shoots several of his pursuers before they set
fire to the barn. His desire to cheat them of their lynching party
by shooting himself with his last bullet does not bring about the

peaceful exit for which he had hoped. The mob rushes into the burning barn to get at this violator of taboo, and they are not content to leave his body to the flames:

> The mob dragged the body hastily into the open. The roof of the old barn was about to fall in. Before dragging it forth, they had taken no chances. A hundred shots were fired into the dead body. Partly in anger at being cheated of the joy of killing him themselves. They tied it to the rear axle of a Ford. Howling, shouting gleefully, the voice of the pack after the kill, they drove rapidly back to town, the dead body, riddled and torn, bumping grotesquely over the holes in the road. . . .
> Back to the public square. In the open space before the Confederate Monument, wood and excelsior had been piled. Near by stood cans of kerosene. On the crude pyre they threw the body. Saturated it and the wood with oil. A match applied. In the early morning sunlight the fire leaped higher and higher. Mingled with the flames and smoke the exulting cries of those who had done their duty— they had avenged and upheld white civilization. . . .
> The flames died down. Women, tiny boys and girls, old men and young stood by, a strange light on their faces. They sniffed eagerly the odour of burning human flesh which was becoming more and more faint.
> . . . Into the dying flames darted a boy of twelve. Out he came, laughing hoarsely, triumphantly exhibiting a charred bone he had secured, blackened and crisp. . . . Another rushed in. . . . Another. . . . Another. . . . Here a rib. . . . There an armbone. . . . A louder cry. . . . The skull. . . . Good boy! Johnny! . . . We'll put that on the mantelpiece at home. . . . Five dollars for it, Johnny! . . . Nothin' doin'! . . . Goin' to keep it myself! . . .
> The show ended. The crowd dispersed. Home to breakfast.[23]

Kenneth, in Atlanta to perform an operation when Bob's body is burned and mutilated, returns to his own fate the next day. On a late night distress call to attend the daughter of one of the prominent whites in the city, he is victimized by the select members of the Ku Klux Klan who have just had a meeting near the home Kenneth is visiting. The Klansmen, who have decided that the best way to bring about Kenneth's "accident" is to accuse him of insulting a white woman, have a perfect set of circumstances created for them in Kenneth's visit to his patient. No one but the family knows Kenneth is attending the woman (black doctors attending Southern white women was also a taboo), and the father is away seeking aid from the governor to protect Kenneth from the Klan. Therefore, his wife and daughter are alone when Kenneth is called to perform a second operation. The Klansmen wait outside, attack Kenneth when he emerges from the house, and take him out into the woods for his summary hanging. The newspaper article which reports the incident asserts that Kenneth was "charged with attempted criminal assault on a white woman" (p. 300) and that Bob, who was lynched earlier, "had run amuck and killed two young white men. No reason could be found for their murder at the hands of the Negro, as they had always borne excellent reputations in the community" (p. 300).

Reminiscent of Chesnutt's *The Marrow of Tradition*, in which a black doctor who is called in to save a white person suffers at the hands of a mob, and of Chesnutt's *The Colonel's Dream* with its similar projects scheduled for Central City, *The Fire in the Flint* is ultimately a pessimistic novel. Lynch law reigns supreme, and the Blacks do not have any redress against it. White's bleak view may again have been inspired by his own work to stir the nation's conscience about lynching. The NAACP had worked to get a national antilynching law passed for the five years preceding the publication of White's novel, but with no success. Perhaps to White, there was little black people, educated or otherwise, could do to halt the brutalities perpetrated against them through lynchings and burnings. They were victims when they defended themselves and victims when they did not. Kenneth's plight, in particular, anticipates that of Roy Williams in Langston Hughes's "Home."

The Ritual as It Results from Violation of Sexual Taboo

A primary concern motivating the rituals in postslavery settings is the myth of Southern white womanhood—its purity, and therefore, its untouchability. Langston Hughes recounts in "Home," a short story from *The Ways of White Folks* (1933), the tale of an accomplished black musician who is hanged as a result of speaking to his former teacher, an elderly white woman. The whites have already defined Roy Williams, who has made his reputation in Europe and returned home, as an "uppity nigger," one who has education, clothing, and talents that should be reserved for whites only. But because Roy is law abiding and generally stays out of the way of whites, they have no rational excuse for doing him violence (rationality instead of legality, because the law is never a concern). This excuse comes in the implied mythical threat to white womanhood:

> The sidewalk filled with white young ruffians with red-necks, open
> sweaters, and fists doubled up to strike. The movies had just let out
> and the crowd, passing by and seeing, objected to a Negro talking
> to a white woman—insulting a White Woman—attacking a WHITE
> woman—RAPING A WHITE WOMAN.[24]

Under the guise of protecting a white woman, the mob can kill Roy
and thus eliminate the threat to its image of white superiority in
education and art. The roles they play are predetermined by the
traditions, real or implied, that they uphold. The men in the crowd
respond in the only way they deem appropriate; their ritualistic
roles have been·decided by their culture:

> So they knocked Roy down. They trampled on his hat and cane and
> gloves as a dozen men tried to get to him to pick him up—so some
> one else could have the pleasure of knocking him down again. They
> struggled over the privilege of knocking him down.
>   Roy looked up from the sidewalk at the white mob around him.
> His mouth was full of blood and his eyes burned. His clothes were
> dirty. . . .
>   Some one jerked him to his feet. Some one spat in his face. (It
> looked like his old playmate, Charlie Mumford.) Somebody cussed
> him for being a nigger, and another kicked him from behind. And
> all the men and boys in the lighted street began to yell and scream
> like mad people, and to snarl like dogs, and to pull at the little
> Negro in spats they were dragging through the town towards the
> woods.
>   The little Negro whose name was Roy Williams began to choke
> on the blood in his mouth. And the roar of their voices and the scuff
> of their feet were split by the moonlight into a thousand notes like a
> Beethoven sonata. And when the white folks left his brown body,
> stark naked, strung from a tree at the edge of town, it hung there all
> night, like a violin for the wind to play.[25]

Roy's superior education and clothing have made the whites look
ridiculous; such an affront cannot be tolerated. Therefore, Roy's
body is left as a parody of his accomplishments; he has been used
as an instrument for revenge, and his very body is reduced to a
thing that the mobsters can play with.

    Hughes's story was published following a decade of "scientific"
studies—biological, anthropological, and psychological—to prove
or disprove the inferiority of Blacks and may have been inspired by
these.[26] After reviewing these studies, Walter White concludes:
"Discrimination, injustice, brutality, and even lynchings are beyond all doubt due in part to the racial self-esteem of whites and

their attitudes towards those whom the pseudo-scientists have dubbed inferior, which has sprung from such false conclusions."[27]

The protection-of-white-womanhood theme is stated just as explicitly in Charles W. Chesnutt's *The Marrow of Tradition* (1901), in which a middle-aged black servant is erroneously accused of raping and murdering a seventy-year-old white woman:

> "Burn the nigger," reiterated McBane. "We seem to have the right nigger, but whether we have or not, burn *a* nigger. It is an assault upon the white race, in the person of old Mrs. Ochiltree, committed by the black race, in the person of some nigger. It would justify the white people in burning *any* nigger. The example would be all the more powerful if we got the wrong one. It would serve notice on the niggers that we shall hold the whole race responsible for the misdeeds of each individual."[28]

Any scapegoat becomes necessary for symbolic statement. The punished will take upon himself the committed evil, whether or not he is guilty, and the world will be set right again. The gods of vengeance will have been appeased. It should be pointed out that one of the major concerns in the novel is "nigger domination." With the voting power of Blacks during Reconstruction, black majority was a real threat in some areas, a threat which encouraged lynching-bees on any pretext. Although the servant escapes burning in this instance, the motive behind such threats is nevertheless apparent.

Paul Laurence Dunbar explores the justification for defending white womanhood by having his white protagonist express the traditional way of looking at black threats to that womanhood. In "The Lynching of Jube Benson," Dr. Melville relates how Jube is falsely accused of murdering his mistress, who is also the doctor's fiancée. The doctor recounts his feelings once Jube is discovered: "I saw his black face glooming there in the half light, and I could only think of him as a monster. *It's tradition*" (emphasis mine).[29] Similarly, Theodore Dreiser's narrator emphasizes the effect of tradition in the lynching he witnessed of a black man accused of attacking a white girl in "Nigger Jeff": "Still, also, custom seemed to require death in this way for this. It was like some axiomatic, mathematic law—hard, but custom. The silent company, an articulated, mechanical and therefore terrible thing, moved on. It was also axiomatic, mathematic."[30]

Once captured, Dunbar's Jube is taken back into town to await his death.

> Hungry hands were ready. We hurried him out into the yard. A rope
> was ready. A tree was at hand. Well, that part was the least of it,
> save that Hiram Daly stepped aside to let me be the first to pull the
> rope. It was lax at first. Then it tightened, and I felt the quivering
> soft weight resist my muscles. Other hands joined and Jube swung
> off his feet. [P. 7]

At this moment the doctor cannot remember that Jube is a man
and a friend; he can only see a raging black monster out to destroy
white women. He blames his "false education" in this traditional
way of viewing Blacks with causing him to take part in the hanging-
murder of his loyal and trusted friend, one who had faithfully
nursed him through a bout with typhoid. The doctor can analyze
his action in retrospect (and after a white man is found to have committed the crime), but he could not resist the traditional, "mathe-
matical" role he willingly played at the time the black man was
accused.

The predetermined roles, the community spirit, the picnicking
atmosphere, the Sunday finery, the trophy gathering—all these familiar elements are brought to a height in the punishing of a violator of sexual taboo in James Baldwin's "Going to Meet the Man."[31]
Related in a flashback, the picnic/burning still has all the elements
of ritual. The story opens with Jesse, a white deputy sheriff in
charge of a small Southern town during a civil-rights demonstra-
tion, at home trying to make love to his wife after a particularly
frustrating day. He is unable to perform sexually, and his mind
roams back over the day's events; these, along with a remembered
incident from Jesse's childhood—that in which a black man was
burned to death—will serve as the sources of sexual arousal for the
momentarily impotent Jesse. Several Blacks have been jailed that
day, including a young man Jesse knew years before and who is
clearly the leader of the group of demonstrators. Jesse beats the
youth in an effort to get him to stop the other Blacks from singing
in jail. The young man refuses and Jesse applies a cattle prod to
various parts of his body, including his testicles. Staunch in his refusal, the young man suffers intense physical pain, but it is Jesse
who suffers psychologically as a result of the experience and who
responds sexually to it.

It is clear from the few thoughts Jesse has before he begins reflecting upon the day's events that he views Blacks as sexually different from himself, and that he holds them on the same level with
animals, assuming that they breed with abandon, without any
sense of morality. The sexual difference initially centers upon the

distinctions he makes between his wife and black women. He meets his failure to perform with his wife Grace with a patience he would not exhibit with a black woman: "He could not ask her to do just a little thing for him, just to help him out, just for a little while, the way he could ask a nigger girl to do it" (p. 198). A "nigger" girl, since she already approaches the level of the animal, cannot be further degraded if she is requested to do something "whorish" in bed. Jesse's thoughts of what a black woman can do cause "a distant excitement in him, like a far away light," but the thought by itself is not enough to renew his sexual strength.

His belief that marital infidelity can be discounted if it merely takes the form of sexual release with black women illustrates the considerably devalued position he accords such women. He and other white men in the town use their positions and their color to overcome black women sexually whenever they are in the mood for a different sexual experience. He regrets that, with the demonstrations, those times have changed:

> Sometimes, sure, like any other man, he knew that he wanted a little more spice than Grace could give him and he would drive over yonder and pick up a black piece or arrest her, it came to the same thing, but he couldn't do that now, no more. There was no telling what might happen once your ass was in the air. [P. 199]

His sexual stereotyping of the races causes him to view black women as wild and free, harbingers of delight which can only be concocted by a perverse imagination.

To Jesse, black women are clearly antithetical to his wife Grace. As her name suggests, she represents that bearer of culture we have identified earlier in this study; her role in perpetuating the white race demands that she be pedestalized, so Jesse cannot "degrade" her by asking her to help him perform sexually.[32] Blacks, on the other hand, "are no better than animals" (p. 200), and they exist as "a whole tribe, pumping out kids, it looked like, every damn five minutes, and laughing and talking and playing music like they didn't have a care in the world" (p. 200). It is only logical then, to Jesse's way of thinking, that one can get sexual stimulation from a people who are so naturally free with their bodies.

Jesse turns from these reflections to the day's events, and it is further clear that he uses the pain he inflicts upon the leader of the demonstrators as a sexual stimulus. If the beating can arouse him, it is understandable that the killing and castrating of a black man would make him experience complete sexual fulfillment. As he be-

gins relating the day's events to Grace, who is or is pretending to be
asleep, he provides graphic details of the beating scene, and, "as he
talked, he began to hurt all over with that peculiar excitement
which refused to be released" (p. 201). A couple of things are happening here. First of all, the twinges of excitement Jesse feels are
comparable to those he felt in thinking of the black woman; they
are both little stirrings in the face of his temporary impotence.
There is also a vicarious pleasure in remembering the excitement
he experienced at the moment he was beating the boy. The scene
then shifts, and Jesse is acting out again what he has done earlier
in the day. He applies the cattle prod to the young black man, hears
him scream, and feels again the joy he felt at that time. He culminates the beating by applying the cattle prod to the young man's
testicles and by kicking him when he consistently refuses to make
the other Blacks stop singing; he calls the boy a "bull" as a way of
separating himself from the human being he is treating so viciously.
So emotionally involved in the violence that he cannot control his
own shaking, Jesse stands over the unconscious boy and feels "very
close to a very peculiar, particular joy" (p. 202). That joy, of a sexual nature, is what triggers in Jesse the memory of the lynching/
burning he witnessed in childhood and the particular pleasure he
had felt then.

In the jail cell, though, he feels himself involved in a competition
with the leader of the demonstrators, one in which his very manhood is called into question. When the now-conscious young man
calls to Jesse, he instinctively "grabbed his privates" (p. 202), as if
whatever the young man would say would be a direct threat to
what he has just tried to destroy in the youth. And indeed there is a
challenge, for Jesse remembers that this is the young man who refused, even at ten years old, to accept chewing gum from him when
he had gone to collect money from the boy's grandmother. When
the young man now insists that Jesse and other white men will
learn to respect black women like his grandmother by calling them
Mrs., Jesse's response is both intimidated and sexual:

> "You lucky we *pump* some white blood into you every once in a
> while—your women! Here's what I got for all the black bitches in
> the world—!" Then he was, abruptly, almost too weak to stand; to
> his bewilderment, his horror, beneath his own fingers, he felt him-
> self violently stiffen—with no warning at all; he dropped his hands
> and he stared at the boy and he left the cell. [P. 204]

This memory of earlier sexual arousal must be set against Jesse's
current impotence and judged on the basis of how it, along with

other things he remembers, finally enables him to perform sexually with his wife.

That "peculiar, particular joy" he feels in the prisoner's cell, and the vague memory it evokes in him, is tied to the incident in his life in which he had perhaps first identified Blacks with a special sexuality. As his impotence lingers, his mind wanders back to his early childhood when his father and mother took him to the burning-execution of a black man. Hundreds of their neighbors gather in the just dawning hours to punish the black offender; women and children are an integral part of the group. The occasion is used as a very special social outing. Jesse remembers that they carried food: "It was like a Fourth of July picnic" (p. 210). His mother had combed her hair and put on "the dress she wore to church" (p. 211). In answer to his questions about a picnic, his father had said, "That's right, . . . we're going on a picnic. You won't ever forget *this* picnic—!" (p. 211). His family and the neighbors sing joyously on the way to the picnic grounds.

In the early morning arrival at the scene, Jesse is "handled, hugged, and patted, and told how much he had grown" (p. 214). The casual, festive atmosphere continues and the black man who "knocked down old Miss Standish" is brought chained before the crowd. A mood of delightful anticipation develops. The fire is started and the black man is lowered and raised above it as if the men are roasting a pig or barbecuing a chicken. Jesse observes the group anticipation: "There were two older men, friends of his father's, raising and lowering the chain; *everyone, indiscriminately, seemed to be responsible for the fire*" (emphasis mine, p. 215). All must protect and defend what Miss Standish represented.

Here the specific threat to Miss Standish, black male sexuality, must be reduced and controlled. Control that was only implied in works by earlier black writers is made explicit in Baldwin through the process of castration. It is necessary to quote a long passage to illustrate orgiastic group involvement, the propensity to ceremony, and the transferral of sexual power from the black man to the white males present.

> He [Jesse] turned his head a little and saw the field of faces. He watched his mother's face. Her eyes were very bright, her mouth was open: she was more beautiful than he had ever seen her, and more strange. He began to feel a joy he had never felt before. He watched the hanging, gleaming body, the most beautiful and terrible object he had ever seen till then. One of his father's friends reached up and in his hands he held a knife: and Jesse wished that he had been that man. It was a long, bright knife and the sun

seemed to catch it, to play with it, to caress it—it was brighter than
the fire. And a wave of laughter swept the crowd. Jesse felt his father's hands on his ankles slip and tighten. The man with the knife
walked toward the crowd, smiling slightly; as though this were a
signal, silence fell; he heard his mother cough. Then the man with
the knife walked up to the hanging body. He turned and smiled
again. Now there was a silence all over the field. The hanging head
looked up. It seemed fully conscious now, as though the fire had
burned out terror and pain. The man with the knife took the nigger's
privates in his hand, one hand, still smiling, as though he were
weighing them. In the cradle of the one white hand, the nigger's
privates seemed as remote as meat being weighed in the scales;
but seemed heavier, too, much heavier, and Jesse felt his scrotum
tighten; and huge, huge, much bigger than his father's, flaccid,
hairless, the largest thing he had ever seen till then, and the black-
est. The white hand stretched them, cradled them, caressed them.
Then the dying man's eyes looked straight into Jesse's eyes—it
could not have been as long as a second, but it seemed longer than a
year. Then Jesse screamed, and the crowd screamed as the knife
flashed, first up, then down, cutting the dreadful thing away, and
the blood came roaring down. Then the crowd rushed forward,
tearing at the body with their hands, with knives, with rocks, with
stones, howling and cursing. [PP. 216–17][33]

By its laughter, the crowd gives its approval to the knife wielder to
reduce the black man's potential sexual power to insignificance.
(The knife wielder's anonymity—"the man with the knife"—rein-
forces his group role; he acts for the will of the crowd, not as an
individual.) Stereotypes about black male sexuality inform the
whole scene. The "heavier" weight of the black man's privates is
the weight of the white stereotypical myth of threatening black
male sexuality. Treating the popular white attitudes toward such
subjects spanning a period of nearly three centuries in America,
Winthrop D. Jordan comments that

> castration of Negroes clearly indicated a desperate, generalized
> need in white men to persuade themselves that they were really
> masters and in all ways masterful, and it illustrated dramatically
> the ease with which white men slipped over into treating their
> Negroes like their bulls and stallions whose "spirit" could be sub-
> dued by emasculation.[34]

The whites can thus control Blacks and experience their own sexual purgation at the same time. There is clearly a kind of communal orgasm at the death of the black man in Baldwin's story. Jesse

sees this effect upon his father, whose "eyes were very peaceful" (p. 217) and in the general sense of sharing the crowd experiences.

Baldwin's passage illustrates not only the whites' desire for mastery over Blacks, but also the desire of whites, especially white males, to harness black sexuality and use it for their own purposes. After reminiscing on the scene, Jesse wakes his now sleeping wife and asserts: "Come on, sugar, I'm going to do you like a nigger, just like a nigger, come on, sugar, and love me just like you'd love a nigger" (p. 210). His eagerness suggests that he is depending upon stereotypes that not only he, but Grace as well, holds about black people. She may be prudish in her own sexual responses, but she has undoubtedly been made aware of what "they" do. That she does not resist her now aroused husband shows how willing she is to use stereotypes to her own advantage and for her own satisfaction, for she "moans" with pleasure under Jesse's renewed activity. He has succeeded in transferring the black man's sexuality to himself, a transferral that is partially suggested by the intensity of his eye contact with the dying man. Calvin Hernton offers an insightful comment on the need in white males to appropriate black male sexuality to themselves by castrating black men:

> Castration represents not only the destruction of that mythical monster, but also the *partaking* of that monster. It is a disguised form of worship, a primitive pornographic divination rite—and a kind of homosexualism in reverse. In taking the black man's genitals, the hooded men in white are amputating that portion of themselves which they secretly consider vile, filthy, and most of all, inadequate. At the same time, castration is the acting out of the white man's guilt for having sex with Negro women, and of the white man's hatred and envy of the Negro male's supposed relations with and appeal to white women. And finally, through the castration rite, white men hope to acquire the grotesque powers they have assigned to the Negro phallus, which they symbolically extol by the act of destroying it.[35]

The black man is considered bestial, possessing animalistic passion. But at the same time, ironically, Jesse goes to meet "the Man"; the sexual capacity might be thought bestial, but such prowess is the basis on which all *true* men are judged. From a psychosexual point of view, Jesse sees the "beast" as a man. The difference in calling sexuality bestial on the one hand and manly on the other is the difference between black and white. Here again is the evidence of the ritual nature of the act: if the white man can attribute his own basest sexual desires to the black man, as Jordan observed, then he can remain clean, pure, and morally superior in the eyes of his society. The crowd not only evinces solidarity in protecting Southern womanhood, but in protecting its image of itself.

This image, according to Baldwin and other black writers, has remained basically unchanged during the past century, and hence, the whites' need to destroy Blacks has remained unchanged. The cruelty persists; the lawlessness persists; the warped defense of eroded values persists. The forms of oppression may change, but the basic structure which they support is still in place.

Thus, the lynching is a ritual in support of the preservation of values, and, for Jesse, it is a rite of passage, an indication that he is being prepared to take his place in a society whose values are sanctioned. The lynching/roast occurred when he was a tiny boy riding on his father's shoulders and has served the purpose of initiation for Jesse. He had sensed that at the time and "had loved his father more than he ever loved him. He felt that his father had carried him through a mighty test, had revealed to him a great secret which would be the key to his life forever" (p. 217). Jesse's perception was correct, for he has been initiated into all the ugliness of power and control over Blacks that the mobsters would have thought his just due. The frame story, set in the present, shows Jesse exhibiting all the values he was so graphically initiated into accepting. Jesse has adopted, as Peter Freese asserts, "his whole view of life from his father." [36] He beats the black youth and jails his fellows because they have stepped out of their place. True to the lessons he has learned about considering Blacks somewhat less than human and certainly not deserving of respect, he refers to the black leader's grandmother as "Old Julia" and cannot condone the youth's need to assert: "You might know a Old Julia someplace else, white man. But don't nobody by that name live here" (p. 203). Jesse considers the youth a "crazy kid," one who obviously does not know how to act with white people.

Though Jesse may have forgotten his little black friend Otis, whom he had known at the time of the burning, how he treats Blacks in the present parallels what his father had hinted should be Otis's fate. The two boys, still innocent in their childhood, had been frequent playmates until Jesse noticed one day that he had not seen Otis for a couple of days. This is after the "crime" for which the black man will be roasted has been committed and before the man is caught. When Jesse's father maintains that Otis is absent because he is probably afraid, the boy retorts: "But Otis didn't do nothing!" (p. 209), to which his father responds: "Otis

can't do nothing . . . he's too little. . . . We just want to make sure
Otis *don't* do nothing" (p. 209). Thus the killing functions both as
an example to other Blacks and as an initiation for Jesse into his
future role in relation to Blacks. They should be confined and kept
in their places, and vivid lessons should always be taught to them
if they dare to refuse the order under which they must live.

Jesse's reference to doing his wife "like a nigger" reflects the
place of subservience, sexual abandon, and general disrespect to
which he has relegated all black men and women. Ironically, and
subconsciously, it also reflects his envy of the sexual and spiritual
manhood he attributes to black men. However, on the conscious
level, his society has taught him well in terms of his position in relation to Blacks. He is the person of power and authority; Blacks
exist for his control and exploitation, and at the mercy of his whims.
The ritual has been crucial in inculcating this.

Baldwin uses the lynching scene in his story for structural as
well as thematic considerations. It serves to develop the plot of the
story by exposing the earlier antagonism between Jesse and the
black leader and by showing the black youth's dissatisfaction with
the position he has been assigned. The scene characterizes Jesse
and provides necessary information about his acceptance of a role
defined by his group, an acceptance which has been exhibited by
his treatment of the marching Blacks. In spite of these traditional,
customary attitudes of whites towards Blacks, however, Baldwin
suggests that a part of the structure may be crumbling. The disintegration is not due to a change of attitude on Jesse's part, but on
the part of the black leader who sets out to overturn traditional
white ways of viewing Blacks. Even while the young black man is
being beaten senselessly, he continues to maintain:

> "My grandmother's name was Mrs. Julia Blossom. *Mrs.* Julia
> Blossom. You going to call our women by their right names yet.
> —And those kids ain't going to stop singing. We going to keep on
> singing until every one of you miserable white mothers go stark
> raving out of your minds." [P. 202]

Although the ritual still works for Jesse, the potential for its destruction, Baldwin suggests in the story, is already in the making;
even as Jesse is doing his wife "like a nigger," the sound of cars
bringing black demonstrators to town echoes on the gravel road
outside Jesse's house, and the dogs which have barked incessantly
throughout the story continue to indicate that all is not as well as
Jesse now assumes it to be. The ironic overtones of the title also
imply that Baldwin sees the ritual as threatened; there has been

positive progression from Johnson's "brute" and McKay's "dreadful thing" to Baldwin's "Man."[37]

Freeing themselves from the shackles of restricting definitions is a major part of the struggle in which all of these characters are engaged. To move from dehumanization to the claiming of manhood or womanhood often proves too great an effort for them, yet they do make the attempt. It is that slight effort at resistance, one which usually ends in death, that points the way to the larger purpose of these scenes. The black characters always desire instinctively to act as human beings; they will wear their fancy clothes, get their educations, and strike back—as best they can—when struck. Though they may die in the process, such intuitive responses presage possibilities for racial survival. They want to live, even in the face of death, as we shall see with the unusually repressed characters in Richard Wright's works.

CHAPTER 4

Ritual Violence and the
Formation of An Aesthetic

Unlike many of the writers whose works are discussed in the preceding chapter, Richard Wright uses the lynching and burning ritual, and historical and social connotations surrounding it, to shape the basis of his aesthetic vision of the world. Metaphoric lynching, along with literal lynching, permeates his works. Together they set a pervasive tone of fear and apprehension. The ritual also determines communal and individual character and provides the symbolic unifying structure for "Between the World and Me" (1935), "Big Boy Leaves Home" (1938), *Native Son* (1940), and *The Long Dream* (1958). Much more centrally integrated into the whole of his works than in that of works by writers preceding and following him, the lynching metaphor becomes for Wright's characters the stimuli in reaction to which their life responses are made. The male characters live, eat, and breathe the threats perpetually hanging over their heads, and the women in their lives are forced to share their anxieties or be dismissed from consideration.

Wright's preoccupation with ritual violence paralleled in part the increased concern in the 1920s and 1930s over the lynching of Blacks and the brutality with which they were killed; there was a corollary increase in the thematic treatment of lynching by black writers who were sensitive to black history and circumstance in the United States. Richard Wright joined Langston Hughes, Sterling Brown, and other black writers in a heightened attention in their literary productions to one of the prevailing dangers to black life. In 1930, a few years before Wright's works began to appear, twenty black persons were lynched in the United States, which means they were accused of crimes, pursued, captured and either summarily executed by hanging, burning, or shooting, or executed after they were given a mock trial, or taken from jails and summarily executed in a similar manner. Twenty is not a substantial number for one year's victims in the history of the lynching of Blacks in the United States; the number exceeded two hundred a year in the peak years of the 1890s. What is glaring is the year—1930—and what is curious about twenty is that it represents an increase of al-

95

most two hundred percent over the number of black lynch victims for 1929 (7), fifty percent over 1928 (10), and twenty percent over 1927 (16). In 1931, there would be a decline again to twelve victims and to six in 1932.[1] Economic disasters concomitant to the Depression obviously had an effect upon the rising number in 1930; increased idleness and irritability were probably additional factors. Blacks, who had always been an irritation to whites, now found themselves in an even more precarious position for receiving the effects of white frustration. Not only, therefore, did the number of black victims increase in 1930, so too did the brutality with which lives were taken. Arthur F. Raper points out that "a number of the victims were tortured, mutilated, dragged, or burned," which suggested "the presence of sadistic tendencies among the lynchers."[2]

If twenty Blacks could be lynched in 1930 and the known lynchers could escape punishment for their barbarities, then something was still seriously and drastically wrong with a country which promised equality for all. Wright began to attack the problem in his works and to formulate from this one historical pattern an aesthetic which grew out of oppression.

Wright would incorporate the gruesome details of historical lynchings again and again in the development of his fiction. His portrayal of the atrocities parallel almost exactly those of real-life events. One such historical event will serve as comparison for the details Wright presents in "Between the World and Me" and "Big Boy Leaves Home." From his tabulations and descriptions of lynchings which occurred in 1930, Raper includes one from Ocilla, Georgia. Under a heading, "The Extremes of Mob Action," Raper recounts that, during the execution of James Irwin of Ocilla, Georgia on February 1, the victim

> was jabbed in his mouth with a sharp pole. His toes were cut off joint by joint. His fingers were similarly removed, and his teeth extracted with wire pliers. After further unmentionable mutilations, the Negro's still living body was saturated with gasoline and a lighted match was applied. As the flames leaped up, hundreds of shots were fired into the dying victim. During the day, thousands of people from miles around rode out to see the sight. Not till nightfall did the officers remove the body and bury it.[3]

The victim had been accused of rape and murder. The mutilations Raper finds "unmentionable" include such items as cutting off ears and castration. There were also instances, the Ocilla case included, in which souvenirs were gathered from the lynched and burned

bodies. The reporter who is timid about the "unmentionable mutilations" joins many historians and others writing about lynching
in the United States. Barbarities were not reported in the name of
delicacy. By contrast, Wright would not find the details unmentionable; he would record the killing and the over-kill, as well as
the ceremonial aspects of both.

The hangings and burnings of the Ocilla variety that Raper and
Wright treat are literally and figuratively lynchings. Wright would
formulate his aesthetic based on a literal, historical level and would
take it to a symbolic level. The two levels also existed historically
in the 1930s. Ocilla, Georgia, provided a literal lynching, but Scotts-
boro, Alabama, in 1931 provided a figurative one. There was no
rope, but the nine young black men who were accused of raping
two white women aboard a freight train were clearly lynched.[4]
They were lynched as certainly as Bigger Thomas is lynched in *Native Son*. Again, in both instances, the victims are accused of rape.
Wright would take the implications of this accusation and use
them repeatedly in his artistic works to make statements on the
conditions of black life when it is necessarily antagonistically pitted
against white life in this country.

In "Between the World and Me," Wright introduces the lynching/
burning image which would hold an acute fascination for him in
later years; it would become the center of his aesthetic for the remainder of his literary career. Careful examination of the poem
will reveal the artistic use Wright makes of historical violence—
how he sets tone, shapes dramatic tension, uses detail for connotative associations, and links past with present. He also uses contrasting imagery (light and darkness, and warmth and cold as
parallels for life and death) and other contrasts (the individual
against society, man and animal). He further depends upon audience (reader) participation and creates an artistic storytelling tradition by lifting his victim to the level of conscious artist. The
speaker in the poem becomes an artist who shares with Wright a
historically based approach to the creation of literature. A long
poem, "Between the World and Me" was published in *The Partisan
Review* in 1935. The poem is not usually anthologized or as well
known as are Wright's other works, yet Wright critics consider it of
significant value. For example, Keneth Kinnamon calls it Wright's
"most successful early poem" and claims that Wright's career as a
poet was important because it produced a "poem of unmistakable
merit, 'Between the World and Me.'"[5] The text of the poem is as
follows:

And one morning while in the woods I suddenly stumbled upon
    the thing,
Stumbled upon it in a grassy clearing guarded by scaly oaks
    and elms.
And the sooty details of the scene rose, thrusting themselves
    between the world and me . . .

There was a design of white bones slumbering forgottenly upon a
    cushion of gray ashes.
There was a charred stump of a sapling pointing a blunt finger
    accusingly at the sky.
There were torn tree limbs, tiny veins of burnt leaves, and a
    scorched coil of greasy hemp;
A vacant shoe, an empty tie, a ripped shirt, a lonely hat, and a
    pair of trousers stiff with black blood.
And upon the trampled grass were buttons, dead matches,
    butt-ends of cigars and cigarettes, peanut shells, a drained
    gin-flask, and a whore's lipstick;
Scattered traces of tar, restless arrays of feathers, and the
    lingering smell of gasoline.
And through the morning air the sun poured yellow surprise into
    the eye sockets of a stony skull . . .

And while I stood there my mind was frozen with a cold pity for
    the life that was gone.
The ground gripped my feet and my heart was circled with icy
    walls of fear—
The sun died in the sky; a night wind muttered in the grass and
    fumbled with leaves in the trees; the woods poured forth the
    hungry yelping of hounds; the darkness screamed with thirsty
    voices; and the witnesses rose and lived:
The dry bones stirred, rattled, lifted, melting themselves into
    my bones.
The gray ashes formed flesh firm and black, entering into my
    flesh.
The gin-flask passed from mouth to mouth; cigars and cigarettes
    glowed, the whore smeared lipstick red upon her lips.
And a thousand faces swirled around me, clamoring that my life
    be burned . . .

And then they had me, stripped me, battering my teeth into my
    throat till I swallowed my own blood.
My voice was drowned in the roar of their voices, and my black
    wet body slipped and rolled in their hands as they bound me to
    the sapling.
And my skin clung to the bubbling hot tar, falling from me in
    patches,

And the down and the quills of the white feathers sank into my
  raw flesh, and I moaned in my agony.
Then my blood was cooled mercifully, cooled by a baptism of
  gasoline.
And in a blaze of red I leaped to the sky as pain rose like water,
  boiling my limbs.
Panting, begging, I clutched childlike, clutched to the hot sides
  of death.
Now I am dry bones and my face a stony skull staring in yellow
  surprise at the sun . . .⁶

On the literal level of the poem, the speaker presumably takes a
walk in the woods and uncovers the scene of a lynching and burning. He views the evidence of death and identifies vicariously with
the lynched/burned man. He imagines himself in turn being killed
by a white mob. In his observation and choice of details, the speaker
recreates on one level the motivation and atmosphere for the lynching, ones grounded in historical black experience in the United
States and, on another level, he uses detail for expression of an artistic statement he shares with Wright.

The speaker's walk is as abruptly interrupted as is Myop's in
Alice Walker's "The Flowers";⁷ both discover the evidence of a
black man having been lynched, and both lose their innocence as a
result of what they experience. Myop, who loses the innocence of
girlhood, does not encounter in as sharp detail the way in which
the man has died. With Wright's speaker, on the other hand, who is
himself a black man, there is identification with the victim as a
black human being and particularly as a black man. That identification enables him to become much more involved in imaginatively
recreating what has happened sometime before his arrival.

Representing a violation of human life and nature, the first few
details the speaker observes indicate that the mob has executed
a blasphemy against all living things. There is a general belief,
which Billie Holiday alludes to in "Strange Fruit," that the tree
upon which a man has been hanged will die because the "fruit"
it has been forced to bear is so unnatural. The "charred stump"
which points "a blunt finger accusingly" at the sky begins a series
of pathetic fallacies which produce an effect of nature's crying out
to higher powers for allowing such a cosmic outrage to occur.
"Torn tree limbs" and "veins of burnt leaves" further extend the
connection between nature and man; we can also speak of human
"limbs" being "torn," just as we can call an amputated leg or arm a
"stump." Man and nature have died together, and even as they
cushion each other, there is no peace. They cry out together for

some justice, and one kind of justice they receive is the artistic telling of their story so that the speaker, as artist, has the possibility of
affecting his audience to bring about either change or sympathy.

The declarative listing of details sets an initial tone which approaches detachment, a kind of calm after the storm. Items are catalogued as in a shopping list, and the extensive use of forms of the
verb "to be" control the speaker's emotional involvement at this
point. Only in the next stanza is the calm broken by a second
storm, the one in which the speaker's identification with the dead
man makes him live the scene all over again. He must work through
the same rage to a cathartic emotional "death," one which will
leave him wiser in the ways of the world in which he lives. Details
of calm and storm are selected for their connotative associations.
To anyone who has a passing acquaintance with violence done to
black men in America, much will be revealed beyond the simple
cataloguing.

In his seemingly casual observation of details, the speaker lists a
"whore's lipstick." Keneth Kinnamon asserts that the lipstick "suggests, to one familiar with southern mores, the ostensible motive of
the lynching."[8] Prompting Kinnamon's assessment is this historical assumption: a white woman judged to be free with her sexual
favors, or one who simply has a black lover, *must* cry rape when
discovered with the black man and *must* join the mob in pursuing
and killing him.[9] This might be the case in the poem; after all, the
speaker is careful to assign an identity to the owner of the lipstick.
It might also, however, be an instance of women joining the lynching festivities (they were very prone to do so) and prostitutes, who
are presumably less inhibited than some females, would perhaps
be in the forefront. Wright's assigning of the lipstick to a whore
also imaginatively undercuts the claims white men usually made
to the sanctity and "purity" of Southern white womanhood. A man,
who may or may not have had sexual contact with her, must die for
a woman who sells her virtue for profit. Such twisted reasoning
underscores the unmatched irrationality involved in lynching for
presumed crimes of a sexual nature; it enables the speaker to imagine a "hungry yelping of hounds," indicative of the chase scene
which developed once the "crime" was discovered. Since charges
of alleged rape were the most emotional causes of lynching of
black men, the connotations of the whore's lipstick provide historical and creative dimensions to the explanation of motive in
the poem.

The speaker's observation of the details of evidence before him also recreates for the reader the historical atmosphere of a holiday. Matches, cigars and cigarettes, peanut shells (especially), lipstick —all indicate the casualness and festivity, the sadistic desire for pleasure, with which a life has been taken. The activity might easily have been a baseball game, at which the home team won. Historically, lynchings were often holiday and dress-up affairs. One historian records that for the famous lynching/burning of Henry Smith in Paris, Texas, in 1893, "excursion trains were run for the occasion and there were many women and children in the throng which watched the sufferings of the victim."[10] A reporter following a lynching in the South recalled that farmers drove their wagons into town from the surrounding farms: "Their wives and children and dogs were along. Many brought lunches—big six-layer cakes and fried chicken."[11] Wright's crowd seemed to have had a similar festive air. Yet, in the midst of the innocent holiday accoutrements, a man has been castrated ("a pair of trousers stiff with black blood" —black as in dried and black as in race), tarred and feathered, lynched and burned. To the speaker's mind, the crowd has indeed had a holiday of vengeance, one obviously designed to right the wrong it deems to have been committed against it. There is no evidence of regret or remorse, only the pathetic fallacy of "a sapling pointing a blunt finger accusingly at the sky."

The speaker's imaginative supplying of details to the lynching and burning is thorough, and his first reaction is universally human; he feels "a cold pity for the life that was gone." Contemplation sharpens the general response into specifics. His sorrow for humanity is redirected, and he begins to focus upon himself as an individual; he becomes afraid—"my heart was circled with icy walls of fear." But his fear is vague at this point; it has no direction. Further contemplation sharpens the vague fear even more in the direction of the specific; the general human degradation becomes the specific degradation of the *black* individual. The "I" becomes central for the speaker. As it becomes centralized, or specific, the "I" reverses itself and becomes simultaneously generalized again. The speaker is alone, but he is alone with the community of his race. Individual black tragedies become racial tragedies.

> The dry bones stirred, rattled, lifted, melting themselves
>   into my bones.
> The gray ashes formed flesh firm and black, entering into
>   my flesh. . . .
> And a thousand faces swirled around me, clamoring that
>   my life be burned . . .

What has happened to the victim can happen to the speaker. He then takes us to a higher level of imagination in transcending time and space and recreating with his own body what happened to the dead man sometime before.

The silence of the first part of the poem is transformed to what can be compared to the noise of a football stadium immediately after the singing of the National Anthem. As the speaker creates, we hear the roar of the voices drowning out his own, the hissing and bubbling of the tar, the mournful cries of his agony. In the realistic identification with his pain, we try to remember his crime. To his mind, his crime is his blackness, his racial identification with his dead brother. Since he does not know what crime the dead man has committed, he accuses himself of the only crime for which, in the eyes of whites, all Blacks are individually and racially guilty —that of blackness. David Demarest offers further comment on this racial and individual consciousness in the poem:

> On its most general level, the poem exemplifies a personal encounter with Donne's often-paraphrased words: no man is an island; ask not for whom the bell tolls, it tolls for thee. But in the black and white context of a lynch scene, a much more specific statement is implied: racial violence done to any single black involves all blacks, a compelling consciousness, a pity and fear, that is unavoidably involving, that can become an obsession. Such a consciousness of violence and threat must stand forever between the speaker and the world. No black can escape awareness of white violence; no black can avoid an identification with the victims.[12]

Imaginatively recreating the death scene with himself as victim, the speaker thereby becomes the artist. What he so vividly visualizes enables the reader to witness the horror and to be drawn into the experience. From the passive scene he has observed, the speaker actively creates a lifelike replica. The gin bottle no longer lies idle; it is "passed from mouth to mouth." The discarded lipstick becomes a grooming instrument. Blood is no longer "stiff" and dried; the speaker chokes on it. He portrays and experiences the horrors of being beaten, bound, tarred and feathered. He experiences the helplessness at the hands of the mob and the instruments which they use to "kill" him. His skin clings to the tar; the tar does not cling to him.

His use of alliteration, simile, metaphor, and hyperbole as well as the analogy to baptism extend the speaker's role as artist. The analogy, especially, adds artistic, historical, and racial dimensions to the speaker's creative endeavor. Baptism is assumed, first of all, to be reinforcing; it soothes the penitent in his belief in God and his union with the church. Ironically, the speaker's baptism is one of hatred, not one of love. It is administered by gasoline, not the life-giving substance of water. It is a baptism of fire, like Claude McKay's in "Baptism" and resembles, not the work of heavenly forces, but that of the Devil. The ironies of the baptism analogy are increased by its association with Christianity. Needless to say, there is nothing Christian about the act which is being envisioned unless it is viewed as a crucifixion, in which case the speaker, like Christ, is executed for upsetting the status quo. By choosing a metaphor that works on more than one level, the speaker enhances his stature as a budding artist.

The speaker's religious overtones also suggest something about the Christlike suffering Blacks have had to bear in America. They are murdered innocents, like Christ. In each case, "guilt" is inherent—in skin color for Blacks and in ethnic background, in part, for Christ. Also, both are killed for going against established order; the speaker has presumably violated sexual taboo and Christ dared to present Himself as king of the Jews. Claude McKay makes a similar comparison between Blacks and Christ for his portrayal of ritual violence in "The Lynching"; both he and Wright's speaker see the ironies of the religious connections between a "Christian" country and its unChristian actions. Again Demarest comments:

> The implications of the poem are amplified by religious sugges-
> tion—the "dry bones," the "baptism of gasoline," the general effect
> of crucifixion and saintly martyrdom. One result is to magnify the
> martyrdom blacks have suffered in America, and the point is under-
> scored that each victim—like dry bones—will rise and live again
> in the consciousness of other blacks. But part of the effect is also
> an attack on a "Christian" white America that crucifies men for
> sport.[13]

Perhaps, too, in the speaker's reference to baptism and dry bones there is an additional irony connected with black people being historically tied to such a brutal religion. They believed in baptism and waited patiently for the dry bones the preachers fed them from Sunday to Sunday to rise again. Is there no deliverance except in death? Or perhaps, just perhaps, the speaker turns the symbolism around. He says: "Now I am dry bones and my face a stony skull staring in yellow surprise at the sun . . ." By identifying himself as dry bones, the speaker defines himself as potential, potential not to rise up recreated in flesh to save a race, but the potential of the artist to become spokesman for that race and to assume a certain amount of responsibility toward it. His are the dry bones of creativity, the skeleton from which his body of works will grow. His has become a mission of revelation; he moves from observer to carrier of news, from the innocence of unordered observation to the accumulation of experience from which art flows, from the casual observer of related details to the ordering of details into literature.

The speaker has not only experienced a baptism of fire; he has had his epiphany and moved from the lack of artistic expression to the creation of art. Kinnamon also discusses the move from passive to active in the poem, but not in the context presented here.[14] The speaker has moved from pity and fear—emotional responses to the scene—to a calculated, systematic ordering of events. He allows the seemingly casual details to become the substance and formation of his first artistic creation. The sun no longer stares at the scene; he stares at the sun. He no longer allows details to act unconsciously upon him; he is in control of them.

Wright's speaker has made history the substance of art. He has looked into one of the experiences of black people in America and made that experience the motive in a search for truth. The truth of his, and indeed all black experience in America, is that the country is oppressive, its values are perverted, and it is basically immoral. In addition, whites will never view Blacks as their human or social equals, and they will continue to be powerful and destructive. Still, although one black man is victim, another is also on the scene—surviving. His survival is another undeniable truth. And, as Jean Toomer suggested in *Cane*, there is a beauty even in the ugliness of survival.

Wright, who gives his speaker life and manipulates his artistic growth, shares the same aesthetic with the speaker (if indeed at this point they can be said to exist apart from each other). Racial memory, Wright maintained, is a living thing; the history of Blacks in America and before that is an everpresent part of their ongoing lives and is a root from which artistic expression grows. He articulated this point in *12 Million Black Voices*:

> We black folk, our history and our present being, are a mirror of all the manifold experiences of America. What we want, what we represent, what we endure is what America *is*. If we black folk perish, America will perish. If America has forgotten her past, then let her look into the mirror of our consciousness and she will see the *living* past living in the present, for our memories go back, through our black folk of today, through the recollections of our black parents, and through the tales of slavery told by our black grandparents, to the time when none of us, black or white, lived in this fertile land.[15]

It is the role of the artist to keep those experiences and memories of the past a consuming part of the present. The black writer must become as Wright's speaker in mastering the details of black experience in America and ordering them for a consistent artistic statement ("the witnesses rose and lived"). In an essay written in 1937, Wright presented what he had worked out artistically in the poem in 1935; black writers must have a nationalistic bent to their work and black history must be a major part of the themes they should develop. "Theme for Negro writers," Wright wrote, "will emerge when they have begun to feel the meaning of the history of their race as though they in one lifetime had lived it themselves throughout all the long centuries." [16] Living the racial experience and recreating it is certainly what Wright's speaker does in "Between the World and Me" and what Wright used as a guide for all of his work.

Historically and socially, black people in the United States will forever experience a division between themselves ("me") and the rest of the country ("the world"). That division of the individual against society, or the minority against the majority, will never be looked upon with the nostalgic sweetness which defines the experiences of Huck Finn; it will always be viewed with hostility. Blacks in America will always run the risk of being treated as "things," or debased to the level of animals; rarely will their humanity be given room to blossom. As mediator, the artist can hope to bring about some changes in this condition, and he may discover, as Charles W. Chesnutt did at the turn of the century, that most of his mediating efforts are looked upon with a questioning or a debunking eye. Still, he has his calling, and Wright believed he had to do what he could.

The lynching as presented in "Between the World and Me" serves as a model for literal and metaphorical lynchings which occur throughout the corpus of Wright's work as well as a model for discussion of the psychology of repression used historically against Blacks. From "Big Boy Leaves Home," which was written in 1935 and revised in 1936, to the other stories in *Uncle Tom's Children*, to *Native Son* and *The Long Dream*, lynchings appear at various levels of treatment in Wright's work. Wright uses this central metaphor to follow the pattern established in "Between the World and Me," to play upon it, and to extend it to additional levels of symbolic interpretation. For example, in "Big Boy Leaves Home," written immediately after "Between the World and Me," another literal lynching and burning occurs. In the short story, however, Wright has increased the possible dimensions of interpretation.

Motive that was ambiguous in "Between the World and Me"

is made explicit in "Big Boy Leaves Home." Big Boy and three of his companions, Bobo, Lester, and Buck, go swimming nude in a forbidden waterhole and encounter a white woman momentarily separated from her escort. The woman screams. The myth of the threat to white womanhood raises its ugly head, and in the ensuing events, during which the boys are only trying to get their clothes, the white man fatally wounds two of them. He is then overpowered by Big Boy and Bobo; Big Boy shoots him when he tries to regain control of the gun. Big Boy, Bobo, Buck, and Lester have violated sexual and racial taboo by putting their nude black bodies in the presence of a white woman (although the soldier is killed, the "real crime" relates to the white woman). In this scene, Wright evokes many aspects of racial repression and denial. Literally, the woman's body cannot be touched by the black boys (and that is not their desire); to do so, or even to put themselves in the position of being *accused* of doing so, is a violation of racial taboo that is punishable by death. Figuratively, the white woman becomes a symbol of denial. The boys have already violated taboo by swimming in the forbidden waterhole. To have a white woman appear at that scene as an additional untouchable object further emphasizes restrictions placed upon the boys because of their blackness. They must stay in their physically defined worlds, away from even the thought of emotional encounter with white women. The woman here is *not* a whore, as the one in the poem is assumed to be; therefore, the position the boys find themselves in, in relation to her, is infinitely more dangerous.

When Big Boy kills the soldier who comes to the woman's unneeded rescue, he and Bobo are awakened to a sense of their personal and racial danger as acutely as the speaker in "Between the World and Me" is awakened to his. Blackness is enough of a "crime" without adding a real one to it (justification of innocence or guilt is irrelevant in the historical scheme of things). As a result of initiation into awareness of vulnerability, Big Boy and Bobo attempt an escape immediately; Big Boy is successful, Bobo is not. The "hungry yelping of hounds" the speaker has imagined in "Between the World and Me" becomes a group of men running along a hillside with guns and "coils of rope slung over shoulders," and with dogs baying at their heels.[17] The chase that was only suggested by evidence in the poem is brought to its climactic finish in the story. The speaker in the poem can only surmise what the chase might have been like, since he is locked in a specific moment. From Big Boy's limited perspective, we witness the end of the chase as it culminates near his hiding place in a kiln on the hill where Bobo is burned. Only in *Native Son* will the full chase be presented, where "the hungry yelping of hounds" becomes an extended police hounding through a concrete jungle, with glaring searchlights and modern "lynching" equipment.

The picnic, ball-game atmosphere that could only be reconstructed imaginatively in the poem is made central to the story. Big Boy witnesses the gayety, the spirit of festivity with which the burning of Bobo is carried out. The members of the mob (men and women) sing as they bring Bobo up the hill—"*We'll hang ever nigger t a sour apple tree . . .*" (pp. 47, 48), after which there is "hard laughter." Bobo must be burned as quickly as possible, not only as an example to other Blacks, but to soothe the insecurities of frightened and mythically threatened whites. One member of the group remarks: "Ef they git erway notta woman in this town would be safe" (p. 46).

The burning of Bobo is carried out in community spirit. One man brings wood, another tar and feathers, still another gasoline. Women are vocal in their desire to see everything and are as eager for Bobo's death as their men.

> "Jack! Jack! Don't leave me! Ah wanna see im!"
> "Theyre bringin im over the hill, sweetheart!"
> "AH WANNA BE THE FIRS T PUT A ROPE ON THA BLACK BASTARDS NECK!"
> "Les start the fire!"
> "Heat the tar!"
> "Ah got some chains t chain im."
> "Bring im over this way!"
> "Chris, Ah wished Ah hada drink . . ." [P. 48]

There is a sense of hurry necessitated not only by the desire to placate the crowd, but by impending rain. When the rain does come, Bobo is a "writhing white mass gradually growing black, . . ." (p. 49).

White women, the most potentially threatened according to the mythical structure, join their husbands in making the burning a community ritual. Two Wright critics are perceptive in tying the sexual elements of the story together as they relate to both white males and white females. One comments:

> The myth of Negro sexual superiority is linked with the myth that every black male desires a white woman. Together they work to create the fear and hatred revealed in "Big Boy Leaves Home." The fear of being sexually inferior produces jealousy and the neces-

sity for vengeance in the white men. The act of burning and mutilating the black youth is basically an act of sexual revenge. Concomitant with the fear of rape held by the white women is sexual
desire and curiosity. The burning of the Negro is a vicarious sexual
experience for the women who watch.[18]

And clearly, too, the white males equally experience a kind of sexual purgation; however, the above quotation is unusual in the
critic's willingness to see an active, participatory role for the women
who witness the lynching. In his observation that there is ambigu-
ity in whether the white woman is "frightened" or "fascinated" as
she stands paralyzed before the nude black boys is further recognition that the women were at times not as innocent as they and
their white consorts insisted.

Another critic suggests that the behavior of the white woman "is
composed of sexual come-on and paralyzing fear"; it leads to the
lynching of Bobo, an act which takes the place "of the sexual act
itself." The women who cry out for their husbands not to leave
them and to wait so that they can see Bobo are crying out "in ec-
stasy." The analysis continues:

> At the beginning of the story nature smiled, in light, over the free,
> uncontaminated sexuality of the black boys dancing naked; nature
> now sags low, heavy with clouds, as the white community reaches
> its sexual consummation. The orgasm is a burst of fire, and then the
> quiet afterplay of rain. . . . The desire is not merely to punish—a
> bullet could do that— . . . The desire, much more than a desire to
> punish, is a desire to enjoy. The desire is desire. . . . the story, on
> the surface a tale of hurt and death and pain and physical dis-
> comfort and terror, is a story about pleasure. . . . The white com-
> munity, man and woman together, achieves the release of a huge,
> black pain.[19]

The white women also join their husbands in making the lynching song "round and full," and they, like their husbands, eagerly respond to the shout, "LES GIT SOURVINEERS!" Someone does
manage to get a finger and an ear before being driven back by the
intensity of the heat. Dan McCall suggests that "the plucking off of
the 'SOURVINEERS,' fingers and ears, becomes, symbolically, the
act of ripping off the black penis."[20] This gathering of trophies completes the transformation of the lynching/burning scene from one
of simple killing to one of ritualistic execution. The whites have
gone beyond the mere expiation of sin; they have gone to extremes
in making their power felt and in consolidating themselves against

any threats to that power. Wright is again drawing upon historical occurrences to make his point about suppression. Many lynching victims had their remains chopped or broken up and parceled out to the executioners.[21] Historically, and in "Big Boy Leaves Home," that which had the power to harm, here Bobo specifically, but represented by his ear, is reduced to a trivial thing, the ownership of which restores the carrier to a position of control over that thing. The same kind of transference of power or good luck to ward off threats works in just the opposite manner with rabbits' feet and black cats' bones. Collecting souvenirs from black victims gives whites a physical symbol of superiority and power, epitomized by their ability to crush anything or anyone who dares to defy a taboo of the group.[22]

By working with his central metaphor of a lynching, Wright moves it from the implied ritual of "Between the World and Me" to the specific implications of primitivism and the ritual of the expulsion of scapegoats in "Big Boy Leaves Home." One Wright critic, Blyden Jackson, has recognized the ritual dimension of the crowd's behavior, but in a slightly different context.[23] The burning of Bobo, Jackson asserts, is a rite of castration.

> Wright, whether wittingly or not, gathers up the essence of that which he is struggling to express and stores it all into one symbol and its attendant setting. For the spectacle of Bobo aflame at the stake does constitute a symbol. It is a symbol, moreover, the phallic connotations of which cannot be denied. Indeed, the particularity of its detail—the shape of its mass, its coating of tar, the whiteness of the feathers attached to its surface or floating out into the surrounding air— are almost too grossly and gruesomely verisimilar for genteel contemplation. Whether Wright so intended it or not, the lynching of Bobo is symbolically a rite of castration. . . . In the lynching of Bobo, thus, all lynchings are explained, and all race prejudice. Both are truly acts of castration.[24]

Jackson's position is tenable when racial power is viewed in sexual terms. This approach adds many more complications to the psychosexual realm of race prejudice, as Baldwin is astutely perceptive about in "Going to Meet the Man." To suppress the black man, in this analogy, is to put him in the feminine position of the sexual act; his manhood is stripped from him; he is "castrated" (black women presumably join their men in being powerless and oftentimes submissive, but must suffer additionally from the male-oriented analogy). It is no wonder, continues Jackson, that the

grinning, hat-in-hand, bowing and scraping darky so resembles a
eunuch.

Castration, from the larger view of lynchings and burnings, is
only one element in a series of elements (beating, shooting, gathering of trophies) designed to convince Blacks that white power is
limitless. Jackson does not consider the larger dimensions of expulsion of evil and setting the world right again, especially for white
women ("Ef they git erway notta woman in this town would be
safe"), but in his recognition of how the crowd functions for the
smaller rite, he also glimpses the larger view. Of the crowd, he
writes:

> Its members know what they are supposed to do, and they do it,
> as if they were performing the steps of a ritual dance—which of
> course they are. . . . They are acting tribally, even as every lodge
> brother, black or white or yellow or red, who ever gave a secret
> handshake and every Babbitt who ever applauded a toastmaster's
> feeble attempts at jollity at the luncheon of his service club.[25]

Doris Lorden, Norman Meier, and others have repudiated sufficiently the tribal excuse in their studies of crowd behavior.[26] Tribal-
ism might be universal, but its *manifestations* are not. To compare
a secret handshake or a response to a toastmaster's speech to the
inhuman taking of Bobo's life is perhaps the overextension of an
analogy. Yet Jackson's observation of how the crowd functions as a
group executing a rite is more than many critics studying this
story have recognized.

In "Big Boy Leaves Home," Wright has been able to move his
central and recurring metaphor to a new level of creativity and
symbolic suggestion. In other stories in *Uncle Tom's Children*, such
as "Down by the Riverside," he moves away from the literal scene
of a lynching and develops his metaphor purely on symbolic levels.
The symbolism is perfected in *Native Son*, where psychological, social, and historical implications of the metaphor of lynching are
intricately interwoven for forceful artistic expression. He would return to the symbolism again in *The Long Dream* and set it in operation on both literal and figurative levels, in a manner reminiscent
of "Between the World and Me." That poem was crucially important because it established early in Wright's career the pattern
most of his works would take and the central metaphor that would
become the basis for his aesthetic.

In both "Down by the Riverside" and "Long Black Song," a black
man is figuratively lynched by a blood-thirsty white mob. In both
instances, the men have committed the crimes of which they are

accused, and in both instances, there are enough extenuating circumstances that their actions, if the world in which they live could possibly judge them fairly, could be forgiven. In "Down by the Riverside," a man steals a boat from a white family so that his brother, Mann, can take his pregnant wife to a hospital. The action occurs during the height of a flood and is compounded by the fact that stealing the boat, which is the white family's only means of escape from the rising waters, is tantamount to stealing a man's horse during frontier days. On the other hand, Mann's wife has been in labor for four days and obviously cannot deliver the child without the aid of a doctor. Seeking help before his arrival at the hospital, Mann mistakenly calls out at the home of the boat's owner, who, recognizing his boat, demands its return and begins shooting at Mann and his family. Mann returns the fire, killing the white man. Arriving at the hospital only to discover that his wife is dead, Mann is pressed into service on the levee and works for several hours rescuing people from the flood, the last of whom are the wife and two children of the man he has shot. They recognize him, and he is summarily killed by soldiers who have been called in to assist during the flood.

Mann's actions during the flood had been commendable, so much so that the colonel in charge had asked him to look him up later—possibly for a job or a reward. He works out his grief for his wife by assisting others, but it is the irony of black existence in this country, Wright suggests, that no amount of expiation will assuage the sin of having killed a white man and come into contact with a white woman. It is the summary justice, rather than the specific threat to white womanhood, that links this story to Wright's lynching aesthetic. Still, the woman has ultimate power over Mann's life; although her young son identifies Mann as the "nigger" who has shot his father, it is the white woman who must make final, positive identification. She quickly forgets that Mann has risked his life to save those of herself and her children, and she has not an ounce of potential to forgive. Furthermore, it is only her word which saves Mann from a charge of rape, for the white men in charge clearly want to suggest that Mann may have had a sexual interest in the woman:

> "Did he *bother* you, Mrs. Heartfield?"
> "No; not *that* way."
> "The little girl?"
> "No; but he came back to the house and got us out. Ralph says he had an axe . . ."
> "When was *this*?"

"Early this morning."
"What did you go back there for, nigger?"
He did not answer.
"Did he *bother* you then, Mrs. Heartfield?"[27]

The questions stretch even a classification of absurdity. Flood waters have risen over twelve feet, a levee has recently broken, and
more rain has poured down during most of the night. In addition,
Mann has suffered through losing a wife and a child, and he has
been forced to work without food, sleep, or compensation. Yet, the
stereotypical notions in the minds of the arresting soldiers center
upon upholding the purity of Southern white womanhood. No
mention is made of the dead white man; in this story, he is merely a
subsidiary catalyst to the execution of Mann.

Mrs. Heartfield's positive identification leads to a planned lynching of Mann, which he manages to escape by running and forcing
the soldiers to shoot him. He has no defense that will be acceptable
to the unforgiving, quickly forgetful whites; he can only choose his
manner of dying. He has thought constantly after shooting the
white man that he will enlist the aid of other black people in trying
to make an escape sometime during the night's activities. Like
many other Wright characters, though, he finds himself finally
alone, for those who would risk helping him will be just as vulnerable to punishment as he is. He remembers at one point "hearing tales of whole black families being killed because some relative
had done something wrong" (p. 104—many homes are burned in
the search for Big Boy in "Big Boy Leaves Home"). Ultimately, he
concludes that he cannot share his secret with anyone; his isolated
position highlights the irony inherent in his name, and the death of
Mann becomes yet another insignificant, naturalistic tragedy in
the unrelenting world of white hatred which Wright depicts.

No less is that true of Silas, in "Long Black Song," who kills the
white man who has slept with his wife one afternoon.[28] Thinking
that a man's home should indeed be his castle, he sets out to punish
his wife as well as the intruder. He bullwhips the man and fatally
wounds him with a rifle; as Sterling Brown says, "*they come by
tens.*" The avenging crowd, ever ready to show this black human
being who wants to be a man that he must retain the classification
of "thing," sets the cabin into which Silas has barricaded himself on fire and watches it burn down around him; his wife also
watches from the safety of the hillside to which he has forced her to
escape. Her careless action has brought about her husband's death
and her too-early widowhood. Again, the only choice her man has

is the manner of his death, and the cycle of ultimate impotence in the face of white mobs continues, for Silas has violated a taboo no less exacting in its demands for blood than is that of actually raping a white woman.

The crowds which gather into mobs to execute Mann and Silas share a kinship to the "legal lynchers" who hunt Bigger Thomas down in preparation for killing him in *Native Son*. He, like Mann and Silas, is unquestionably "guilty" of the action for which the men hunt him down. Equally unquestionable are the extenuating circumstances surrounding his actions. Mobs have no ear for such things, so Bigger Thomas becomes yet another "nigger" rapist and murderer who must be chased, caught, and killed for daring to come into contact with the most untouchable of taboos. This added dimension ties the mob which pursues him to the one portrayed in "Between the World and Me" as well as to that portrayed in "Big Boy Leaves Home." With Bigger Thomas, Wright shows not only the fear his character has of Mary Dalton, but also the attraction he feels toward her. On that fateful night when she gets drunk and he must take her home, a history of approach and avoidance as far as white females are concerned wells up in him, and he is as much attracted to the possibility of making love to her as he is frightened by the possibility of being discovered in her bedroom.

> He lifted her and laid her on the bed. Something urged him to leave at once, but he leaned over her, excited, looking at her face in the dim light, not wanting to take his hands from her breasts. She tossed and mumbled sleepily. He tightened his fingers on her breasts, kissing her again, feeling her move toward him. He was aware of her body now; his lips trembled. Then he stiffened. The door behind him had creaked.[29]

For fear that he will be caught in the most compromising of positions with a white woman, Bigger Thomas smothers Mary Dalton to death. His action is informed by his history just as surely as are those of the boys in "Big Boy Leaves Home" and in the conclusions the black men draw about their fates being sealed in "Down by the Riverside" and "Long Black Song." To be in the presence of a white woman is bad enough, but to be caught in her bedroom is the height of criminality. Bigger Thomas, if discovered, will have to pay just as Chris does in *The Long Dream*. There is no innocence for black men so uncovered. Bigger Thomas knows that, and his action is as much informed by that history as it is by his immediate desire to keep Mary quiet so that he will not be discovered.

Pursued in an urban version of the chase the speaker had envisioned in "Between the World and Me" and that which Bobo is victim of in "Big Boy Leaves Home," Bigger Thomas shares with his literary forebears the isolation, the state of being lost. He quickly learns from trying to share his experience with Bessie that to be violent and black is to be alone; other Blacks, because of their knowledge of what whites do to guilty parties and those close to them, really can offer very little assistance to Bigger. The dragnet the police spread around that concrete jungle will destroy anything which stands in the way of its capturing its one big fish.

Since the scenery has changed from the rural areas in which trees are so readily available, and since the times, too, are somewhat beyond the era of widespread lynching, the police take Bigger to the courts to exact the justice that is almost as summary as a lynching would have been. They draw upon "sexual mythology," Noel Schraufnagel points out, and thereby encourage the press to paint "vivid images of the bestiality of the already condemned black youth. In the minds of the white bigots, Bigger is the brute Negro incarnate who should be eradicated in any way possible, preferably by lynching."[30] Buckley, as prosecuting attorney, is allowed to stir up emotional reactions to Bigger which parallel those of any leader of a mob. In his summation at the trial, he refers to Bigger as a "miserable human fiend" (p. 372), a "half-human black ape" (p. 373), a "bestial monstrosity" (p. 373), a "black lizard" (p. 373), a "black mad dog" (p. 374), a "sly thug" (p. 374), a "subhuman killer" (p. 373), a "hardened black thing" (p. 374), a "rapacious beast" (p. 374), a "beast" (p. 375), and a "piece of human scum" (p. 375). Primarily echoing the subhuman categories which defined the lynched man as a "thing" in "Between the World and Me," Buckley's descriptions serve as the battle cry to action. If the mob is prevented, because of the eyes of the world, from taking Bigger out and stringing him up, then they *must* kill him legally. To do otherwise is to deny kinship to culture, humanity, and whiteness, and it would mean failure to make the world safe for white women and children again—the same psychology which prevailed in the lynching of Bobo.

Though there is a legal system and courts, Bigger has no more access to a fair trial than his counterparts in the earlier works, and no more than Chris will have in *The Long Dream*. From Wright's point of view, there can be no justice because there can be no understanding, and there can be little understanding from people who refuse to see part of their number as fully human. As long as Blacks are separated from whites, and caged in ghettos of denial, then many of their actions will be rapacious. When Bessie points out to Bigger that the whites will accuse him of having raped Mary, he is momentarily shocked, then realistically understanding:

> Bigger stared. He had entirely forgotten the moment when he had carried Mary up the stairs. So deeply had he pushed it all back down into him that it was not until now that its real meaning came back. They would say he had raped her and there would be no way to prove that he had not. That fact had not assumed importance in his eyes until now. He stood up, his jaws hardening. Had he raped her? Yes, he had raped her. Every time he felt as he had felt that night, he raped. But rape was not what one did to women. Rape was what one felt when one's back was against a wall and one had to strike out, whether one wanted to or not, to keep the pack from killing one. He committed rape every time he looked into a white face. He was a long, taut piece of rubber which a thousand white hands had stretched to the snapping point, and when he snapped it was rape. But it was rape when he cried out in hate deep in his heart as he felt the strain of living day by day. That, too, was rape. [Pp. 213–14]

Bigger's symbolic rapes are just as powerful as those situations in which whites rape black people in general—from stripping social and political power away from them to the very stripping away of their humanity. Their assumption that the white woman has been raped and their own rage to punish that "crime" will lead them to continue the emasculation of Blacks in general and of black men in particular. That symbolic and real loss of power in *Native Son* is picked up again in the last novel Wright published before his death.

The Long Dream (1958), a lengthy, sometimes unwieldy novel, overburdened with racial rhetoric and heir to as many contrivances as *The Outsider* (1953), is at times embarrassingly repetitive for such a late work in Wright's life. Developed chronologically with the age of protagonist Rex (Fishbelly) Tucker, the novel keeps turning back on itself in the first couple of hundred pages in terms of what Fish learns. A traumatic, potentially enlightening scene has to have an equally enlightening counterpart in the next chapter or the next year of Fish's life. Only when Fish quits school at sixteen, and eleven years after the novel begins to chronicle his life, is Wright able to sustain a dramatic incident beyond a few pages. Wright's Fish is too adult, interpretive, and analytical for his adolescent years, and his ability to analyze and maturely interpret his experience strains credibility again and again. Guided too self-consciously by its author, the novel depends upon violence and

shock value to engage the reader, and that engagement is elicited
by less intrinsically dramatic methods than those employed in earlier Wright novels and short stories. The novel fails, for the longest
time, in Wright's inability to move his characters beyond the deterministic mode of race relations and philosophizing; when that
mode is broken, it is done so at the expense of solid preparation for
it—though the motivation may be strong enough. Echoing scenes,
tones, nuances, and many discussions of the previous novels and
stories, *The Long Dream* is nonetheless an important work.

In the context of this study, the novel intrigues precisely because
of Wright's obsession with the idea of an undercurrent of violence
always threatening to burst forth in black/white relationships. The
central metaphor of the white woman as the ultimate taboo for
black men surfaces again here to shape practically all of Fish's responses from the time he is about ten years old. Wright's use of the
metaphor may properly be called an obsession because of the persistence with which it occurs in his works and because of the intense psychological space it occupies in *The Long Dream*. The word
"obsession" is not intended to suggest a negative evaluation; rather,
it is used to show how determined Wright was to shape that historical reality which defined his race into the substance of art.

Before Fish is twelve, he somehow knows that, as a black boy/
man in Southern white Mississippi, the threat of death by exagger-
ated violence at the hands of white men is something to which he
must be particularly sensitive. He quickly learns that his mere existence is reason enough for the whites in his community to take
offense with him if they so desire. Consequently, his early education, through parental teachings and reinforced by experience,
points out to him that he must fear whites first and foremost. Fear
leads to scheming and lying, to humility, and finally to self-hatred,
because one is forced to degrade one's self so thoroughly for reasons difficult to understand. And yet there is ambivalence in the
education, for it is the nature of human experience that that which
is most frequently pointed out as being forbidden is that which is
most frequently desired. To Fish, the "adoring hatred" he develops
for the white world centers upon what it holds most dear and what
it teaches him is most out of his reach—the white woman.

Fear, guilt, shame, humility, deception, hatred—all come to be
centered upon the image of the white woman which white men
have used to teach black men that the latter are not worthy to
touch the hem of her garments. Fish's attitude toward her is similarly shaped by the attitude he has been taught to adopt toward
the white world in combination with the self-hatred which has also

been externally imposed. General distinctions between Blacks and whites shape Fish's initial response to the world in which he lives. Sent on an errand to his father's undertaking establishment when he is six, he is forced into an alley to bring luck to a white man shooting dice. "Niggers are born with luck," the man maintains in an emotional kinship to plantation owners who believed that their illnesses could be transferred from their own bodies into those of the slaves who were forced to surrender to the touching process. "You ain't shot no dice," the man continues telling the child, "so you got *all* the luck. I'm going to borrow some of it."[31] Powerless not only against whites, but against adults in general, Fish learns that he is without significant human worth to the man who holds on to him and forces him to throw the dice again and again. He can be used against his will, discarded when he is no longer of use, and paid without consultation about the value of his "work" or the compensation it should bring. His six-year-old experience mirrors in large part the role his father plays in running whorehouses for the chief of police; when the father is no longer of use to the chief, he is discarded. Fish's microcosmic experience points out the separation between the races and his powerlessness to do anything about his own position.

Fish's experience with the gamblers is reinforced by two early incidents in the novel; both serve as further learning experiences about the value whites place on black people as well as that black people place on themselves. The incidents also illustrate the power of language to control reality and the power that accrues to a group of individuals acting together (like a mob). Black people, seemingly in acceptance of definitions whites bestow upon them, devalue themselves further by calling each other "nigger." Sam, one of Fish's adolescent playmates and ten-year-old spokesman for Wright, maintains that the boys are not really American because they ride Jim Crow trains and busses, and go to Jim Crow restaurants, schools, and churches. They are neither African nor American; they are "niggers" and therefore "*nothing*" (p. 35). Although Fish wants to reject Sam's thesis and fights him because of the statements he makes, he quickly concludes that he is a "nigger," forever outside the mainstream of the white American world. Later, he looks at himself in a mirror, then "sucked a volume of hot liquid from his saliva glands and spat, sputtering the glass. 'Nigger,' he whispered in a voice that was like an escaping valve" (p. 37).

Throughout the novel, characters will comment upon Fish's good looks—even the white policemen who arrest him for trespassing at the waterhole during the mud fight. Surely some evidence of those good looks must be apparent at this point. Yet Fish accepts the evaluation of repulsiveness he and his friends associate with "niggerishness," and he rejects himself. Such an early rejection is altered slightly when he rejects sniveling, "niggerish" behavior in his father, then solidifies when he himself is forced to respond with sniveling and crying after his own arrest.

Fish early learns that "niggers" are characterized by powerlessness and subservience, that they are groveling creatures easily emasculated—both physically and psychologically—by the forces over which they have no control. The extent to which he has learned his lesson can be illustrated, in the second incident, in how Fish, Sam, Zeke, and Tony treat Aggie West, the identifiable homosexual in their neighborhood. When he tries to join in one of their games, they label him "pansy," "fruit," and "fairy" (p. 38) and join together in beating him into a bloody departure.

Still in their pre-teenage and teenage years, the boys have nevertheless formed prejudices as irrational as those whites hold toward them. Aggie is a weaker creature who can be bullied by the "mob" of four players in ways similar to the destructive play white men sometimes direct at black men, such as in the incident in which Sonny's uncle is killed in James Baldwin's "Sonny's Blues." They feel power over Aggie by virtue of their masculinity, their group solidarity, and their physical prowess, so they do to him together what almost any one of them could have done alone. They differ from white mobs in that they are mutually ashamed of their violence, and Zeke, one of the older boys, is able to realize not only the shame, but the model from which their violent actions flow: "We treat 'im like the white folks treat us," he "mumbles" "with a self-accusative laugh" (p. 39).

With Aggie, the boys act out dominant, aggressive roles in imitation of the whites whose world lies just beyond the reach of theirs. Self-effacing in the presence of whites, the boys, like Fish's exploitative father Tyree, act out their aggressions on Blacks who are still weaker than themselves. Tyree will bow, scrap, cry, and crawl before the white police chief Cantley, but he exhorts rents from his black tenants with all the tolerance of Attilla the Hun. He does not respect black people in his community because the majority of them are beneath him financially and socially. As established undertaker and owner of much property, he has managed to coexist peacefully with the whites by exploiting Blacks in clubs and whorehouses. He passes along a share of his profits to the chief in exchange for having his bit of black "dignity." The boys, who have not yet experienced the world in the same way Tyree has, nevertheless have formed notions of the kinds of relationships that exist there; this is evident in their discussions of "niggers" and Africa as well as in their vicious treatment of Aggie.

The final component of Fish's education is more felt than articulated by him, for it is dangerous even to give conscious thought to it. Since he has learned that he is a powerless "nigger," one who is denied access to the white world, and he has equally learned what the white man holds most dear in his world, that is the one thing he finds most attractive. Images of white women become for Fish, both in his dreams and his waking state, the pinnacle of that which he is denied. He begins to dream about them and to fantasize that he will somehow transcend that invisible barrier which has been placed in his path to keep him from them. As early as the age of twelve, he is so attracted to a newspaper picture of a white woman that he tears it out and carries it around in his wallet.

Yet, he knows within his heart of hearts that he is committing what white men would consider a sin, and he has also been taught the consequences of that sin. Especially vivid examples of his education occur on the occasion when the boys go to the circus on "colored" folks day. They stop before "a girls show where five half-nude white women" dance "swayingly" and listen to a barker invite customers to "the greatest sex show on earth" (p. 42). Fish and Zeke, who contain their "suppressed excitement," are nonetheless "entranced" by the sensual movement of the white women, and they, with Tony, resolve to buy tickets. Abruptly Sam, usually the most racially conscious, points to a sign that the other boys have not seen. It simply says: "NO COLORED." Sams adds the commentary which goes beyond his years: "White men don't want you looking at their naked women." Ironically, even on "colored" folks' days at the circus, the restrictions which are designed to keep them in their places are still in effect.

Comparable to the battle royal scene of Ellison's *Invisible Man*, the incident here equally tantalizes the boys and moves that temptation beyond their grasp. As boys on their way to becoming men, they are shown what they lack, forced to desire that lack, and forced to watch it being snatched away from them. Just as Tantalus could never drink from the receding stream or eat fruit from the tree kept just out his reach, the black boys must learn that they can never really expect to have what the white man sets up before them as being most desirable.

They share the confusion of Ellison's characters in that, when an opportunity presents itself and they are actually in the presence of a seminude white woman, they bolt away in fear. Their lessons op-

erate like a two-edged sword; whether or not white men are physically present to prevent them from making contact with white
women, the psychological controls which have been instilled in
them work just as well to keep them in place.[32] Such is the case as
they leave the circus ground and look around the tents where the
performers live. One of the white women whom they have seen
dancing earlier asks them if they have any money, then she begins
"unbuttoning her blouse and baring her big white breasts in the
half-light" (p. 48). The boys run instinctively. Certainly we can say
that a part of their discomfort rests in the fact that they are twelve
to fifteen years old and that the woman is much older. They are all
without sexual experience at this point, and that, coupled with
their knowledge of the possible consequences of being caught with
a white woman, makes them bolt away into the darkness. Even as
they run, they are less creatures of individual wills than of predetermined reflex. Zeke yells out "in panic" almost immediately
that they must stop running: "If a white man see us running like
this, he's going to think something's wrong, sure as hell!" (p. 48).
The specific wrong of possibly being caught in the white woman's
presence is quickly generalized into the constraints that serve to
keep Blacks, and especially black males, forever acutely conscious
of the risk of unpleasant contact with white males. To be caught
running is to be guilty of something; no explanation would be requested before punishment would be meted out.

Sam correctly points out that the woman is "lynch-bait," and his
nervous fear combines with that of the other boys to make them
pledge never to mention to their parents what has happened to
them. Their evaluation that "both *colored* and *white'd* think we
bothered the woman" (p. 48) is a testament to how potential violence shapes black community character and to how ingrained a
part of the black psyche the taboo of white women really is. The
boys are generally apprehensive about their position in the world
in relation to whites, and Fishbelly in particular feels an increase
in the consuming fear which is becoming more and more a part of
his life: "Fishbelly watched his friends leave, then he remembered
too late that they had been too nervous to say good-by. A cold sweat
covered his skin as he walked with downcast face through the hot
dark" (p. 48).

The education which has come to him in bits and pieces and the
vague fear he has sometimes felt are crystallized into one huge
image of oppression on the night Chris, an older friend to Fish, is
caught in a hotel room with a white woman and is killed by a mob

as a result of that encounter. What happens to Chris becomes the central image to which Fish will return again and again throughout the novel as he tries to understand the violence which often defines relationships between Blacks and whites. The power of Chris's action, and the gripping effect it has upon the black community, is reflected in the way in which the fathers of the boys near Fish's age drive to school to take them home after Chris has been discovered; they know that the mob will descend upon any black boy or man it deems capable of having committed the offense or any who shares racial affinity with Chris. Carrying a gun does not give Tyree Tucker the comfort it should, and even after he and Fish arrive at their house, he is still extremely agitated and fearful, and his wife is no less uncomfortable. Fish, ashamed that "these scared and trembling people" are his parents, is still somewhat confused as his father tries to explain: "You twelve years old and it's time you know! Lissen Fish: NEVER LOOK AT A WHITE WOMAN! YOU HEAR?" (p. 64). Not yet able to bring all the bits of his education together, Fish nevertheless senses what is happening: "This was a ceremony. He did not think it; he felt it, knew it. He was being baptized, initiated; he was moving along the steep, dangerous precipice leading from childhood to manhood" (p. 64). Listening to shots being fired near his house, seeing his parents crouching in the darkness, noting the anxiety of his father's repeated admonitions, feeling his own insecurity—these things ultimately do not shock Fish completely into manhood. A move toward that state will occur later that evening when he is forced to look upon Chris's mutilated body. For the time being, however, he is still attracted enough to the mystery of Chris's action and to the object of his conquest to take the newspaper picture and stuff it in his pocket.

Calling attention to itself because it happens while the Tuckers and the rest of the black community are under siege, Fish's action at once highlights and dramatizes the lure of that forbidden fruit. Not allowed to turn the lights on to go to the bathroom, he gropes his way and strikes a match to locate toilet paper. His attention is immediately riveted to a stack of newspapers and the woman's picture:

> On the front page of the dusty top sheet was a photograph of a white woman clad only in panties and brassiere; she was smiling under a cluster of tumbling curls, looking straight at him, her hands on her hips, her lips pouting, ripe, sensual. A woman like that had caused Chris to die . . . The woman in the photograph was

> pretty; there was no hint of evil or death about her . . . His match
> flame dwindled flickeringly and, at once, he scratched another to
> life, stood, snatched the newspaper from the top of the pile, ripped
> the face from it, then folded that paper face and jammed it into his
> pocket. He didn't know why he had done that; he had acted before
> he had been aware of it. But he knew that he wanted to look at that
> face again and he would never be able to stop thinking of what had
> happened to poor Chris until he had solved the mystery of why that
> laughing white face was so radiantly happy and at the same time
> charged with dark horror. [Pp. 68, 69]

So far, Fish has only been told that Chris is probably dead, and,
because his father owns a funeral parlor and he has seen dead
people, death is not especially frightening to him. He has seen
nicely embalmed, familiar black people laid out in velvety lined
coffins. Similarly, though the threat of a foreboding white presence
has been felt, it has not touched Fish yet except, in an aggressively
playful way, with the gamblers; thus, he has education without the
concrete personal experience to make it gospel. After all, even if the
boys had gone into the trailer with the white woman at the circus,
there is no guarantee that they would have been discovered and en-
dangered. Now, with Chris's death, Tyree Tucker thinks it is time to
give his fast-growing son firsthand knowledge of the brutality about
which all of his forebodings have warned him. He insists that Fish
accompany him to the funeral parlor when the call comes to announce that Chris's body has been brought there. With the picture
of the white woman still tucked away in his pocket, Fish goes to
view the results of the "picnic" and "circus" the whites have had
with Chris. Tyree's helper turns the body for Doctor Bruce to examine it:

> Chris's bloated head and torso turned first, then the legs followed,
> violently, shaking rigidly for a few seconds, as though the body still
> lived. Tension gripped Fishbelly; the conflict in his mind between
> the lifeless, torn form before his eyes and the quick, laughing image
> of the Chris he had known was too much. He swallowed, ran his dry
> tongue over his lips, staring disbelievingly at the blood-clotted,
> bruised face showing distinctly in the unshaded bulb's blatant
> glare. . . . Dr. Bruce's fingers probed delicately into the mass of
> puffed flesh that had once been Chris's cheeks; there was no expres-
> sion on those misshapen features now; not only had the whites
> taken Chris's life, but they had robbed him of the semblance of the
> human. The mouth, lined with stumps of broken teeth, yawned
> gapingly, an irregular, black cavity bordered by shredded tissue

that had once been lips. The swollen eyes permitted slits of irises to
show through distended lids. [P. 75]

The torture twenty-four-year-old Chris has suffered includes lynching as well as having been dragged through the streets of Clintonville behind a car. One ear is missing, perhaps "eaten away by the
friction of asphalt against the side of the head" (p. 76); the "mangled
neck . . . might've been broken in *two* places or more" (p. 76); "the
nose is almost gone" (p. 77); "the left cheek has been split by a
gun butt" (p. 77); a hole has been kicked through his side to reveal
his intestines; and "the *genitalia* are gone" (p. 77). Mutilation has
achieved its objective in robbing Chris of almost everything that
marked him as human, and certainly that which marked him as a
man. For violating the ultimate taboo, he is now reduced to a
harmless monstrosity.

As Dr. Bruce correctly points out, Chris's death is not only intended as punishment for his assumed crime; it is also intended as
a warning to the other black males in Clintonville: "While killing this boy, the white folks' actions were saying: 'If any of you do
what this nigger did, you'll end up like this!'" (p. 76). The Blacks,
powerless to retaliate or to bring the guilty parties to trial, are in
some ways relieved that the killing is over. White blood-lust has
been satiated, and Blacks have indeed had the lesson reinforced for
them: they cannot expect to trespass upon the most sacred of white
properties without being brutally and summarily punished for it.

Guilt and innocence are again irrelevant. While Chris was actually caught in the room with the white woman, several Blacks in
the community know that she had pursued him until he could no
longer resist her efforts. Then, finding herself simultaneously ful-
filled and "compromised," her guilt led her to cry out for destruction of the very thing she had so recently desired. The role she
plays in the drama is just as historically determined as is the role
Chris plays. Her upbringing has made it just as clear that she must
consider herself superior as it had made clear to Chris that he
should consider her taboo. Both violated the sanctions which had
been placed upon them by white males, but, as the pattern goes,
only Chris is forced to pay with his life for the violation. Both fearful, yet both desiring each other, it was destined before their births
that only one of them could survive such an encounter; Chris has
gambled and lost.

Overpowering, subliminally consuming, the lure of the white
woman remains for Fish as strong a pull as is the fear manifested

in what has happened to Chris. And that is the fate of black men in Wright's world. Like moths, they are drawn to those powerful lights which will not only singe their wings, but will tear them apart membrane by membrane. What happened to Chris became the tangible image to reinforce the mental ones Fish had accumulated year after year about the precarious state of his existence in the black and white worlds of Clintonville. Yet, it is his fate to want that which he knows he may have to die for.

Embedded within that possibility for death is also, from another point of view, the potential path to manhood. If a black man can indeed conquer one of those untouchable white women—and escape in the process—that could represent his freedom and his maturity; that possibility is what Wright develops in *Native Son*, and what William Melvin Kelley executes so playfully in *dem* (1964). Though Bigger Thomas will indeed finally be killed, he is nonetheless freed through his act of violence. Fishbelly Tucker, like Kelley's protagonist, Cooley, does not think in terms of freedom through violence; he is attracted to the possession of a white woman as a way of severing himself from the fear and subservience which so disgust him in his parents and other Blacks he sees in his community. The forbidden photograph he carries in his wallet becomes his identification with something beyond the stifling definition which is thrust upon him as his father prepares him for his version of manhood. On the morning following Fish's release from jail, he listens to his father explain that white men want to see black men either "crying or grinning" (p. 114); that is how Tyree has effected Fish's release. Instead of being grateful, he concludes that the whites will not have to emasculate his father, for Tyree is already emasculated. It is a childish observation, born of pride and the betrayal of the need to believe that parents are invincible, and it is one born of naiveté, not experience. No matter how different from his father he would like to be, Fish is still a boy whose dreams of escape from emasculation are merely that; they cannot stand him in good stead when he is arrested for trespassing, and he, like so many other black men who have found themselves in similar positions, believes that the very thing which whites so fear about him—his manhood—will be taken away.

During the incident in which Fish and Tony are arrested for engaging in a mud fight on property belonging to a white man, Fish's behavior is more "sniveling" than any he has seen his father exhibit thus far. He is fifteen, still without sexual experience, and still fascinated by white women. Caught staring at a white girl, he faints when one of the officers flicks open "a long, gleaming blade," and declares, "Nigger, I'm going to *castrate* you!" (p. 111). For the remainder of the trip to the stationhouse, the policemen give their attention to this joke while Fish cringes with memories of "Chris's bloody, broken body" (p. 113). His mind triggered by visions of castration, he suddenly remembers the connection between the night Chris has been killed and the photograph he has in his wallet. In panic, he stealthily retrieves the bit of newspaper and, with unusual determination, chews and swallows it.[33] The strength manifested in that effort surfaces again at the stationhouse when, threatened with castration a third time, he resists the urge to faint, even when the officer maintains that he will "cut 'em off and sew 'em in your goddamn mouth!" (p. 120).[34] He finally concludes that they can kill him, but he will not faint anymore. That resolve, which seems to represent a kind of progression, will be undercut later when Fish again finds himself in the hands of the police.

What is important here is that the general fear of white males is combined with the specific fear of the violence that can result from contact with white women, a violence localized in castration—which is what white men usually do to black men they catch with white women. Thus, even when a portion of the equation may seem to be missing (Fish has not been accused of "bothering" a white woman), the ingrained fear still localizes in the dread of castration. It is a threat which is so demoralizing that Fish cannot tell his father what has happened, and it is typified by the shame which both boys feel so intensely (Tony has been reduced to hysterical crying) that they form the pact to keep their shame a secret. It is a secret which can only engender more fear, so the vicious circle continues. Black boys and men who are ashamed because they cannot do the things which are usually identified with their gender form secret unions to keep their humiliation from black men not so humiliated as well as from black women; the irony is that those secret pacts are probably so common that the need for secrecy is imaginary.

To Fish, Chris becomes the touchstone for gauging his own fear as well as for inspiring some determination to transcend fear and symbolic castration. Fish thinks of Chris's example continually: when he is in the police car with the forbidden picture of the white woman, when he is in jail and a white trusty recounts how Chris's cries of innocence matched those of Fish and Tony, when he is released from jail and Tyree warns him that he cannot help him if he gets "into trouble like that Chris" (p. 143), when he is about to have his first sexual experience, when he dates a black woman who looks almost as white as the one he knows is responsible for Chris's death, when he tries to explain to Gladys how white folks hate enough to kill (because they have killed Chris), when Tyree is threatened with jail, when he is arrested the second time, and when he lingers in jail thinking of the control the white people have over him. Chris becomes a Christ figure who should have been able to expiate the sins of black men by his demise, but whose brutal death has only momentarily staved off the lust for blood. Failing to save, he serves instead to point out how vulnerable the black community and black males really are.

Fish sees that vulnerability when Cantley has Tyree killed when he tries to use canceled checks from the chief's portion of the bribe to show that city hall approved of the fire violations. Expected, at sixteen, to take over where Tyree has left off, Fish fails because he is not convincingly able to effect the "crying and grinning" facade Tyree has put on for years for the whites with whom he has had to deal. Believing that Fish is a threat and that he has still more of the canceled checks, Cantley frames him by sending a white girl to his room to cry rape. Suddenly, Fish is caught in the realization of the fears which have provoked his imagination throughout the novel. He finds himself in the "waiting-all-my-life-for-something-like-this-to-happen" syndrome that so characterizes Bigger Thomas; all his fears are made manifest when the girl tears off her clothes and screams, and the guilt that has preceded fear somehow makes the confusing situation perversely appropriate.

Fish's long road to a different kind of maturity begins during the two years he spends in jail. He might have been released earlier so far as the rape charge went, but he beat up a stoolie Cantley planted in his cell and was consequently sentenced for that. Because of what has happened to Chris and because of Fish's identification with it, we are led to expect lynching and castration in his case as well. Instead, Fish manages to escape from the South. He does not produce the checks for Cantley, resolving, perhaps as his only means of defying Cantley, to stay in jail as long as necessary. When Cantley is finally convinced that Fish will indeed follow in Tyree's "crying and grinning" footsteps, he releases him, giving him his three-thousand-dollar share of the take from the whorehouses and sanctioning his return to the collection business. Swiftly retrieving the checks, Fish hastily makes his getaway by train and plane to Paris, where two of his childhood friends are serving in World War II.

While in jail, however, he has tried to place that peculiar relationship between black men, white men, and white women into some kind of perspective:

> White men made such a brutal point of warning black men that they would be killed if they merely touched their women that the white men kept alive a sense of their women in black men's hearts. As long as he could remember he had mulled over the balefully seductive mystery of white women, whose reality threatened his life, declared him less than a man. In the presence of a white woman there were impulses that he must not allow to come into action; he was supposed to be merely a face, a voice, a sexless animal. And the white man's sheer prohibitions served to anchor the sense of his women in the consciousness of black men in a bizarre and distorted manner that could rarely ever be eradicated—a manner that placed the white female beyond the pitch of reality. [P. 363]

Unable, perhaps, to envision himself ever escaping such conditioning, Fish resolves to leave the country. But as the plane glides over the ocean toward Paris, the conditioning which is such an ingrained part of the psyche of black males in Wright's works rears its head once again.

> His knees were held stiffly together, as though he expected his presence to be challenged. For more than two hours he had avoided looking in front of him, had always kept his eyes to left or right. Finally he stared directly at the object that rested under the dreadful taboo: the young woman ahead of him had a head of luxuriant, dark brown hair, the wispy curls of which nestled clingingly at the nape of her white, well modeled neck. His Bowman Street experiences made the rounded firmness of the woman's throat a symbolic stand-in for the exciting, hidden geography of her body and he grew tense, for that simple image, just two feet from him, was the charming trap that could trigger his deepest fears of death. [P. 378]

His effort to make the woman "unreal" and "remote" is not convincing. He may have grown, but he still has a long way to go.

By allowing Fish to leave the country, Wright is able to evade the deterministic philosophy which has pervaded the book. Escape, however, comes at the expense of rejection of America, and if America must be rejected, if indeed it has been a "long dream," then the philosophy has not changed, rather Wright has decided to lift his character beyond its control. To be in America, as Sam pointed out early in the book, is to be "nothing" if one is black, and any claim to Americanness is simply dreaming. Tyree, too, continued this imagery by describing young black men in America as being so many dreams; the dreams were blotted out as each young man like Chris died for some insane reason. To fulfill the dream, or to wake from the dream into reality which is not a nightmare, is to leave the country. For black men, the threats of lynching and castration leave few alternatives. Unfortunately, for the majority of them, who cannot escape through the efforts of upper-class fathers, literal or symbolic castration awaits them, and who can say that there is a meaningful distinction between the two?

CHAPTER 5

An Aborted Attempt at Reversing the Ritual

The extent of Wright's preoccupation with lynchings and burnings, both in the metaphorical and literal senses, sets him apart from the writers preceding and following him who deal with the subject. His aesthetic concerns are at once unique but also reflective of those shared by other writers in the tradition. Though Baldwin's presentation of the burning in "Going to Meet the Man" is powerful, no writer following Wright would allow the subject such a central place in the corpus of his or her works. Yet, these writers continued to show, through their occasional treatment of lynching, that it had not completely been eradicated from the psyche of the black American writer. One writer who takes the subject of lynching beyond its gruesome brutalities to a level of philosophical reflection is John Wideman; he uses it as a vehicle through which to explore the inspiring as well as the debilitating effects the idea of lynching can have upon the human imagination. His black characters plot a lynching, themselves, that is a monument of brilliance, daring, and sardonic political statement, but the horror of the crime they plan still ties them historically to the very brutes whose actions they wish to repudiate.

For Wideman, lynching serves as a metaphor for the psychologically and physically destructive ways in which Blacks and whites have interacted with each other; the long-term effects of those interactions can either stifle the growth of his characters or allow them the means for self-expression—if they have the ability to control the extent to which the past influences them. In their desire to find a symbol for their own liberation by reaching back into the past for one which usually meant degradation and death for them, they play simultaneously with the possibility for freedom as well as for further enslavement.

Wideman's *The Lynchers* (1973) is a fascinating study of four black men who plot the lynching of a white policeman. By resorting to this reversal, they intend to dramatize what has happened to Blacks historically and, through their action, galvanize the black community into a renewed energy and self-respect. Wideman begins his novel, not with the plotters, but with an extended section

129

of "Matter Prefatory," which paints in nineteen pages the graphic details of the brutality and violence surrounding the history of Blacks in America. Taken from historical sources, collections, newspapers, folklore, books, petitions, and autobiographies, the materials provide a background against which the novel is set. Beginning with general descriptions of the conditions of Blacks during slavery, the passages progress to focus on violence done against Blacks, particularly as that violence relates to lynchings and burnings.

In structuring his novel in such a way, Wideman freely admits his debt to history in the creation of his fiction, and he goes further than many black writers in setting the two up side by side. Questions immediately occur to us after reading the Matter Prefatory. Will the characters created against this backdrop see themselves as much related to their history as Wideman sees himself? Will they be able to carry out their planned lynching? Are they capable of enough hatred, enough determination to mirror in their actions what whites did without conscience to the characters' black ancestors? Wideman heaps on enough violence to rivet the readers' eyes, and the historical atrocities are stamped on our minds as we read the novel. Such a device forces us into more active participation in the novel by stirring our anger and imaginations and by setting up the justification for revenge; we are thus prepared to be led through the violence of retaliation if that is where the characters will lead us.

Wideman's choices in the Matter Prefatory are all effective, but some are particularly so. One passage will suffice to show the sort of example Wideman records.

> More than 500 persons stood by and looked on while the Negro was slowly burned to a crisp. A few women were scattered among the crowd of Arkansas planters, who directed the grewsome work of avenging the death of O. T. Craig and his daughter, Mrs. C. P. Williamson.
>
> Not once did the slayer beg for mercy despite the fact that he suffered one of the most horrible deaths imaginable. With the Negro chained to a log, members of the mob placed a small pile of leaves around his feet. Gasoline was then poured on the leaves, and the carrying out of the death sentence was under way.
>
> Inch by inch the Negro was fairly cooked to death. Every few minutes fresh leaves were tossed on the funeral pyre until the blaze had passed the Negro's waist. . . . Even after the flesh had dropped away from his legs and the flames were leaping toward his face, Lowry retained consciousness. Not once did he whimper or beg for mercy. Once or twice he attempted to pick up the hot ashes in his hands and thrust them into his mouth in order to hasten death.

> Each time the ashes were kicked out of his reach by a member of the mob.
> As the flames were eating away his abdomen, a member of the mob stepped forward and saturated the body with gasoline. It was then only a few minutes until the Negro had been reduced to ashes. . . .[1]

Though this passage describes a burning without the traditional lynching and souvenir-gathering, it, together with a couple of other examples Wideman has chosen, provides the details of the lynching-and-burning ritual which we have identified historically and in the literature. Wideman's research to locate just the passages which would serve his purpose illustrates that he had a keen awareness of the significance of ritual within society; that awareness is expressed more clearly in the novel, as the characters go about their daily lives and as they plan the lynching death of the policeman.[2]

Willie Hall, called Littleman by his fellow plotters Thomas Wilkerson, Saunders, and Rice, is the man with the plan for the execution of the policeman. His plan springs from what he sees as the need to clarify race issues in the big city of Philadelphia, where people have perhaps unintentionally forgotten their historical roles, or rather, the places history has assigned to them.

> —What this town needs is a good old fashioned lynching. The real thing. With all the trimmings. It would be like going to church. Puts things in their proper perspective. Reminding everybody of who they are, where they stand. Divides the world simple and pure. Good or bad. Oppressors and oppressed. Black or white. Things tend to get a little fuzzy here in the big city. We need ritual. A spectacular. [P. 60]

Littleman begins by comparing his plan with the ritual of going to church, but soon broadens it to the realm of the spectacular and the political.

His interpretation of ritual is the same as that with which this book began. Everyday activities do become ritualized, and only the more so should special occurrences. Wideman sets the plan for the lynching, then—the unusual ceremony—against the backdrop of the smaller rituals in which almost all of his characters engage. Repetitive actions and activities inform their lives with a sameness similar to the existence of slaves.

Thomas's mother, for instance, is described as going about the "neat ritual" (p. 31) of planning meals for her family and watching them grow up and leave her. As Wilkerson is dressing to meet Tanya, a fellow teacher whom he has worshipped from afar and whom he would like to impress, he is described as planning and going through a ritual to score with her (p. 89). Willie Hall meets a young lady who had spent some time watching him one night as he walked along the beach. It is a routine he follows to soothe himself, usually ending it by urinating into the sea. He then wonders what the girl would have thought "if she had peeked at that particular finale to the ritual" (p. 122). Saunders remembers the pain of his mother's lessening mental powers and recalls her crying and pantomiming "the ritual of shutting down a large house for the night" (p. 143). When Willie is hospitalized, he refers to "the rituals of pissing, shitting, having my body washed" (p. 160). And, on a visit to a bar, Saunders observes the owner being served his breakfast in a routine that is repeated every day; "both Fats and the baby faced woman serving him spoke slowly, softly, in no hurry to finish the ritual" (p. 235). Thus the concept of ritual is not new to the community in which Littleman plans to execute the policeman; getting the Blacks to move from one level of ritual to the other will be the greatest challenge.

The question becomes, then, whether or not Littleman and his fellow conspirators will be able to draw the black community from the routine of its lives to focus upon the momentous event which has been designed to bring about some change in their lives. If he can get Saunders, Wilkerson, and Rice to realize that they are not inventing something new, just heightening a pattern in their own community which was commonplace in others decades before, he may be able to succeed with his plan. In his efforts to convince them, he provides the historical context and tries to instill in it a kind of pageantry which will appeal to the others. He maintains that he is "not talking about grabbing just any old body and stringing him up to the nearest lamp post," but that he is calling for a "formal lynching" (p. 60). Such a lynching would be characterized by "style" and "power" and would be modeled on those carried out by Southern whites. The whites did not shy away from "real blood" and "undignified screams and writhing"; rather, there was a "communal hard-on" when the black person was lynched and burned. If Littleman can convince the others that they, too, have the power to execute a lynching, that all it takes is creative as opposed to pedestrian thinking, then he may be able to inspire them to adopt the methods of their oppressors in righting a historical wrong. If he can convince them of the power to be assumed by exacting blood in a communal, controlled orgy, then perhaps together they can effect much-needed social changes.

That is the rationale. The plan for the lynching is equally de-

signed for its sense of drama and showmanship, almost in the
sense that Marcus Garvey used such inducements to attract people
into his movement during the 1920s. Initially, there would be a picnicking atmosphere about the lynching, comparable to many we
have seen historically.

> —You know if it was done right, if tradition, nuance, imagination
> were consulted, the victim would have to be a white cop.
> —And in the middle of the afternoon. And everybody standing
> around. Not looking at the beast but eating chicken from picnic
> baskets, sitting on fences munching watermelon. Dancing, singing,
> playing ball. Blasé as could be. [P. 62]

Littleman's detailed laying out of the plan for the others is designed to convince them, especially the skeptical schoolteacher
Wilkerson; at the same time it provides an outlet for his fanciful
imagination.

The four conspirators are to kidnap a black woman, Sissie, who
is a prostitute for a white policeman. The woman is to be held for a
few days, then killed and mutilated. They plan to blame the killing
on the policeman, circulate rumors to that effect, and try to get an
article in the local black newspaper making the same claims. Their
intention is to get the community so inflamed that it will readily
respond when the conspirators produce the policeman as the guilty
person. They will then go through the ritual of publicly executing
the policeman on a warm day ("*has to be warm to bring our folks
out*), . . . *preferably a holiday that has special meaning for black folk*"
(p. 64). A sack of flour will be thrown over the policeman's head
just before he is lynched to complete the final mocking gesture. The
plan may be far-fetched, but Littleman's rationale for it is politically astute. His planned creative act of violence will convey to
whites that they can no longer set limits upon and control Blacks.
The lynching of one cop will be used to deny "a total vision of reality" (p. 114). Through their example, Littleman and the others will
show that suppressing a few black people or killing one as an example to the others will not suffice to contain the race as a whole,
for a new breed of black man is coming who will disregard the consequences taught by lessons of the past and who will "deny any
future except one conditioned by new definitions" of Blacks "as
fighters, free, violent men who will determine the nature of the reality in which they exist" (p. 114).

For Littleman, the potential contained in his plan becomes "*a
goddamn regular Fourth of July powder keg just waiting*" (p. 65) for
someone with the imagination and the stamina to carry it out. He

plans for it over a period of years, more than thirteen months of
which are covered in the novel. He understands that "the symbol
matters, the ritual" (p. 61) of lynching, and he wants to capture the
imaginations of his people by publicly reversing something they
have feared throughout history. If he can show that black people,
represented by the conspirators, can also work together to accomplish a symbolic goal, then perhaps the community can be inspired
as well. "Every black man," he tells Thomas Wilkerson, "carries a
fear of death in his heart, a fear of death at the hands of white men.
Each is isolated by his fear of death. It's that terror we must release
our people from" (p. 116). That fear is tied to the history of Blacks
in America, to the fact that "if a white woman was molested or a
slave struck his master and ran away, the South reacted by killing
any niggers who happened to be handy. No question of justice, of
catching the offender. All black men were responsible and the rules
of war meant all were guilty" (p. 115). If that collectivity into which
they have been placed historically can now draw the Philadelphia
community into a different kind of collectivity, one which, from
Littleman's point of view, is positive and constructive, then the
basis of that nation of black people he envisions can begin to become a reality.

   Littleman sees the planned lynching as a way of unifying the
black community in which he lives; he does not consider the problems inherent in his idea. The major problem with the plan, Wideman seems to suggest, is that Littleman too consistently uses
whites as the model for change. No matter how effective he may be
in what he wants to accomplish, he is still doing it in reaction to,
not in spite of, the white community. And no matter how powerful
reaction may be, it is still imitation, not creation. His exposition on
the concept of nationhood shows his imitation: "When one man
kills it's murder. When a nation kills murder is called war. If we
lynch the cop we will be declaring ourselves a nation" (p. 115). The
declaration will probably lead to war with the whites, because
they will not be able to ignore the policeman's death. If they did so,
it would be declaring the black community equal to theirs, declaring the right of the Blacks to mete out justice and punishment.
Since the whites are not likely to do that, Littleman's plan has the
potential to destroy his community weighed equally in the balance
with his hope that it will unite the Blacks.

   One of the problems with Littleman's plan, we quickly begin to
discover, is that the planning is perhaps more attractive to him
than is the possibility of its execution. And as the novel goes along
for so many pages without a concrete move toward selecting the

policeman and working out the details of the execution, it becomes clear that something else is also at fault. A part of that something else is the absence of historical motivation for the plotters. From their position of secondary status in a country with a large white majority, it is difficult for them to feel the same urgency to preserve purity and uphold standards that motivated many of the historical lynch mobs. For those historical participants in mobs, intellect was sacrificed to feeling. They thought on a simple and emotional level—something is threatening the purity of our womanhood and the authority of our laws; it must be crushed before it spreads. With Littleman, the intellectual exercise of planning a lynching is perhaps more appealing to him than the actual death of the policeman.

It is a measure of his brilliance, and of his role as the leader who must be aware of all possible twists and turns in the plan, that Littleman recognizes this limitation in himself. Littleman recruits Wilkerson, whom he believes to be a practical intellectual, as a safeguard against his own tendency to think too much. Littleman feels at times that he cannot "trust" his mind because it is "lazy and preening" and can be deceptive (p. 110). Wilkerson is brought in to keep as much of an element of reality in the plan as is possible, or at least to force Littleman to think with a purpose instead of for the sake of the art of thought. Even with this precaution against thinking himself into inertia, the success of the plan is not ensured.

About two-thirds of the way through the novel, we realize that the men will not carry out their plan. Several reasons provoke this conclusion. First of all, the young men live in the North, and their location does not provide psychological impetus comparable to that which might have developed on Southern soil. There is no repression immediate enough to mid-twentieth century Philadelphia to make the black men feel the wrongs committed against them as acutely as would a black community which had, say, witnessed a lynching in Mississippi around the same time.

In addition, the four plotters are all men who, by standards of the black community as well as those of the white, have "made it" to some extent. Though we are not given extensive information on Littleman's background, it is clear from his speech that he is college educated, or at least substantially well read. Thomas Wilkerson, though the son of a garbage collector, has gone to college and become a teacher; he may have a job in a black community, but he is far removed from the first-hand knowledge of white brutality which might prompt other Blacks, not so fortunate, to be more re-

sponsive to Littleman's plan. Wilkerson, the most middle class of
the four, is also the most skeptical. Saunders, who has lived his
early life among hustlers who made their living in the streets, has
nevertheless abandoned that livelihood to become a safe, secure
postal worker. Though he is more prone to violence than are the
others, he has still essentially escaped the threats of physical violence which might have been his lot on other territory. And Rice,
the reclusive janitor, more silent and reserved than the others, has
also made his compromise with power by accepting a job in the
basement of a building where rich whites live. Although he has
been advised to stay out of the tenants' way because his presence
might make them uncomfortable, he is not threatened with violence either. Thus the plotters do not represent the most repressed
members of the black community or the most threatened.

The importance of their social positions cannot be overestimated
in explaining why the plan cannot be carried out. Initially, none of
the plotters is married and none has property. Secondly, none has a
position significant enough in the community to exert influence
upon other members of the community. Consequently, they have
not the *tangible* motivations to inspire violence against the policeman. Their plan becomes theoretical and abstract, offered in the
name of righting wrongs and changing morality, in the name of a
notion of nationhood, rather than in the urgent need to protect
what one already has. Littleman asks his friends to kill for what
may be, not for what already is; and perhaps Wilkerson, at least,
thinks he can accomplish as much through his own efforts as a
teacher as Littleman can through the plan to kill the policeman.
Philosophical about an issue in a world which does not lend itself
to his brand of philosophy, Littleman is less an anachronism than a
curiosity. Wilkerson listens to the plan as much out of a fascination
with Littleman as out of an interest in the actual possibility of the
execution.

As leader of the group, Littleman also becomes a curiosity for us
as readers. He gets his nickname from his slight stature and from
the fact that he is crippled; when he is observed from a distance, he
is literally a little man. It is ironic, therefore, that this tiny man is
the one with the idea about lynching a policeman. Since the plan
never comes to fruition, perhaps Wideman is suggesting that the
tiny man is misdirecting his large brain. Perhaps, in the final analysis, he is to be viewed as a big-headed little cripple who has grandiose ideas. Still, he seems to be able to draw individuals one
would assume to be reasonably intelligent into his plan. Weird
Rice and malleable Saunders are not crazy, but they are more

easily convinced than Wilkerson; Littleman therefore focuses his attention on convincing Wilkerson that the plan will work. He knows that the other two will not have second thoughts if he succeeds in convincing this college-bred black man.

Littleman gives such an impression of largeness in the early scenes of the novel that we are somewhat surprised when, briefly, we are given an objective view of him. Out of frustration and an acute sense of the injustices in the society, Littleman goes to a local junior high school and makes a political speech from the steps. The police are called, and Littleman is forcibly removed, but not before one of the policemen yells out: "*Get the crazy black dwarf off the fucking school steps*" (p. 118). The pointed incongruity between the man's size and his ideas, coupled with the demeaning facts of his arrest and hospitalization, signals to us that both the man and his vision may be less impressive than we had thought. Two other incidents similarly reduce Littleman's stature and raise questions about the soundness of his mind with regard to the planned execution; both scenes contain fantasies in which Littleman imagines doing violence to someone and, in both cases, the intended victims are black. He thinks of raping a girl on a beach in Atlantic City because he believes she has seen only his crippled legs. He wants to "remain concealed in whatever pocket of shadow he stood. Leap out and strike her down with the leaded cane. Pin her body to the sand. A man taking what he wished" (p. 121). His projection and his overreaction here, and his not wholly explained mental aggression, raise questions about the plan. It, too, may be a way for him to achieve some semblance of manhood by doing what people who look him over casually would assume that he is incapable of doing.

In the other scene, equally specific in its imagined violence, Littleman imagines using a razor blade to kill Anthony, the reserved young black man who cleans his hospital room, because he may be spying to uncover the plan. The absurdity of Littleman's thoughts is blatant. How could he possibly expect to kill a strong young man with a mere razor blade, especially since he has been made helpless by the taking away of his crutches? And how could he expect that the man would be in reach long enough for him to make several slashes with such a flimsy weapon? If Littleman was sane at the moment he conceived the plan, these thoughts suggest that he may be slipping somewhat in his mental capacities, although there is still a certain amount of rationality in his thinking.

Incidents also occur with each of the other characters that indicate that the plan will remain in the realm of the imagination. There are flaws in each of their personalities that signal their potential for error and their potential for turning against each other. Thomas Wilkerson, first of all, wavers between a sense of superiority and one of insecurity. Although he is attracted to the idea of Littleman's plan, he is perhaps equally moved by gratitude that someone has noticed him and wants him to be involved with something. His father has turned into a drunken roustabout, his mother has retreated into the self-righteousness of old age, and Tanya, the woman he admires, really does not see him. Littleman selects him, cultivates him, and spends time trying to convince him of the validity of the plan. Yet, Wilkerson quickly falters in belief and conviction. He is self-conscious when he must assume the leading role while Littleman· is hospitalized, and he allows his imagination to control him when he has to make a visit to jail (he thinks the jailers know of the plan and are going to keep him there under arrest). Fear, timidity, conscience, and guilt would all prevent Wilkerson from carrying out the plan. Also, his inability to trust the men who are to work with him would lead perhaps to violence among them even before they could think of committing violence against the policeman.

Wilkerson's conscience, however, is his greatest stumbling block. He resolves to visit Sissie and her family, then, after traveling a long way, fails to confront them; instead, he turns away from the daughter's stare and hurries "toward the glitter of South Street" (p. 215). His guilt, combined with his weak personality and his worry over his father's incarceration for murder, also leads him, on a drunken visit to Tanya, to reveal the plan. It is only her lack of interest in Wilkerson and in what he has to say that prevents her from acting upon what he tells her or even from seriously questioning him about it. Things have indeed fallen apart; whether Tanya is curious about them or not, they will not be carried out as planned.

Wilkerson shows through his actions that he lacks both the necessary coldness to think of committing murder and the imagination to realize that there will be casualties in any revolution. Rice, on the other hand, whose reclusive residence in the basement of The Terrace Apartments parallels his closed state of mind, is an individualist who hides under the guise of cooperation. He hopes, by going along with the others, or by seeming to, that things will eventually happen in his favor. What little we know of him comes through his reaction to the killing by Thomas's father. He is "indignant" that Orin Wilkerson "had to go out and act a nigger" (p. 189) just when the group is about to bring the plan to fruition. His frustration heightens his already frenzied imagination, and he soothes his nerves and his ambition by playing with the guns left in his keep and by plotting his own rise to head of an interim government. In the midst of his reveries, a knock comes at the door. The drunken Wilkerson, as he told Tanya he would, comes for the guns, only to be met by a crazy Rice whose imagination tells him that he has been uncovered. Instead of answering the door, "he aimed where he thought the center of the door should be then made a fiery shambles of the darkness as he pulled the trigger" (p. 230). And that takes care of three of the four conspirators; Littleman is hospitalized, Wilkerson is dead, and Rice will shortly be in jail.

Isolated from any community to the point that he could not imagine intense involvement with it, Rice is clearly not the stuff of which lynchers are made. Without the calculation and the necessary coldness, and without a specifically directed hatred, he can only become a victim of the insulated circumstances under which the plot has been laid out. His lack of a clearly defined motivation for participating in the lynching makes him search for reasons for involvement along the lines of personal advancement. And since personal advancement is not even something he can envision in realistic terms, he does not pass as a minimally worthy appendage to the intended new nation.

Saunders, the fourth conspirator, seems to have the qualifications necessary to commit violence. Littleman has recruited him specifically to kidnap and kill Sissie when it is time to do so. He recognizes that Saunders has the ability to move "quietly," with "assassin's feet." His family background and his life of pimping and hustling would suggest that he can commit acts without caring about the individuals against whom the acts are directed. As a young boy, Saunders had watched his mother, who had seven children by "various fathers," lapse into a physical and mental condition which "the doctors at the clinic felt it superfluous to name" (pp. 142–43). He had been witness to the "incoherent fantasies" which characterized her existence and had stood in curious fascination as she had on one occasion stripped her clothes from her body and writhed on the floor. Completely detached from human sympathy with her, he continued that detachment through his hustling and pimping life, which suggests that he does have the cold-heartedness necessary to participate in the lynching.

As he goes through the night trying to find Sissie's apartment, he imagines himself on a hunt, "stalking" his prey, studying "the habits of his quarry." He compares his intended murder to those carried out by Jack the Ripper, and he resolves to "read more about the Ripper" (p. 148). If Saunders were content to locate the apartment of the woman and study her from a distance, he might be

able to commit murder. Instead, he decides to make personal contact with her. Since Raymond, Saunders's brother, is the father of
Sissie's child, Saunders uses the pretext that Raymond has sent her
money in order to get into the apartment. While he certainly has to
know who he is planning to kill, he is not quite prepared for what
he finds. Not only is the child present, but so is an older woman,
who seems to have responsibility for the child when Sissie is away.
More surprising, Sissie is not the monstrously overweight, unattractive black woman he has envisioned her to be. If she were
dressed to go out, Saunders can imagine her looking "as soft as the
pampered redbone girls his new post office job and status made
him eligible to court and fondle" (p. 156).

The problem with our potential Jack the Ripper, then, is that he
reflects too long upon the personal level about his intended victims. Seldom did the lynchers of history feel the necessity to make
such sustained, and understanding, personal contact with their
victims. Saunders is impressed by the fact that the two women and
the child are living in an abandoned apartment building (perhaps
because of the convenience for prostitution rather than because of
financial necessity) and, though he tells us otherwise, by the stoical
resignation to life which shines through the child's eyes. Consequently, though he had intended to give the child a few dollars, he
gives her all of the near hundred dollars he has in his pocket.
He tries to rationalize that it is his urge to get out of the apartment
which causes him not to select out a portion of the money instead
of handing it all over, but he tries too hard to convince himself. And
though he concludes that he will kill them all if necessary, we cannot help but believe that the fact of his kinship to the child will
negate that possibility.

His test by fire occurs on the morning he must wait in the bar for
the first phase of the plan to begin. He does not know that Rice has
shot Wilkerson just a few hours before and that Wilkerson will not
be showing up to meet him. He is so conscious of the imminent
changes which will result from the lynching that he almost expects
some change in the people he meets on the streets and those he
sees in the bar. Though seemingly not as prone to nerves as is Rice,
Saunders nevertheless becomes more and more anxious as time
passes and it is clear that Wilkerson is inexcusably late:

> He called Wilkerson's apartment. If the phone had been a funnel he
> would have spit through it. As he listened to the futile ringing, the
> black receiver become a club. He squeezed it, felt his knuckles
> sting. He cursed Wilco through his teeth, slammed the receiver like
> a club on Wilkerson's eggshell skull. [P. 238]

Tension continues to rise as Saunders realizes how much Wilkerson's tardiness is jeopardizing the plan; he is "primed" to get Sissie that evening.

Although Saunders maintains that he can sit in the bar all day waiting for Wilkerson, and pick the plan up again the next day if necessary, he is clearly not capable of doing that. When a man opens the doors of the bar, then retreats to the outside, Saunders has been so hopeful that the opening doors meant Wilkerson's entry that he becomes almost catatonic to discover that it is not. He imagines choking Wilkerson to death, and he becomes so angry he literally cannot move or speak:

> If he moved a fraction of an inch in any direction, the whole incredibly inflated structure would crash down. Seas of blood, of bile and phlegm and sickly meandering whiskey were waiting to flood from his body. Saunders remained on his feet after the door had shut. To speak would be to scream. To touch, murder. [P. 243]

Thus Saunders is left with any potential for violence directed only at himself. If he survives the pressure of this day with an ulcer, he will be lucky. He seems as near to insanity in his anger as Rice is in his fantasies and as Littleman is approaching in reality. In fact, the final image we are given of the lynchers is that of Littleman, who has been moved to that dreaded seventh-floor ward, whose eyes blaze "on nothing," and whose wonderfully articulate speech is reduced to sounds, "almost like gagging" (p. 251). Thus ends the tale and the fate of the lynchers. They have failed for reasons of personality, but they have also failed for other reasons.

Although Wideman prefaces his book with the detailed accounts of the atrocities committed against Blacks by whites throughout American history, accounts which would justify some retaliation, he finally espouses a different morality from that which has guided the actions of the whites. His novel becomes an exploration of the desire for revenge on the part of those who lack the depravity necessary to effect that revenge. To take life, for whatever purpose, goes ultimately against the grain of the concept of nationhood, and Wideman stops his characters short of completing their plan. It is understandable, he seems to suggest, that any black person, and especially black men, should want revenge for what has happened to their ancestors. Finally, though, it is not within their will or within their sense of community to effect the revenge. And it is certainly not permissible to plan to kill a black person as a prelude to the killing of a white policeman. To illustrate how thoroughly antithetical such actions would be to black human nature, Wideman allows the mere contemplation of them to drive almost all of his characters mad. What they imagine doing may be attractive as a political gesture, but they can only destroy themselves by persisting with the plan.[3]

On the other hand, by showing the mental breakdown of these imitators of white lynchers, Wideman may be suggesting that insanity is precisely the condition of the society which, through so many generations, continued to kill other human beings in such a violent way. How, then, can black people really justify aspiring to whiteness, even at the level of imitating their violent acts? To do so is to join forces with powers which are against nature, because vengeance can merely change the color of the oppressor; it does not make the violence any more palatable. Wideman denies Baraka's thesis in *The Slave*—where it is suggested that black men probably will not be more humane in positions of power than the whites were, but they should have their turn—by positing that violence in kind cannot liberate, cannot form the basis on which a new nation of happy people is to be founded.

The failure is also tied to the immediate victim they have chosen: Sissie, a black woman. Historically maligned, misused, and devalued by the whites, the black woman is now to be similarly degraded by the men of her own race. Saunders suggests that Sissie is already dead because she works for the white policeman; his memory is short on the black women he had working for him during his hustling days. Does the color of exploitation make it any less exploitation? His judgment of Sissie and her work for the policeman is tied to his own fragile ego; Sissie becomes not of value in herself but as something the policeman has taken away from black men. So Saunders and the others still give her no intrinsic worth, and they never suggest the possibility of trying to reclaim her for the black community. It is easier to judge her, just as it was easy for Saunders to sit by and watch his mother go through her painful fits without lifting a hand to aid her.

If the potential lynchers place such an expendable value on Sissie, why do they believe the black community will be stirred to respond to her disappearance? Saunders himself points out that it would take at least ten killings of black prostitutes for there to be any serious public notice. That is why they plan the extra feature of mutilating Sissie. What they lack in numbers, they plan to make up for in atrocity. And that plan is no more horrifying, Wideman suggests, than the atrocities which were committed against black men who were castrated, burned, and had their fingers cut off and eyes gouged out.

The role Sissie is scheduled to play in the lynching is also a parody of the role white women traditionally played in lynchings. Mobs were called to heap vengeance upon black offenders who dared to rape and murder white women, or who just happened to be in their presence when the ladies screamed. Can a black woman, a prostitute, serve the call to vengeance that Littleman and the others are expecting? Will her community place the same value on her that the lynchers have by simply ignoring what is planned for her? As the plotters themselves recognize, the nature of Sissie's work and her isolated apartment will ensure that her disappearance will not be noticed for some time (her daughter and the old woman will simply think she is away with the policeman), and certainly not before they plant the rumors about her. But even after that is done, it is questionable as to how much response they will be able to evoke.

The moral distinctions to be made between Wideman's lynchers and those of history can also be seen in the reaction of the former to Sissie. Saunders, who works hard to win a medal for coldheartedness, cannot help but observe and sympathize with the conditions under which Sissie is raising her daughter. And Wilkerson, who has a much more active conscience than any of the others, cannot even bring himself to face the woman, let alone to think about having an active part in her death. Though the group's plan to kill her places them in the same role as whites who historically devalued black life and took it freely, their actions and thoughts show that they are not the cutthroats they would have to be to follow through with everything they have planned.

Wideman suggests, through his characters, that abstract hatred is not sufficient to motivate the taking of a life. His characters, through Littleman, are attracted to the spectacle of the ritual lynching, but must be pepped up repeatedly or their resolve will fail. All of their reluctance, their hesitation to get on with the plan, is tied to the lack of intensity in their hatred. They cannot reduce either Sissie or the policeman to the total level of subhumanity which would be necessary for the lynchers to act without compunction. If they would indeed follow the lynching models from the South, they must be able to view their victims as animals who do not deserve any special consideration. The policeman is never really real to them, but even after Littleman is beaten almost to death by two officers, the plotters cannot manage to use that injury as a motive for dehumanizing the policeman. Sissie is too close to Saunders and to a way of life all of them have witnessed within the black community for her to be less than human. Willing themselves to hate therefore turns out to be a more formidable task than any of the lynchers have planned; they may have spurts of hatred, but they cannot sustain the emotion.

The time setting is a further factor in the failure of the plotters to carry out their intended lynching. Lynchings in the form they advocate were almost nonexistent in this country in the third quarter of the twentieth century, and they had been nonexistent long before that in the state of Pennsylvania. The absence of historical immediacy, therefore, and the lack of recent models, force the lynching more into the realm of the imagination, which must draw on far-distant materials. Also, if the setting for the novel is the same time as that of its composition, the action occurs just after the great bursts of energy of the civil rights movement and the liberal atmosphere which pervaded the 1960s. Thus, it is questionable whether or not they can resurrect enough of the pre–1960s animosity between Blacks and whites to accomplish their purpose.

Another major factor in the failure of the planned execution is the absence of a community structure to support it. The lynchers must *solicit* community support; the responses they hope for will not be automatic. This, too, differs from the historical model. One thing which is consistently clear in historical lynchings is that entire communities were aware of acting out roles which their very places in society assigned to them. A community was threatened; it was called upon to respond in a ritual manner to the threat. As Wright and Dunbar point out, the roles were more important than the individuals; and when the calls came, they had to respond whether they, as individuals, wanted to or not. There are no comparable violent acts to which all members of the black communities in the United States are expected to respond. It is not certain, therefore, that Littleman and the others will be successful in creating one.

The examples of black people shown from Littleman's community do not suggest that he will be successful. While he is in the hospital, he contemplates recruiting Anthony to join the plotters. What becomes clear, however, is that Anthony, who is only in his teens, has made his peace with the world. He refuses to smoke in areas forbidden to him, and he sneaks quietly away to the floors like the seventh where the nurses do not complain about his smoking. He is visibly shaken when Littleman insists that he light a cigarette in his room and a nurse enters just as he completes the lighting. He has no interest in the history Littleman tries to share with him, because he cannot see the relevance of such information to his already predetermined life. The black people in the bar which Saunders visits exhibit the same inertia, as does little Lisa.

The only people with the energy to contemplate a future are those who are working exploitative games, such as pimps and prostitutes. In a world in which the hourly concern is most important, it is questionable whether Littleman and the others will get the black people to think two or three years or decades into the future.

Finally, that pervasive fear Littleman recognizes as existing among Blacks, especially black men, would have to be eradicated if the plan is to accomplish its objective. The chances of doing that, of changing history so drastically, will probably not materialize through a hundred lynched white policemen. Fear and inertia can kill ideas, especially when those ideas are presented at the level of the philosophical in a world given to the brutal realities of existence. One of those brutal realities provides the backdrop for the novel and suggests, in its pervasive stench, that Littleman and the others have ignored too drastically what the world around them is really like.

The novel does not begin with the lynchers; after the Matter Prefatory, it begins with Orin Wilkerson, father of Thomas, garbage collector ("sanitary engineer") for the city of Philadelphia. Just home from a drunken night on the town with his garbage collecting buddies, Orin Wilkerson is the antithesis of everything the lynchers envision in terms of nationhood and unity. Orin has neglected his wife and abused her mentally, if not physically, by his carousing. Instead of trying to resolve their differences, he remains locked away in some world which has little meaning even for him, and his wife similarly keeps herself beyond reconciliation. We do not know how these two have arrived at this state in their marriage, but we do know that there are slight chances for great improvement.

The scene then shifts to a garbage-collecting run, in which Orin "Sweetman" Wilkerson and his buddies exchange stories of their sexual exploits and the freakiness of the white women they have encountered. The virtue that white men defended historically and the ritual which Littleman is planning—which grew out of that defense of virtue—are thus parodied by these working-class men who seem to get all the white women they want and for whom there seem to be none of the barriers Littleman articulates so well. We can certainly speculate on whether the men tell each other the truth about their escapades, but even allowing for a degree of exaggeration, they seem ultimately more healthy in their basic tastes and actions than are the men who plot and plan. Or perhaps Wideman is suggesting that these men are the men who need to be recruited for a change of attitude.

What becomes clear with the garbage collectors is that, though

they may handle the filth of the city in their underworld, almost
underground existences, they are nevertheless men of action rather
than men of ideas. When they see women they want, they go after
them—unlike Thomas with Tanya and Littleman's initial insecurity with Angela. Their activity indicates that they are also men of
passion, and they provide immediate contrasts to the calculating,
thoughtful men Littleman and Wilkerson are. It is therefore ironic
that these garbage collectors are the ones who can be stirred immediately to violence, without any pep talks or justification. And
while that is also their tragedy, it nevertheless provides a contrast
to the lynchers. While they plot and plan a murder of grandiose
proportions, Orin Wilkerson kills his best friend for a few dollars;
he thereby makes mockery of the plan which provides the major
focus for the novel:

> Radcliff had his car parked there and we were carrying a can of gas
> to get it started. Me and Childress and Radcliff. I bought the gas and
> Radcliff was supposed to pay me but Childress screaming Radcliff
> better give him the money because I owed him. And Thomas, I
> swear to God I didn't owe him nothing, but he got mad. I told him
> Radcliff was giving money to nobody but me and Radcliff said I
> was right since I bought the gas and I didn't have anything that day
> anyway, hardly enough to get me a taste of something after work
> but Childress he just keeps shouting and getting madder. . . . He
> went running and when he came back had his knife open. . . . I kept
> trying to talk to him. Backing up and saying wait a minute, man,
> wait this is your man I remember trying to get him to say some-
> thing but he was staring wild right in my eyes and circling with
> that knife. I knew he meant business. Too late, he was too close.
> I tried to run but tripped over a log. I was down when I got it out
> remember opening it with my teeth and pushing myself up and
> him on top of me I shoved with it in my hand and fell on him.
> [Pp. 196–97]

This is the pathetic drama of reality, not the pageantry of a planned
symbolic execution. Orin stabs his friend, then holds him in his
arms on the ride to the hospital, only to discover that he will die
shortly thereafter. There had been no pageantry, only Orin vomit-
ing beside the car and being viewed as "an ignorant razor fighting
nigger, stinking of sour wine" (p. 198). While the death does serve to
bring Orin and his wife to a kind of peace with each other that they
have not known for years, it does not serve any larger, communal
purpose. Yet, it is violence to match that the others conceive.

It is perhaps in part because of hearing his father's story that
Thomas Wilkerson goes to see Tanya and decides to get the guns

from Rice. Their plan must seem decidedly far-fetched and unreal to him after he has heard his father's story. Between the planned death and the actual one, there is the difference between illusion and reality, between symbol and object. The knifing of Childress must make the planned lynching of the policeman seem like the diversion of a hyperactive mind.

The incident with the garbage collector strikes a realistic tone, and that realism undercuts the quirky idealism of Littleman and his cohorts. We acquiesce in the undercutting, but still are desirous of retaliation for the historical violence. Still, we do not leave the novel feeling that Wideman is advocating the status quo; rather, he has very persuasively shown us what will not work to solve the racial animosities in this country. He is not willing to give up black humanity for racial revenge; nor is he willing to compromise realistic objectives for fantastic ones. Most importantly of all, he is not willing to create a new mythology in the black community which would be based on violence sanctioned by political rhetoric and unbridled imagination.

CHAPTER 6

Beyond the Ritual?

The decline in lynchings of black persons in the United States did not presage a similar decline in the portrayal of lynchings and burnings in literature created by black American writers. Yet, as we have seen with John Wideman, it did eventually lead to a change of focus. After the 1970s, an additional change developed within the literature. There is an undermining of the primary emotional cause for lynching in the literature by portrayal of physically nonviolent interactions between black males and white females. In several works, the effects of integration are reflected in these interracial relationships. The black man's fear of being caught in the presence of the white woman is exchanged for his public and private confrontation with this figure whose counterparts in history have caused so many deaths. Black writers are now more willing to bring the myth to light for the purposes of examining it instead of simply perpetuating or denying it. Interestingly, more black women writers are now involved in this trend. The threat of castration obviously did not affect them as it did black men, and few of them historically have depicted scenes in which black men are hunted down, lynched, burned, and castrated for presumed crimes against white women.

With the arrival of the early 1980s, two black writers, one male and one female, wrote novels in which a black man comes into the forbidden presence of a white female and manages to survive in spite of the history surrounding them. In one instance, the aura of the myth of sacred white womanhood surrounds the novel, and, in the other, the ancient fear is briefly hinted at, then dissolved. Toni Morrison, in *Tar Baby* (1981), and David Bradley, in *The Chaneysville Incident* (1981), are both concerned, but in different ways, with the effects of history upon their characters. Morrison is more concerned with the mythical aspects of history while Bradley is concerned with the factual history which leads to myth, but both allow their characters to come to grips with who they are through confrontations with history and with the white women who are a significant part of that history.

148

Denial of the Ritual

Toni Morrison's *Tar Baby* (1981) has all the ingredients which could lead to an accusation of rape and the summary execution of a black man; however, those potential outcomes are short-circuited by the location in which they occur, by the personality of the major white protagonist, and by Morrison's undercutting or transformation of several mythic ideas which pervade the novel. Morrison sets her novel on a privately owned island in the Caribbean, in a chateau-like dwelling called L'Arbe de la Croix; the island and the house are the retirement home of Valerian Street and his wife Margaret. Having made a fortune in a family-owned candy business, Valerian has consented to retire early and leave the running of the business to newer heads. Now approaching seventy, he has transported his music collection, his love for flowers, and his reluctant wife, many years his junior, to this self-imposed exile. He has also transported his faithful servants, Sydney and Ondine, to continue his conception of domestic tranquility and the good things in life. Most of the scenes on the island occur around Christmastime, when Sydney's and Ondine's niece, Jadine (Jade), is home from Paris for the holidays. Educated at Valerian's expense, and providing for him a peculiar kind of entertainment, Jadine is farther removed from black culture than the island is from the United States.

In this world apart from the larger one in which the roles for all the characters have been defined, Valerian's has indeed extended beyond that of leader to that of god. He controls his wife, Jade's education, Sydney's and Ondine's future, and the livelihood of the islanders who work as cooks, washerwomen, and gardeners around his home. He is not required to appeal to any higher power; nor is it necessary for him to get the sanction of his peers—considerations that affected many of the mob actions we have seen earlier. His absolute control is important for what happens when the black man enters this idyllic setting, and some of the ugliness which Valerian and his household have escaped by leaving the United States again becomes prominent. When Son, the potential black rapist, is found in Margaret's bedroom, the response is surprisingly casual. On one level, the reaction is ironically appropriate because the setting is so far removed from the American soil which engenders many of the stereotypical notions about race relations. That those stereotypes do remain on another level suggests how impossible it is for American Blacks and whites to move completely beyond traditional attitudes toward each other, no matter what their location in the world. Valerian, who could very easily kill Son, or have him killed, instead decides that, in the spirit of adventure and the lack of restraint which defines his retirement, he will treat the matter playfully. His game, conducted on the mental level rather than the physical level of abuse and castration which would generally accompany the discovery of a black man in a white woman's private quarters, will eventually backfire.

Valerian's reaction cannot be due simply to his age and his physical infirmity; he still has the power to command the death of a man who has invaded his wife's bedroom, and there are forces nearby which would support that response to the invasion of privacy no matter what the color of the individuals involved. Rather, Valerian, who has had as much experience in shaping people as in acquiring wealth, perhaps sees another opportunity to shape someone. Also, we cannot deny that the element of boredom perhaps plays a part in his reaction to Son; after all, Valerian's primary activities are sitting in the greenhouse listening to music, taking care of the flowers, and having Sydney wait upon him. Son's entry is a diversion from that routine and a change of pace from Margaret, whom Valerian finds tolerable at best and in whom he has no sustained interest, other than embarrassing her at the dinner table for her forgetfulness and lack of knowledge about table manners.

Thus the black "beast" who is found in Margaret's closet is domesticated into a pet by Valerian who, through that action, continues to play with people's lives on his fantasy island. Indeed, Valerian's attitude toward Margaret is such that he is inclined to believe she has been drinking too much when she comes trembling downstairs struggling to reveal what she has discovered in her closet. Son, who has jumped ship and has been hiding around the house and stealing food for days, crouches in Margaret's closet when she unexpectedly leaves the dinner table following an argument with Valerian. Later, screaming with fear, she returns to the dining room only to have Valerian bark rather harshly, commanding her to explain what is happening. Margaret is so terrified she can only say, "in my closet," "black," and "in my things."[1] Valerian accuses her of histrionics ("this is not the Met") and suggests that she has had too much to drink. He is only convinced that Margaret is not hallucinating when Sydney returns from his upstairs quest with Son, at gunpoint, preceding him.

Margaret's reaction is understandably human. What woman would not be shocked to proceed to her closet and discover an uninvited, funky, unshaven, and unkempt male lurking in it? I contend, however, that for Margaret the fear is greater because she is a white female and the intruder is a black male. She may be on the island, but she is one of the characters who has brought some of her Americanized mythological thinking with her. The phrases she whispers out in her fear all indicate that she has received, from her point of view, not just an invasion of privacy, but a personal threat. Her most private space has been violated; indeed, we might not overextend the image by suggesting that the shape of the closet itself and the idea that it has an unwanted individual there has overtones of rape. Even without that extension, however, Margaret's few utterances convey violation. The emphasis is on possession; what is uniquely Margaret's has been trespassed upon ("*my* closet," "*my* things"—emphasis mine). It is reasonable to be upset at finding an intruder in one's closet without emphasizing the "things"; yet Margaret's iteration suggests that the offense is almost as great as that of the slave who stuck his hand up the white mistress's dress while she was still wearing it. Margaret's "things," with her perfumes, her body odors, her personality, have been touched not only by an outsider, but by a *black* outsider; that, to her mind, is a kind of rape.

She has been taken over by a force of blackness; when she is initially questioned, she cannot give that blackness any individual identity (when she utters the word, Jade mistakenly thinks that Margaret is simply saying it is "dark" in her closet). Her speechlessness reveals some connection she has made to blackness beyond the fact that a man is discovered in her closet. Why not just say it is a man? Or somebody? She sees the blackness, and that detail is all-important to her. How important will be revealed later when it becomes clear that Margaret is heir to all the racial stereotyping, as far as black men and white women are concerned, which defined many white characters we have seen in works prior to this novel.

While the scene sends Margaret into spasms, it only makes Valerian pause for a moment. Instead of calling the harbor, as everyone else is demanding, Valerian, as surprised as any of them that Margaret has indeed seen something unusual, turns the serious occasion into something he can control with an unexpected reaction: "Good evening, sir. Would you care for a drink?" (p. 80). In Valerian's response to Son, Morrison undercuts the notion of the black man as rapist and that of the white woman as the beauty who needs undue protection. The fact that Valerian invites Son to drink with him shows how lightly he looks upon the possibility that his wife and his home are in need of protection (and he may feel a bit of curiosity about how Son came to be where he is). The major point of his action, though, is to debunk the myth that white women are such sublime creatures that they merit constant pedestalization and protection. Valerian can look lightly upon Son's intrusion because he does not truly value Margaret as wife, mother, companion, or minimally intelligent human being. He married her on a whim, because her beauty appealed to him and because she reminded him of the candy named for him when he was a child. Married to Margaret when he is thirty-nine and she is not yet twenty, Valerian had taken his bride as a complement to himself. Perhaps, in his cynicism and in his aloofness from his own community and family, he never expected her to be anything but the mindless beauty who had attracted him and for whom his interest was lasting but not unwaveringly intense. Nor did he believe the beauty was of the variety which needed any special protection. Frequently left to her own devices, Margaret became more of a useless appendage than a sustaining wife; she was merely another of the molding experiments Valerian added to his collection and gave up on when she turned out not to be especially adept. Because he has devalued her, therefore, he does not expect that anyone else would find her of great enough value to want to rape her.

His attitude toward Margaret combines with the tone of the narrator to devalue her even further. Margaret is consistently and derisively identified by the color of her eyes and the flaming red hair which has so set her apart from her immediate family. Repeatedly referred to as the possessor of "blue-if-it's-a-boy blue eyes" and "the principal beauty of Maine," Margaret is viewed as a hollow woman whose frivolous, transitory claims to special consideration are judged to be small, easily overlooked.

Since Valerian does not come to Margaret's defense, she and the other members of the household are left to perpetuate the myth of the threat to white womanhood that lurking black men are automatically assumed to represent. From the stupefying knowledge that Son has been in her "things," Margaret moves on to contemplate the violation which has presumably occurred there; she provides sexual overtones in the process:

> In her things. Actually in her things. Probably jerking off. Black sperm was sticking in clots to her French jeans or down in the toe of her Anne Klein shoes. Didn't men sometimes jerk off in women's shoes? She'd have the whole closetful cleaned. Or better still, she'd throw them all out and buy everything new—from scratch. [P. 86]

To her, Son has dirtied her most private things, and for that he becomes "this nigger" and "this real live dope addict ape" (p. 87).

Though Margaret makes a sexual connection here and reduces Son to the brutish animal who would readily rape her, she does not yet verbalize that equation. It is through Jade that the issue of rape arises, along with the question of what would have happened had circumstances been different.

In order to understand how the Blacks in L'Arbe de la Croix perpetuate the stereotype of "nigger rapists," two points must be considered. First of all, Jadine and Margaret must be viewed as sharing a kinship as "white" women, and, secondly, a clear distinction must be made, from the point of view of Jadine, Sydney, and Ondine, between "niggers" and the "better" classes of "coloured" people. Through education, severing of connection to black people, and general disposition, Jadine is "white." She has traded a cultural heritage for what she considers the "finer" things in life, and those things are not to be found among a people who are economically and socially deprived. As a "light, bright, damn near white" black woman who has the financial assistance of a powerful white man, Jadine has been given opportunities that many white people do not have. Consequently, she has no reason to identify herself as black; even Sydney and Ondine, her uncle and aunt, are troublesome spots when she considers what her future responsibility to them will be. She has no experience at all in dealing with "street niggers," and she probably would not know what chitterlings were if she saw them. Her upper middle-class leanings place her in a category with Alice Harrison in Chester Himes's *If He Hollers Let Him Go*. She has seen none of the discomfort and the struggle in life, and she does not wish to do so. She is therefore just as "white" in background and social aspirations as Margaret is, and she is almost as white in color. A person like Son affronts everything she believes she is and evokes in her everything she has decided she does not wish to be a part of. She is perhaps more annoyed with Son's presence than Margaret is, and his daring to speak to her makes her as indignant as a Southern Belle who has been proposed to by the gardener.

To Jadine, Sydney, and Ondine, but especially the latter two, Son is a low-life "nigger" who should be shot on sight. He painfully reminds Sydney and Ondine of what they have escaped by volunteering into slavery with Valerian, and he has an uppitiness about him which they believe should be reserved for well-bred black folks. Son is the antithesis of everything they are: he is unmannered, ungroomed, without financial security, disturbingly black, unapologetic, and arrogant even in his poverty and trespassing. In order not to be put into the same category with such vermin, they ag-

gressively advocate his ouster among themselves, but they do not
dare to suggest how Valerian should behave.

Son is what Jadine has escaped in her numerous encounters with
men, and, like the black men who are irresistibly drawn to white
women, despite her distaste, she is similarly drawn to him. It is an
attraction that she will not admit initially, but it finally develops
into a relationship. Throughout that relationship, however, she
views herself as the repository of culture and Son as the diamond
in the rough, the gem which can only be fully appreciated if it is
cut and shaped to the cutter's satisfaction. She wants the man, but
she wants him her way, and she works consistently to try to change
him. All of her efforts reveal that, to her, he is the "nigger" and she
is that "something else" the race has to offer.

As the "white" woman who can be threatened with rape just as
easily as Margaret, Jadine shows an abundance of stereotypical notions, all of which measure how superior and desirable she believes herself to be. It is Jadine who first thinks that Son has lurked
in Margaret's closet "with rape, theft or murder on his mind" (p. 91).
She consistently thinks of him as a "nigger" and equates that classification with rape. To Jadine, Son violates her sense of culture, of
manhood, and of humanity; therefore, he can only be the "ape," the
"baboon," the beast who lurks in the shadows lusting after her as
acutely as Gus did after the heroine of *Birth of a Nation*. Since she
has nothing in common with Son, Jadine can only think that he has
come to take the one thing away from her which so separates
them—that pedestalized elevation which makes her as desirable,
as virtuous and as vulnerable as white women. Son can see what
she has voluntarily given up, and that in part inspires her additional fury against him.

She rushes from her bedroom following her first private encounter with Son with the intention of telling Valerian about Son "trying to rape her" (p. 123), but instead finds herself delaying until,
upon her arrival at the greenhouse, she hears "Valerian and the
man, both laughing to beat the band" (p. 127). No longer able to
share her anxieties with Valerian, Jadine turns to Margaret to discuss the phenomenon of the strange man who has invaded their
privacy. When Margaret asks how much of Son's story about how
he came to the island she believes, Jadine replies: " 'I believe some
of it. I mean I don't believe he came here to rape you.' (Me, maybe,
she thought, but not you.)" (p. 128). She then proceeds to play a kind
of straight man to Margaret's evaluation of the situation. Margaret
begins:

> "I'm going to have it out with Valerian. He's doing this just to
> ruin Christmas for me. Michael's coming and he knows I want ev-
> erything right for him, and look what he does to get me upset. In-
> stead of throwing that . . . that . . ."
> "Nigger."
> "Right, nigger, instead of throwing him right out of here."
> "Maybe we're making something out of nothing."
> "Jade. He was in my closet. He had my box of souvenirs in his
> lap."
> "Open?"
> "No. Not open. Just sitting there holding it. He must have picked
> them up from the floor. Oh, God, he scared the shit out of me. He
> looked like a gorilla!"
> Jadine's neck prickled at the description. She had volunteered
> nigger—but not gorilla. "We were all scared, Margaret," she said
> calmly. "If he'd been white we would still have been scared." [P. 129]

Although Jade has called Son a "baboon" and has supplied Margaret with the word "nigger," she bristles unexpectedly at the word
"gorilla." Perhaps that is a word she has too often heard associated
with black people, or perhaps she believes that if Margaret applies
that description so easily to one black person, it may spill over to
include her as well. The conversation does show, however, how important it is for Jade to establish very clearly an "us" and a "them"
as far as black people are concerned, and she makes her identification with the whites equally clear.

In a later conversation Jade has with Margaret, the woman is still
concerned about Son having been in her closet, and Jade is still the
one to translate that into what Margaret is too timid to confront:
the possibility of rape.

> "Well, Jade, he was in my closet."
> "He isn't there now. What's the matter, Margaret? You think he
> wants your bod?" . . . He doesn't want you, Margaret. He wants me.
> He's crazy and beautiful and black and poor and beautiful and he
> killed a woman but he doesn't want you. He wants me . . . Just be-
> cause he was in her closet, she thought his sole purpose in life was
> to seduce her. Naturally her. A white woman no matter how old,
> how flabby, how totally sexless, believed it and she could have shot
> him for choosing Margaret's closet and giving her reason to believe
> it was true.
> God. . . . I am competing with her for rape! [Pp. 185, 186]

That is the closest Jadine comes to admitting her "whiteness" in
the rape analogy. Though she is initially not flattered that Son has

been in Margaret's room because he mistook it for hers, she nevertheless softens toward him in the days leading up to Christmas.
Her reflections in the passage above occur after she has gone on a
picnic with Son.

Jadine's attitude toward Son changes because she is finally attracted to him as a woman is attracted to a man. For Sydney and
Ondine, however, who also believe that he is infinitely beneath
them, there can never be a compromise with Son. They may be
forced to tolerate him as one of Valerian's extravagant whims, but
they will never like him. Son's "niggerish" qualities and his potential as a rapist are foremost on Sydney's mind, and he wonders
how Valerian could sleep so soundly "with a wife-raper down the
hall" (p. 99). Ondine's softer tone toward Son, her maintaining that
"he didn't rape anybody," though "he's been here long enough and
quiet enough to rape" (p. 99), does not mean that she is willing to
go against her husband's position about the man, and Sydney is
vehemently opposed to him. He is irate that Son sleeps upstairs
with the Streets while he and Ondine sleep "over the downstairs
kitchen." When Ondine tries to remind him that Jadine also sleeps
upstairs, Sydney retorts: "You comparing Jadine to a . . . a . . .
stinking ignorant swamp nigger? To a wild-eyed pervert who hides
in women's closets?" (p. 100). He also asserts that Son is "crazy,"
"liable to do anything" (p. 101). Ondine takes the path necessary for
trying to talk "good sense" into Sydney, but she also has her moments of discomfort about Son:

> She talked sense she didn't know she had about a situation that
> both frightened and disoriented her. But in talking to Sydney she
> knew what it was. The man was black. If he'd been a white bum in
> Mrs. Street's closet, well, she would have felt different. . . . The
> man upstairs wasn't a Negro—meaning one of them. He was a
> stranger. (She had made Sydney understand that.) . . . "Shoot," she
> said aloud. "That nigger's not going nowhere." [P. 102]

Believing that Son, having been exposed to something to which he
is not accustomed, will try to make the very best of a good thing,
Ondine contents herself with going about the business of running
her kitchen. She tries to trust Jadine's good sense to control the extent of her involvement with Son.

Sydney's understandable reaction to Son logically grows out of
his concern for his family; however, the points at which that reaction becomes extreme—in his references to Son as a "crazy"
"swamp nigger"—may have certain unconscious fears informing
them. Before Son's arrival, Sydney has been the only black man

who has access to Valerian's house (Yardman, as the local gardener, Gideon, is called, never comes into the house). Also, as the only American black man nearby, Sydney is also the only one who holds the same relationship to the whites as Son does, and he consequently shares, in spite of his protestations, the same history. If Son, an American black man who is heir to all the stereotyped notions of the racially motivated rapist, is not thoroughly devalued and degraded, Sydney may run the risk of being placed in kinship to him. After all, he has previously had access to all of the places—except Margaret's closet—that Son has made himself so at home with. If Son does indeed perform some unsavory or criminal act around the house, could not Sydney also be implicated? Might not Valerian at that point lump all black males together, and certainly those two who are under his own roof? I would venture to say, then, that Sydney, in spite of his age, is almost as afraid of being discredited as Margaret and Jadine are initially afraid of being raped. For reasons of gender and history, therefore, Sydney must oppose Son with all his strength; these very personal considerations combine with those notions he has about class and social status to make his aversion to Son particularly acute.

Both Sydney and Ondine are aware of Valerian's ability to change moods and of the extent to which he needs digressions to keep him entertained. Part of Ondine's reason for talking good sense into Sydney is that she knows Valerian "might keep [Son] for two days, three, for his own amusement" (p. 102). And Sydney, whose anger has almost made him forget, knows equally well that his employer is capable of changing moods and toying with people. He tells Son:

> ". . . Mr. Street don't know nothing about you, and don't care nothing about you. White folks play with Negroes. It entertained *him*, that's all, inviting you to dinner. He don't give a damn what it does to anybody else. You think he cares about his wife? That you scared his wife? If it entertained him, he'd *hand* her to you!" [Pp. 162–63]

Sydney's last assertion may be a bit extreme, but the general tone of the passage supports the notion that Valerian enjoys playing the role of god on his little paradise island; once he no longer cares to use people as pawns, he will strike them from the playing board.

The problem, though, is that Valerian stays his hand too long and, when he tries to make a play, the players have forgotten their roles. The fateful incident occurs on Christmas Day, when Gideon and one of his helpers are fired for stealing apples Margaret has had imported from the States for the holiday. When Son questions that action, Valerian commands him to leave the house at once. Son's "I don't think so" (p. 206) leads to further rebellion, and Margaret and Ondine end up in a fist fight. Valerian's ineffectual orders to people to leave the room illustrate how far he has lost control of his game: " 'Call the harbor!' shouted Valerian, but again there was no one to do his bidding. He had played a silly game, and everyone was out of place" (p. 208). They continue to be out of place as Ondine reveals how Margaret abused her son Michael as a baby. Thus the skeleton in Margaret's closet is not a black man waiting to rape her, but that she is herself a violent, psychologically destructive abuser of children.

That is the blow which causes Valerian to lose not only his verbal power, but some of his mental capacity as well. He will spend the remainder of the novel being cared for by Sydney in a reversal of roles which shows how pathetic the little god has become. Valerian's loss of interest in things and people around him is in some ways a kind of poetic justice for the molding and shaping he has tried to perform on people's lives. Now, the little god who played with his power to destroy a potential rapist finds himself being nurtured and cared for by Sydney, the person who shares, from one point of view, the closest kinship to the potential rapist.

Ultimately, though, the point of the confusion centers upon Son's role in the sequence of events in which he is involved. Why does he consent to play the role assigned to him for such a long time? Is it sufficient to say that his fear of the consequences of having jumped ship is enough to keep him playfully entertaining Valerian for so long? He must be aware of what the others are thinking, so why does he stay? Initially, the question of his hunger is important. From the point at which he swam from his own ship to the boat on which Margaret and Jadine were riding, he had begun a search for food. And it is logical to accept the fact that he may have continued that search for a few days because he was indeed unsure of what kind of response his presence would evoke. And Thérèse, one of the helpers, had sensed the presence of a "starving" man many days before Son was discovered in Margaret's closet. So, weakness and uncertainty about his reception influence Son initially. But how do we explain his actions once he has been fed, given clothing, and probably has a good chance to escape?

Son turns into a kept man, who, by providing entertainment for Valerian, is able temporarily to make himself at home. He is knowledgeable about plants and music, and wins Valerian's approval by showing him how to make one particularly stubborn flower bloom. He also comes up with a method for keeping ants out of the green-

house. Furthermore, he laughs and jokes and has a rip-roaring
good time with Valerian, including telling him dirty jokes about
black women. The obvious explanation for his behavior is simply
that he wishes to keep in Valerian's good graces long enough to
make a decision about his future actions; therefore, he plays his
own kind of game, executes his own "please the white folks" role.
He also recognizes that Valerian, of all the folks in the house, does
not fear him and does not believe that he had violent intentions
when he arrived at the house: "They are frightened, he thought. All
but the old man. The old man knows that whatever I jumped ship
for it wasn't because I wanted to rape a woman" (p. 133). It is perhaps unusual to assume that logic prevails with white men who
discover black men in the bedrooms of their wives, but Son's non-
chalance suggests that he understands and is reasonably comfort-
able with Valerian's opinion of him. He is so sure of Valerian's attitude and so confident that an accusation of rape would be absurd
that he reveals those "dangerous" private parts to Valerian on his
first trip to the greenhouse:

> [Son] sprayed some of the ant killer on his legs. His kimono came
> undone at the belt and fell away from his body. Valerian looked at
> his genitals and the skinny black thighs. "You can't go round like
> that in front of the ladies. Leave that alone, and go tell Sydney to
> give you some clothes. Tell him I said so." [P. 148]

Certainly Valerian may be concerned with general propriety, but
there is no alarm or fear in his observation, nothing to reveal that
he imagines what he has just seen being used against his wife. He
seems to be satisfied with Son's earlier answers to the question
about how he came to be in Margaret's bedroom. With that matter
cleared up, and with the long-haired, smelly Son cleaned up to
physical respectability at least, he and Valerian can proceed to
share their private jokes and their knowledge about plants and ants.

The larger reason for Son's delay in leaving is his attraction to
Jadine. His many nights of observing her while she sleeps have
made him just as desirous of having her as Bob Jones is of having
Alice Harrison, as Bigger Thomas is attracted to the possibility
of seducing Mary Dalton, and as Fishbelly Tucker is attracted to
white women in general. Son has run up against the one stumbling
block which has impeded the paths of so many of his literary and
historical counterparts; he wants to possess what the society has
consistently taught him is out of his reach. A sailor from Eloe, Florida, which is about as big as a way station to nowhere, Son has a
weak spot for the kind of woman Jadine is in spite of the pride and

self-control he will exhibit about other things. He has been to college for a couple of years, and he has seen many parts of the world, but he has not escaped a desire for the almost white woman who is the antithesis of everything he is.

When they are still on the island together, that Son desires Jadine is made clear through the observations of other characters and from what we surmise from his actions; later, in New York and Eloe, we get more of his direct comments on the matter. Gideon, the yardman, and Thérèse, who first observe the signs of Son's presence around the house and leave food for him, make a bet on how long he will remain hidden: "Gideon said, 'Long as he wants. Till New Year,' while she said, 'No. The chocolate eater's heart would betray him—not his mind or stomach'" (p. 104). Thérèse's prediction proves accurate, and she sees Jadine as a "fast-ass" and a "coquette" (p. 112) who steals Son's heart. Confirmation of her evaluation occurs when Son accompanies Gideon and Thérèse home:

> "You going back?" asked Gideon, "to the island?"
> "I don't know."
> "You want to get in there, don't you, eh? That yalla?" Gideon stroked his chin.
> "Man," said Son. "Oh, man." He said it with enthusiasm but he put a period in his voice too. He didn't want her chewed over by Gideon's stone-white teeth. Didn't want her in Gideon's mind, his eye. It unnerved him to think that Gideon had looked at her at all.
> The old man heard the period in his voice and turned the conversation to serious advice.
> "Your first yalla?" he asked. "Look out. It's hard for them not to be white people. Hard, I'm telling you. Most never make it. Some try, but most don't make it."
> "She's not a yalla," said Son. "Just a little light." He didn't want any discussion about shades of black folk.
> "Don't fool yourself. You should have seen her two months ago. What you see is tanning from the sun. Yallas don't come to being black natural-like. They have to choose it and most don't choose it. Be careful of the stuff they put down."
> "I'll be careful." [P. 155]

For the man who has earlier called Jadine white now to suggest that she is "just a little light" illustrates precisely how caught up in colors Son really is. He had broached the subject when he was trying to put Jadine in her place, so to speak, and his desire to be quiet now approaches the elation of a kid with a new toy which he does not wish to share with his friends. Still, Gideon and Thérèse are

clear about Son's powerful attraction to Jadine, and they know
that part of the attraction is rooted in color.

Ondine and Sydney are also aware that Son is attracted to Jadine, especially after they go on a picnic together, and they see that
Jadine is responding favorably to Son. It is Ondine, however, who,
in the matter of personal relationships, is more opposed to Son
than Sydney is. She has observed him when he thought nobody
was looking and has seen the "wildness. Plain straight-out wildness" (p. 192) in his eyes. She believes Son wants Jadine so desper-
ately that "he'll do what he has to do to get her and what he has to
do to keep her" (p. 192). Under that politely entertaining exterior
Son presents to Valerian is an irresistible passion for the white
goddess. He will stay on the island until he has conquered her, or
until he knows that she will be his elsewhere.

The strongest evidence for the almost reverential attachment
Son has to Jadine is revealed in the scenes in which he stands in
her bedroom before his discovery and watches her sleep. There is
something obsessive about his action and dangerous enough to
cause his emotional if not his physical downfall.

> . . . the first time he entered her room he stayed only a few seconds,
> watching her sleep. Anybody could have told him it was only the
> beginning. . . . he was bound to extend his stay until he was liter-
> ally spending the night with her gratified beyond belief to be sitting
> on the floor, his back against the wall, his shirt full of fruit (and
> meat if he could find any), in the company of a woman asleep. His
> appetite for her so gargantuan it lost its focus and spread to his
> eyes, the oranges in his shirt, the curtains, the moonlight. Spread
> to everything everywhere around her, and let her be.
>   He spent some part of every night with her and grew to know the
> house well, for he sneaked out just before dawn when the kitchen
> came alive. And he had to admit now, standing in the sunlight, that
> he had liked living in the house that way. It became his, sort of.
> A nighttime possession complete with a beautiful sleeping woman.
> [P. 138]

Earlier he has remembered trying to influence her dreams, trying
to give her a sense of reality beyond the ivory tower in which she
lives (pp. 119–20). Both the desire to effect her dreams and the love
for the house as a nighttime possession show the predicament in
which Son finds himself. He knows that Jadine is someone he has
little hope of possessing in the daylight hours, especially in his out-
lawed, unkempt state. She becomes for him a kind of dream woman,

a fantasy, and his desire for her, like his hunger for food, is all-consuming in spite of his recognition of the separateness of their lives. Possessing the dream, and thereby possessing the "white" woman, becomes too strong a motivation for him to even consider leaving the house; perhaps that is what Ondine senses when she maintains that "that nigger's not going nowhere." He is pulled by forces much stronger than himself, but his reach is ultimately much too short to capture a star.

Though Jadine meets Son in New York, goes to Eloe with him, and lives with him for several months, she will not allow him to alter her "whiteness." She remains "gatekeeper, advance bitch, house-bitch, welfare office torpedo, corporate cunt, tar baby side-of-the-road whore trap" (pp. 219–20) who will always inspire desire, but who will never be conquered by her own desire. In Morrison's reversal of color imagery, the tar baby becomes the white woman who lures black men into affection for them, but who can never return that affection. The black man so trapped runs the risk of similarly losing his cultural and racial heritage, and perhaps his very life. As potentially destructive to black men as her historical white counterparts, Jadine serves as a warning for the kinds of traps black people, and black men in particular, must avoid. That Son is unable to do so shows, paradoxically, how much he is tied to a certain part of his history and how susceptible he would be to lynching and burning if Morrison had chosen a different approach in the development of her novel.

Synthesis and Beyond

David Bradley's *The Chaneysville Incident* (1981) is a sustained look at an attempt by a black man, John, and a white woman, Judith, to understand and accept the unusual relationship they have; they will eventually resolve to make it work in spite of the violent history which informs it, including the near lynching of a black man, friend to John's father, because of his romantic pursuit of a white woman. It is important that the relationship is worked out against the backdrop of history, not against the stares and insults of people the couple might meet on the streets (in fact, we never see them in public settings in which other people respond to them). They thus find their strengths privately, and, though we are left to speculate on what their public appearances are like, we imagine they are successful. The novel is therefore as much about the uneasy relationship between a black man and a white woman as it is about the meticulous efforts of John Washington to learn what happened to his father and his connection to that Chaneysville incident. John's attempt to understand the particular burden which is his heritage and his task parallels his attempt to understand the peculiar relationship he has with Judith, with whom he has been living for five years. John, a professor of history at a school in Philadelphia, and Judith, a psychiatrist, have transcended the usual black male/white female relationships by moving their encounter to the level of middle class, liberal open-mindedness that is frequently associated with individuals who have attained a substantial amount of education. What happens to their relationship, therefore, is a consequence not only of their personalities, but of their education, the environment in which they have chosen to live, and their almost reclusive lifestyle.

Philadelphia, far enough above the Mason Dixon Line to bill itself as the "city of brotherly love," allows John and Judith the opportunity to live together more freely than they would have been able to live in a more Southern environment, even though the year is 1979. More than a decade beyond the fervent activity of the civil rights movement, a few years beyond the peak of the women's liberation movement, and psychologically far beyond the flower children's free-love communal living, John and Judith find themselves free to pursue a relationship across racial and cultural lines, but still limited by some of the restraints which would have affected it in earlier time periods and a different territory. Certainly they can share an apartment in Philadelphia, but in five years, there has been little talk of marriage, although it is clear that Judith would like to have a child. The extent to which the two are able to get along is a function of their geography and their era. The extent to which their relationship is, nonetheless, limited is tied to John's search for Moses Washington, a search which has as its basis all the history of racial prejudice in the United States.

We do not see much of John and Judith in their Philadelphia apartment, for most of the novel takes place in southwestern Pennsylvania, in the little town in which John grew up, and in the surrounding areas. We can surmise from what we learn of John and Judith through their conversations, however, and through John's reminiscences about their relationship, that their Philadelphia existence is rather asocial and claustrophobic. In fact, a feeling of claustrophobia defines the tone of the novel in spite of the weaving back and forth through historical time periods and in spite of the actual physical movement of John and Judith from Philadelphia to western Pennsylvania and to the hill country in that area. What the

novel crowds out in terms of physical space is presumably ac-
counted for by John's intellectual exercises, his abilities to trans-
port us as readers back through his father's and his great-grandfather's lives. That, too, will be the route through which he will
overcome the claustrophia of his relationship with Judith and try
to give it new room to breathe.

The Chaneysville Incident, then, is, on one level, the story of multiple journeys, all of which are tied together through and by John
Washington. The dominant journey, both psychological and physical, is that of John's search for the meaning of his father's life. He
discovers that the legendary Moses Washington did not die accidentally, as nearly everyone has thought to this point, but that,
seeking after his own legendary grandfather, one notorious C. K.
Washington, moonshiner and leader of slaves to freedom, he followed African tradition and committed suicide in the belief that
his grandfather was waiting for him just beyond the silence of the
physical body. The present action of the novel occurs when John is
thirty-one, and he has been searching for his father's story since he
was thirteen. Able to conclude his search as a result of materials
he receives after the death of Jack Crawley, his father's last living
friend and John's mentor in woodsmanship, John makes the final
mental and physical journey at first without, then with, the help of
Judith. By searching for his historical connections to his family,
and by immersing himself in that identity, John is able, finally, to
move beyond the restrictions he has placed upon his relationship
with Judith; or at least that is the implication with which we are
left at the conclusion of the novel, for it ends before we see the reso-
lution tested.

Through John's story, and the titillating facts he reveals about his
family's activities during and after slavery, secondary journeys are
revealed in C. K's and Moses's lives. Because Moses sought C. K.—
obviously to the disapproval of his prestigious undertaker father,
who broke the chain of African connection, became Christian, lost
interest in his own father, and denied that there was something
physical after death—and left clues for his son John, it is John's responsibility to seek for Moses and thereby reveal to us not only the
journey Moses made, but that of Moses's grandfather as well. All of
the journeys move from the physical to the spiritual, from distor-
tions of African heritage to reclaiming of that heritage of the belief
in meeting ancestors beyond the grave. John's journey, physical
and mental, will stop short of becoming spiritual because the concerns are now different. C. K. and Moses, who sacrificed their wives
and almost sacrificed their children to the obsessions which con-

trolled their lives, simplified issues even when they may have responded to them in complicated ways. For John, who has no slaves
to attempt to rescue, no moonshine to run or war to fight in, and no
wife or children to neglect, a different purpose emerges. He must
learn his family's stories to free himself of the bone-chilling cold
which resides so prominently in his stomach, but also to understand what his future relationship with Judith will be. Unlike Moses
and C. K. and their women, John and Judith presumably have a
much more traditional relationship even though they are not married. And John has no son for whom he can leave baffling clues as to
why he disappeared one day.

The novel reveals that John is as much victim of as he is seeker
after his heritage, for what will he do with what he learns about
Moses and C. K.? Will he also decide upon suicide and seek both of
them beyond the silence of the body? The answer seems to be no;
therefore, John's search seems to be for information about how to
live, not how to pursue those who have gone beyond living. And
how he will live is really a question of how he will live with Judith.
Though involved with Judith to the point of having made a commitment of time to her, John still holds her outside of the mainstream of his mind and concerns and beyond the emotional center
which his male ancestors stir so strongly within him.

John shares some personality traits with his ancestors: his attitude toward Judith is reminiscent of their arrogant treatment of
their women—especially Moses's—and their general belief that
women should take a backseat to whatever purpose the man felt he
had in life. With John, his intellectual arrogance becomes a way for
him to keep Judith at a distance. For example, on the evening he
gets a phone call from his mother to come home because Old Jack
is dying and Judith sleepily mutters "Phone" in questioning him,
he replies:

> "The telephone is popularly believed to have been invented by
> Alexander Graham Bell, a Scotsman who had emigrated to Can-
> ada. Actually there is some doubt about the priority of invention—
> several people were experimenting with similar devices. Bell first
> managed to transmit an identifiable sound, the twanging of a clock
> spring, sometime during 1876, and first transmitted a complete sen-
> tence on March 10, 1876. He registered patents in 1876 and 1877."[2]

For a man to go through that kind of exercise at eleven thirty at
night, just after he has been roused out of sleep by an urgent telephone call, is a solid measure of his ability to maintain control
over the most troubling parts of his life and to hide his truest feel-

ings from the woman with whom he has lived for five years. He continues his dissertation on the telephone for more than an additional hundred words, illustrating again how convoluted he is capable of becoming. That convolution will be shown throughout the novel as he pieces together, in long diatribes which sustain their interest in spite of their length, the intricate, concentrated minutiae of the lives and dealings of his father and his great-grandfather.

John is proud—too proud to ever let his mask of superiority slip with Judith—and that, combined with his intellectual parrying and love of mental showmanship, leads him to shut down emotionally with Judith. We wonder again and again what Judith finds in John that makes her stay with him despite his seeming detachment and consistent refusal to share his life with her. Certainly, they share their professional lives, but his personal, family life and history remain hidden from her until, in a pattern similar to that Baldwin develops with Ida and Vivaldo in *Another Country*, John draws Judith into the working out of the family history. Bradley also goes a long way to suggest to us that John and Judith are attracted to each other for the reasons that motivate any man or woman who falls in love, that their relationship goes far beyond any curiosity or desire to cross racial lines. Perhaps, then, in those silences and refusals which greet Judith when she questions John, we are to conclude that they have weathered past storms sufficiently that their relationship can take the stress of little rainclouds. However, in the verbal exchanges in which Judith tries to present herself as John's equal, and certainly as his conscience when he refuses to face sensitive issues, the balance that Bradley seems to intend between the two characters is more asserted than convincing. John always seems to have the upper hand, and Judith always to be a bit more submissive than her actual lines would suggest. Consider one of their conversations in which she tries to get John to share some of his life with her:

> "Why don't you ever talk about home?" Judith had said. . . .
> "There's not much to talk about," I said. "It's a one-horse town on the road to no place. They've got five traffic lights now. It used to be four, but they had to put one in to control the traffic on the detour while they built the bypass; now there's nobody to stop at any of them."
> "Well, what about the *history*?"
> I hadn't answered her. I had shivered a little in the cold, but I hadn't answered her.
> "Oh, hell," she said. "I don't care about any of it, really. It's just that you don't *talk* to me."

"I talk all the time," I said.

"Yeah," she said. "About the Ottoman Empire or European nationalism. But you never talk about anything that has to do with you."

"That *is* what has to do with me," I said. "I'm a historian."

"That's what you hide behind. All the Goddamn time. Quotes and anecdotes. Humorous little lectures guaranteed to make you the wittiest fellow at any cocktail party. Only I'm not a cocktail party."

"What do you want to know?" I said.

She stopped suddenly and whirled, spinning out from inside the circle of my arm. "What do I want to know? I don't want to *know* anything. I just want you to talk to me. I just want you to tell me things. I just want you to *want* to tell me things."

"What things?"

"*Jesus!* I don't know. How am I supposed to know? I want you to tell me what you want to tell me."

"I do," I said.

"Yeah. Nothing." [Pp. 71–73]

Against Judith's rising anger at John's refusal to share with her, to open up as one lover might to the other, John stands like the rock of Gibraltar, obviously aware of her dilemma, but refusing to resolve it. Even the controlled description of the outburst—"I said," "she said"—is an indication of how he wishes to keep emotion at the level of fact, to keep their relationship under his control. Judith clearly knows the little games John plays, even when he will not admit them publicly, yet that knowledge does not serve her well in getting inside that wall of emotional exclusion John has set up around himself.

The tone of this conversation is close to that of nearly all of the conversations they have—until very near the end of the novel. John is emotionally aloof from Judith in spite of his being physically in her presence and in spite of their superficial romantic sharing. In many ways, he uses Judith as a measure of his own mental calisthenics; if he can keep Judith involved at one level with his intellectual flights and at another level with curiosity, then he really does not have to reveal much of anything about himself. She will stay because she believes he is eventually worth saving and because his intellectual exercises let her know that there is more to the man than he is willing to show. John becomes, therefore, Judith's most challenging psychological case, for if she can break through his barriers of resistance, she will have affirmed herself in her profession, and she will, as well, have reached the ultimate point of satisfaction in her personal life.

We do not know much about Judith except that her family, many generations before, had been sailors and slaveholders; we cannot therefore derive much of a psychological profile of her beyond what is revealed in her interactions with John. John, on the other hand, makes decisions in his personal life that are based on incidents which occurred when he was growing up. As he pieces together more of his family history, he shows more about himself, especially about how his racial attitudes were formed. We can therefore take those attitudes and stack them up against his interaction with Judith. We begin to surmise the reasons for his aloofness from her and the reasons he seems to want to keep her around in spite of his not being completely open and honest with her. Whatever the degree of his emotional involvement with Judith, she has become for him a trophy to reward the turbulent struggle by which he has come to manhood from a racist town in the mountains of Pennsylvania.

Although Moses Washington had supplied whiskey to the town's prominent white citizens and had become privy to some of the most important occurrences, his actions had not gone far to change the status quo. He had been content, rather, to make his midnight sojourns to the judge's house instead of going there in broad daylight, and he had been content to use his folio of information about his customers to accomplish things on a small, personal scale rather than to work for the progressive good of the black community. The town in which his son John grew up, then, was one in which black boys had to be taken forty miles away to get a haircut, where they had to swim in creeks instead of the local pool, and where they would always be drafted into the armed services before the local whites. It is the bitterness surrounding his brother Bill's induction into the Army that shapes many of John's responses to Judith, to his mother, and to the local whites who knew his father. Bill had been passed through school because he was good in football and wrestling; when he had played out his four-year option, he was flunked and very quickly drafted into the war in Vietnam, where he was shortly killed. Bill's case represents for John not only a personal instance of racism, but a symptom of the structural racism which ties the society together. Allowed into the local school because it was the only one available in the area, Bill, John, and the few other Blacks there had been either barely tolerated or considered only for their athletic prowess, which perhaps approximated most closely the bestial kinship the whites believed they shared. As an athlete, Bill could be controlled, contained, and *used*. When he was no longer of use, he was discarded. John, who had chosen the path of the mind as a way of not being used, of overcoming the obstacles which were placed in his way, came to see Bill's path through school and in the Army as the stifling counterpoint of that seeming freedom Moses Washington had had with the local whites. Whether he will admit it or not, John has learned very early to hate the whites for destroying Bill and for being that looming, potential stumbling block in the lives of all black individuals.

As one way of getting back at the whites, John had decided, at sixteen, that he would take something the whites wanted. That came in the form of Mara Jamison, near-white daughter of the local near-white black prostitute, a high-class madam who had been set up in a house by the local white males. Mara, realizing that she and her sister were being groomed to follow their mother's footsteps in a lifetime of pleasing white men, had come to John to ask him to seduce her so that she would therefore be "unfit" for the white men: ". . . she explained Miss Linda's theory about white men, how they wouldn't want a woman after she'd been with a black man" (p. 300). John sees the requested seduction as an opportunity, and he willingly consents: "I had cheated one of those white bastards out of something. . . . taking something right out from under the lion's nose" (p. 301). John sees Mara for a period of years, sneaking to her house, tapping on the window, and taking her out to the hills for nights of lovemaking. He is afraid to admit that he is possibly in love with her, because he doubts her ability to resist for long her mother's chosen profession for her. He also keeps their relationship quiet because, when Mara does give in, he "didn't want anybody thinking that those white men had gotten something [he] wanted" (p. 303). Thus near-white Mara gets used because of John's ego, and she is finally exploited by those of her own color as well as by the white men who will eventually keep her. John allows a mere possible threat to his self-esteem to shape his reaction to an apparently giving, sensitive young woman. When he goes away to college, she does give in to the white men, but who is to say that it is not in part because of the negation of self-worth she must have felt as a result of keeping her relationship with a man she loved such a closed, strained affair?

Mara is used, but we do not learn her reaction to being used. We can surmise, however, from John's relationship with Judith, that he is also in part attracted to her because she represents something of the forbidden, or that, by living with her, he has kept another white man from having something he may have wanted. Two conversations between them illustrate part of the tension of their cross-racial romance:

> "You're the man with the logic," she said. "Here's some for you.
> You hate white people. I am a white person. Therefore you hate me.
> Only you say you don't; you say you love me. Which seems like a
> contradiction. So I guess you must be lying about something. Ei-
> ther you can't hate so much or you can't love—"
>
> "And you're the psychiatrist," I said. "You know it's not that
> simple."
>
> "I know," she said. "I know. You can hate me and love me at the
> same time. But you see, that's not what I want. I don't want you to
> hate me at all. I don't want to live like that. If I have to, in order
> to be with you, then I will, for as long as I can. But if I'm going to do
> that, I have to know more about the hate, about where it comes
> from. Because you're talking about hating me."
>
> "No—"
>
> "Yes," she said. "Yes, you are. If you think that what somebody
> did or didn't do to a bunch of people who died fifty years before you
> were born is something you ought to take personally, then when
> you say you hate white people I have to take it personally."
>
> I didn't say anything.
>
> "I *am* white, John. You know that? I am. I don't think you ever
> have realized that. Because if you did, then you'd have to hate me—"
>
> "It's not that way," I said.
>
> "Then how is it?"
>
> I sat there for a minute, thinking, getting the words in order.
> [Pp. 287–88]

The words finally are not satisfactory. And Judith continues to stand
before him as a reason for hate and as a reason for veneration; the
mere fact that she is with him is testament that she is not with
some white man, that John has won a competition which, at some
level, he considers important.

In the second conversation, Judith accuses John more directly of
wanting her precisely because she is white:

> "You know, I've always wondered what the hell you wanted with
> me. Why *you* would have anything at all to do with a white woman.
> I thought maybe you wanted to make me suffer, brutalize me in
> some way. But you never did. So I started to think that it was just a
> kind of accident, that you had fallen in love with me in the same
> way I had fallen in love with you, and you were as confused by the
> whole thing as I was, and that what was stupid about it was that
> there should have to be a reason for us, any more than there would
> have to be a reason for two other people—two black people, or two
> white ones. That's when I decided it was all right; there was going
> to be problems, but they weren't the kind of problems . . . Oh, hell,
> you know."

"I know," I said.

"But I was wrong, wasn't I?"

I didn't say anything.

"You wanted me because I was a white man's woman. I was a white man's daughter and when you met me I was a white man's lover, and if you hadn't come along I would have become a white man's wife and probably a white man's mother, and if I wanted you then you could cheat them all. That was it, wasn't it? That's *still* it. I'm just like Mara, only this time you're not just keeping something from them; you're taking it."

I didn't say anything. [Pp. 303–304]

John goes on to explain that he loves Judith for all the "correct" reasons, but her words carry more weight in conjunction with John's history than does his denial.

That ambivalent love/hate response John has to white women and how it relates to his past is revealed in an incident he relates about having dated a white girl prior to meeting Judith. He had observed the girl from a distance for months and had finally gotten up the nerve to ask her for a date. He takes her for drinks and dinner and, back at her apartment, after some heavy petting, she tells him that she likes him, but it is "too soon for her" (p. 76). This special date, which had ended so disastrously, had occurred on the day John learned of Bill's death, and he had chosen to proceed with it rather than go immediately home. Later in the evening, he had hitchhiked home, then attended his brother's funeral the next day, borrowed money and caught a bus back. "I went to see the girl," he says, "and I raped her" (p. 77). Though he felt guilty for a long time and wondered how badly he had hurt the girl, he had "looked at her and saw white" (p. 77) and believed that "it makes sense to blame white people, just because they're white." Therefore, a pattern has been set: he has used a near-white black woman and raped a white woman, and it is not illogical to assume that a part of his attraction to Judith is tied to those earlier feelings of hatred and to a desire for mastery in at least this arena of competition between black and white males.

If the women become the focal point of the competition, then, it may also be assumed that, in spite of his education, John has at some level absorbed the stereotypes about the superiority of black male sexuality over that of white males. The argument for getting back at white men through their women is an old one and as warped as the case Eldridge Cleaver tried to make in *Soul On Ice*; John simply gives it a new intellectual twist. Ironically, though, that which he sees as separating him from the masses of Blacks, namely his education, does not serve to disalign him from black males historically, for he is just as much a victim of that approach/avoidance complex with white women as Bigger Thomas and Bob Jones are. Educational sophistication may add gloss to the old problem, but it does not change the substance of it.

Still, John at least gives the impression of being more in control, more daring than his literary predecessors. He does pursue the white women he wants and, conscience notwithstanding, he does rape one of them. Though the setting for the incident is the mid-1970s, the woman could still make a case against John if she wished to. The notion of the black man as raping beast was still sufficiently prevalent to have worked in her favor if she had desired to prosecute. That John ignores that possibility shows in some ways how he has progressed beyond his forebears in the expression of anger against whites in general, and it also shows how, by choosing a white woman as the vehicle for the expression, he has a clear understanding of what he wants to express, and he is politically daring enough to accomplish his purpose.

What separates John from the Bigger Thomases and the Bob Joneses is that moral issues are not as much a motivating force for him as for the others. Though he may feel guilty about raping the white woman, John shows, in his relationship to Judith, that he does not truly regret what he has done. Retaliation—almost in kind—for Bill's death is the only stimulus to which he had responded. John's attitude, combined with the absence of a social structure surrounding his and Judith's relationship, makes him seem to be a freer agent than the earlier characters—and certainly the era influences that illusion of freedom as well.

John has lived in a community where black men knew the consequences of approaching white women in other than the most superficial and respectful of ways. Yet John's move away from home has also taken him away from a sense of the acuteness of some of those consequences. He is reminded of them when Jack, on his dying bed in 1979, relates one of the stories about a black man, Uncle Josh, and a white woman. The incident had occurred when Moses, Jack, and Josh were young men together, around the second decade of the century. Uncle Josh, a black man light enough to pass for white, had unexpectedly come upon a young white girl walking along the road one day. He had offered her a ride; she had accepted and invited him home for cider in return for the favor. The two had spent a pleasant session talking with each other, and the girl had invited him to return. In their mutual attraction for each other, they had embraced and parted. Underlying that attraction, however, had been Uncle Josh's awareness of the fact that he was a black man and the woman was white; that history informs his initial reaction to the woman just as Old Jack tries to get John to see how it could influence him. Old Jack remembers Josh's story:

> "An' he told me how he whipped them horses over them mountains, half the time thinkin' like a colored man that jest finished kissin' a white girl, wonderin' if maybe hadn't somebody seen it, or if maybe it wasn't some kinda trap, an' the other half thinkin' like a man oughta think about a woman, never mind what color she was." [P. 86]

Uncle Josh's uneasiness comes from the fact that he is in the infamous South County of western Pennsylvania, which, a few miles and no psychological distance from Virginia, had been the site of many slave escapes, captures, and returns. That was the country in which C. K. Washington had his headquarters as he guided slaves through the Underground Railroad, and that was the country where the whites who settled there showed their kinship to their Southern neighbors by voluntarily using their dogs and horses to bring any suspicious black persons back into bondage. Understandably, then, the mood between Blacks and whites had not changed substantially when Uncle Josh went courting in the South County. He became so lovestruck that he forgot everything he knew about the South County, and he took to wearing suits and staring at sunsets at times he had prearranged with the girl. He also went so far as to get a job working for the girl's father so that the two of them could be together through the summer and into the fall.

The girl seems to be responding to Uncle Josh as a man, and her family sees no reason—yet—to raise objections. The black men tease Josh about the drastic changes in his lifestyle, but when they realize the cause of it, they, along with the women, understand the potential powder keg Josh has chosen as his toy, especially in an area where the Ku Klux Klan has elected the sheriff. When Jack learns from one of his white shoeshine customers of the trouble brewing because "some colored boy was nosin' 'round with a young lady down in Southampton" (p. 91), he goes to find Moses, off in the woods tending his stills, for assistance in saving the crazy man's life. Moses, who is reputed to have killed at least eight government agents by this time, and who is known not to have any love for whites, is already a legend in both communities. However, even he knows how retaliatory whites can be in response to this particular violation of taboo. Not only will Josh get his "butt busted," but he will cause the whites to bust "every black butt this side a Pittsburgh" because "the first damn thing them white folks is gonna get to thinkin' is if one nigger can quit sneakin' in the back winda an' start knockin' at the front door, we all gonna be linin' up on the porch" (p. 94). Josh has gone to the front door, so to speak, by planning to ask for the girl's hand in marriage, and this is the fateful day he has selected to make that request. Moses and Jack must therefore race through the early evening darkness trying to catch Josh before he arrives for his own lynching party, for apparently all the whites have made the discovery, including the girl's father and two brothers, and they, along with a party of thirty or so neighbors in white sheets, are waiting for Josh. Moses and Josh accidentally meet up with the hooded party and recognize enough of the mayor's cronies to realize that "whatever they was gonna do to Josh, it wasn't gonna be no lynchin'. It was gonna be damn near as official as the Fourth of July" (p. 101). Certainly the men are planning to string Josh up to a tree; Jack means here that it will not be a disorganized, unsanctioned lynching; the mayor's representatives are planning to make the lynching the law, the official response to the violation of taboo.

They arrive at the girl's house to discover that Josh is already being held captive by her relatives and that she is possibly an accomplice in his apprehension. Overly anxious to help his friend, Jack bursts into the farmhouse and finds himself another candidate for the lynching. His hope that, together, he and Josh can effect an escape is dashed when he observes the condition of his friend:

> "His mind was ruint. On accounta he figgered out—too late, jest like I figgered out too late—that that girl had been settin' him up all along. Maybe he even figgered out that there was folks comin' to lynch him. An' if he figgered that far, he was surely gonna have figgered that when he swung she was gonna be right there, watchin' an' grinnin' and fixin' to go gushy in her bloomers when he started jerkin' around." [P. 104]

The main party arrives and Josh and Jack are taken out together; it gives Jack plenty of time for speculation on what their fates will be. He thinks about the lynching as well as about the castration which may precede it: "I got to thinkin' 'bout what they might do to me 'forehand, things that, well, once they happen to a man, he'd jest as soon die, an' if you come along an' save his life afterwards, it ain't no kindness" (p. 106).

The men who plan the lynching are well aware of their roles and the implications of their actions. Since they want to set an example to the black community, they debate on whether or not they should lynch both of the men ("a nigger's a nigger, an' if you gonna have a lynchin', two's as good as one"—p. 106), or lynch one and send the other back with a message for the rest of the community ("maybe we'll kill 'em both, an' maybe we'll let this one watch so he can go back an' tell the rest"—p. 107). Their awareness of their power overshadows a degree of ineptitude apparent in the mobsters (they bungle and disagree on procedure), but there is no doubt in Jack's mind at the time of the encounter that his very life is threatened. He moves from a state of near hysteria to one of involuntary urination when he realizes that his notion of lynching may not be exactly the same as that of his captors: "we got to the other side a that hill there was a clearin' an' 'leven more fellas in sheets an' a big oak tree an' underneath of it a pile a wood, an' it come to me that when I said lynch I thought about hangin', but didn't everybody think that way, some thought about burnin'" (pp. 107–108).

Uncle Josh, who is still "ruint" from being shocked into awareness of the betrayal, is so spiritually comatose that he almost assists in his own planned lynching:

> "an' then they dismounted an' set about lynchin' Josh.
> It's funny how you see things. Why, a day before all that, if you was to a tole me I could set there an' watch the Klan lynch ma best friend an' not feel a thing, I woulda laughed in your face. But the truth is I can get more riled about it layin' here than I was then. It was jest like watchin' somebody butcher a hog. First they pulled his clothes off him—coat, vest, tie, shirt, pants, long johns, everything—an' they tossed the free end of a rope over the limb a that oak tree an' looped the noose end 'round below his armpits, an' they hoisted him up. Then Parker commenced to make some kinda speech. I couldn't hear what he was sayin' but I knowed what he was gettin' at, on accounta he kept pointin' to Josh's privates an' every time he done it them farmers would grumble. An' then he pulled out a knife an' held it right upside Josh's parts, an' they left out a roar. But Josh didn't. He jest hung there. An' that started gettin' to 'em; I guess it don't make no sense to lynch a man that don't pay you no mind. So Parker said somethin', an' one of them farmers went to his horse an' come back with a whip. I guess they figured to get old Josh's attention." [Pp. 108–109]

Reminiscent of the crowd in Baldwin's "Going to Meet the Man," the group here also seems to be seeking some kind of communal release which can only come through the black man's pain. If he refuses to give in to verbal expressions of that pain, then a part of the climactic purgation is denied to the men. So they bring the whip to try to evoke cries of pain from Josh. That delay is long enough to enable Moses, who has been lurking in the background, to kill the man who has been watching Jack and to enable Jack to get free of the chain with which he has been tied; he then leads the mob on a chase through the woods while Moses cuts Josh down from the rope. Their escape is hampered by Josh's crying and by his consistent refusal to aid in his own escape.

They do succeed in getting away, but the episode changes Josh's behavior for life. He becomes morose, silent, and reclusive. Throughout his long life, he refuses to have an extended conversation with almost anyone, frequently doing his shopping by simply pointing to the items on the shelves that he would like to buy. "Uncle Josh White did not talk. Oh, he *could* talk, and if you followed him for hours you might actually hear him utter a word or two as he bought blackstrap or snuff or some other staple. But apart from those two or three words, Uncle Josh said nothin to anybody besides Old Jack Crawley and Moses Washington" (p. 26). The lynching incident, then, causes him to take his place among the legendary trio who became identified with the other side of "the Hill" in the town where John grew up.

In contrast to what might be expected, since both the hooded and non-hooded parties know each other, there is no violent retaliation from the whites for the escape from the lynching. Everybody agrees to let the situation be, everybody, that is, except Moses Washington.

> "But somebody didn't leave it be, on accounta every month or so something bad would happen to one a them sheets. One went blind from drinkin' leaded shine. One fell in a ditch an' broke his leg an' caught pneumonia an' died. 'Nother one's wife left him. On like that. Jest bad news. Not too much at any one time, but steady; somethin' got every one of 'em. An' inside a 'bout three years wasn't none of 'em around here no more. Some moved on. 'Bout half was dead. Somebody didn't leave it be. . . ." [P. 115]

Jack relates his extended story (covering more than twenty-five pages of the novel) after he discovers that John is involved with a woman. That knowledge becomes clear when he observes the changes in John; though not as drastic as those Moses and Jack witnessed in Uncle Josh, the changes nevertheless represent a visible alteration of what Jack has come to identify as John's personality. And he knows instinctively that John is involved with a white woman. Perhaps, then, the story is designed in part to caution John against such foolhardiness by illustrating what Moses's reaction would have been. For a man who had no love for whites, and prac-

tically none for women, it is almost blasphemous to his memory
that his favored son John would end up being inextricably involved
with a white woman. Jack sees it as a lessening of what he has tried
to instill in John, for involvement with the woman takes him away
from nature:

> "Your blood's got thin from livin' inside a houses all the time, with
> no time in the woods. You walk funny; that's on accounta your feet
> is all flattened out from standin' around on cement all the time.
> You set in a chair like it's home. I don't know what's at the bottom
> of it. Maybe you ain't been eatin' enough fresh-kilt meat, or you
> been drinkin' watered whiskey, or you been messin' with the wrong
> kind of woman. . . ." He stopped. I hadn't said anything, but he
> must have seen something in my face. "That's it, ain't it," he said.
> "It's a woman." . . . He was quiet for a moment. Then he said, "This
> woman a yours. She's a white woman, ain't she?" [Pp. 70, 71]

Appearing early in the novel, before we are aware of the problems in John's and Judith's relationship, and on the eve of Old
Jack's death, the story marks an ending as well as a beginning. It
posits a natural antagonism between the races, especially as far as
black men and white women are concerned, and it sets an uneasy
background against which we must evaluate whatever we learn of
John and Judith. The specifics of Jack's tale may belong to a certain
era, but the general history of racial repression in response to violated taboos does not. The tale therefore sets, as a part of John's
task of learning about his family history, the additional task that he
do something constructive with that knowledge. Aided by Jack,
he could permit racial politics to allow him to reject Judith just
as he has rejected other whites following the circumstances surrounding Bill's death. Yet he chooses, finally, not to use his history
and the information transmitted by Old Jack as reasons for separating himself from Judith. In his determined effort to learn his father's and his great-grandfather's fates, and to reconcile the contra-
dictions in his "hate all whites but exclude Judith" syndrome, he
must draw Judith into learning with him, instead of excluding her
further.

That path to inclusion is a struggle for both lovers. John initially
will not allow Judith to accompany him to Old Jack's deathbed; at
this point in the novel, he is set upon keeping the specifics of that
part of his life to himself—although he had told Judith some of Old
Jack's stories. Nor will he allow her to drive up when he calls to tell
her of Old Jack's funeral. And, on her side, Judith cannot accept the
part of John's background which leads him to mix toddies in the

fashion Old Jack has taught him and, from her point of view, to
drink himself into oblivion. Her psychiatrist's training tells her
that John is hiding something with his drinking, and that the cold
he complains of so constantly is much more psychological than
physical.

The first sign that the two may be able to move beyond the ways
history has taught them to view each other comes in Judith's arrival at Old Jack's cabin. After the funeral, John had sent her a
letter saying he was staying on for a while, which she correctly
read as meaning forever, and he had set out to pursue the hunting
life into which Old Jack had initiated him. Judith's bringing of a
kind of Philadelphia city atmosphere into the cabin on the far side
of "the Hill" suggests that, with Jack's death, some of the old ways
and hatreds may also be ready for burying and that, in the world
John has chosen for himself, she may be able to draw him out
enough so that he will indeed share with her. Judith, like Vivaldo in
Baldwin's *Another Country*, takes the necessary step to be initiated
into that world that whites so seldom see with their black friends.
And, indeed, John will become her guide as Jack has been his, initiating her not only into the world of his personal history, but accepting her fully into his life.

With Judith there in Old Jack's cabin, John pieces together the
story of how his father committed suicide and why. In order to
shape the final pieces of the puzzle, however, he and Judith make a
trip together to the infamous South County where Moses had gone
to take his own life. In looking for the place of his death, they find
stones marking other graves. John surmises that those are the
graves of C. K. Washington and the twelve slaves he had been trying to lead to freedom when they were surrounded by Pettis, a famous slave hunter who had enlisted the aid of almost all the white
men in the South County in order to trap C. K. Instead of being
taken alive, the runaways had chosen to commit communal suicide. John discovers the unusual arrangement of stones which reveal to him that they mark graves, and Judith assists him when it
seems as if he has lost the trail. Significantly, in the new partner-
ship they are forming, it is Judith who stumbles upon the stone
which marks the site where Moses Washington shot himself, and
she knows instantly what she has discovered. It is logical that her
role would become more important at this point, especially since
John has decided to share with her enough to bring her from Old
Jack's cabin, to drive her through hazardous, snowy roads, and to
lead her on a difficult foot chase to the point where he has con-

cluded the graves must be located. The conclusions of his mental analyses lead him to exactly the same place that Moses Washington's physical scouring of the county had taken more than thirty-five years to uncover. So the father and son become one in their search at the same time the son shows the possibility for moving beyond that search by drawing Judith into it.

From the physical evidence of the gravesite, the two return to Old Jack's cabin, where John tells the complete story to Judith, emphasizing throughout that what C. K., Moses, and the slaves have done was not to commit suicide, but to join each other beyond the grave. Judith's reaction is understandable:

> "Oh, great," she said. "So what does that mean? You're going to put on your little Dan'l Boone costume and take your little rifle down there and blow your brains out so you can go hunting with the old men, and sit around the campfire drinking whiskey and telling lies—" [P. 406]

Heir to the Christian tradition which defines the end of breathing as death, Judith has difficulty accepting the African notion of the continuation of the physical which John espouses with his relatives and which he has exhibited very early in the book by burying tobacco, shoes, and a rifle with Old Jack. Judith's role, then, becomes one of trying to move beyond the limitations of her logical, analytical mind, and it is her willingness to make that step which presages a different kind of relationship for the two:

> "You don't think I understand. You're right; I don't understand. But I can believe in you; I do believe in you. If you want to take that gun and blow your head off, I won't try to stop you. And I'll try to understand. And if you say you need something that I can't give you, something you need a toddy to get, then I'll make a toddy for you." [P. 407]

Since the drinking has been such a bone of contention with Judith, this is a major compromise for her. She will continue to supply John with toddies through the telling of his final tale. She cannot hear the singing of the slaves as they pant out their immortality to John in the sounds of the wind, and she cannot hear the voice of Old Jack urging John to tell the last part of the story, but her belief in him is enough to terminate her skepticism, and her presence, in this place and under these circumstances, is a call to him to abandon his factual existence and to use the imagination he has claimed to be lacking throughout the novel. It is only through the mind's eye, the imagination, that he can "see" what happened to C. K. Washington and the slaves on that fateful night they went running through the woods of the South County.

Playing a role similar to that Old Jack has played with him, John says to Judith, in a ritual re-creation of the many sessions in which he has listened to Old Jack tell stories: "You want a story, do you? . . . Fetch the candle" (p. 410). Judith, as initiate, follows the order and accepts the role of being led through the maze of a portion of John's personal history; she also finally sees into a mind which can imagine love, separation, happiness, and commitment and which, in its demonstrated expansion, can also incorporate her. She keeps his toddy cup replenished as John plows through historical facts to a *feeling* for what must have happened to C. K. As he begins to feel, to imagine, to move beyond the intellect which he has used to hide behind, the cold in the pit of his stomach begins to dissolve.

The point at which that dissolving occurs is also significant to John and Judith. The story of C. K.'s life has included a lost love, a woman with whom he fell in love some years after his first wife's death. Before he and this woman, Harriette Brewer, could form a viable relationship, he had gone back to the mountains to run whiskey and she, believing not only in financing slave escapes but actually carrying them out, had gone south to act on her philosophy. The discovery of her action led C. K. to his many daring rescues of slaves; perhaps, as John surmised, he had always been looking for Harriette. Anyway, in the story John now relates, the two of them are reunited a few hours before they will face death together, for Harriette Brewer, the son she has had by C. K., and two daughters she has had by a slave during her many years of sojourn in the South, are among the twelve slaves C. K. had thought would be his final rescue attempt before retiring. He arrives at their hiding place to bring them supplies, recognizes Harriette, "and then she was in his arms" (p. 430). John pauses in his story, expecting questions from Judith, but in contrast to her usual questioning, she remains silent, willing to be led where John leads. That is the position Harriette Brewer also finds herself in, so she and Judith are duplicating roles, in a way, just as John and C. K. are duplicating roles. John's recognition that C. K. is now warm with Harriette (C. K. had led the slavers on a chase to keep them from the runaways, and has become nearly numb with cold and snow) evokes a similar warmth in himself: "And then I realized that something strange was happening. Because I was no longer cold" (p. 430). It becomes clear why the cold dissolves as he resumes the story about C. K. and Harriette:

"He was warm now," I said. "He was warm, and the feeling was strange. Because he had not realized how cold he had been. He had known that his hands and feet and face were cold, even though they were so numb he had lost the feeling in them—he had known that because anyone who knew the weather and who knew how long he had been exposed would have known—and so he had not been surprised when the heat from the fire caused the feeling to come pounding back into them. But he had not known about the other cold, the cold inside, the glacier in his guts that had been growing and moving, inch by inch, year by year, grinding at him, freezing him. He had not known that. But he knew it now. Because he could feel it melting. The heat that melted it did not come from the fire; it came from her, from the warmth of her body that pressed against his back, the warmth of her arms around him, the warmth of her hands that cupped the base of his belly. He lay there, feeling the warmth filling him, feeling the fatigue draining from him, feeling the aching in his ribs easing, becoming almost pleasant, and wishing that he would never have to move." [P. 431]

This wonderful, nonsexual elation C. K. feels parallels the warmth John now feels as he and Judith are rediscovering sharing with each other.

John's awareness of C. K. reveals that he is much more like his great-grandfather than he is like Moses, his father. Moses may have married and had children, but it is questionable as to whether or not he was ever in love. C. K. unquestionably was, as is John, although he has tried to hide that underneath a facade which would resemble Moses more than C. K. John, after all, has spent his time in pursuit of logical answers, just as Moses did in his search for Biblical truth. Now, John must leave the path of his father and return to the path of his great-grandfather by sensing things, by hunting with the feeling in his mind, as C. K. had done in trying to follow the moves of Pettis and the other pursuers. Ultimately, John is much more like C. K. because he finally must admit the central place that love has in his life. He must finally abandon knowledge for intuition and detachment for involvement.

The issues that John is working out in his own life and mind as a result of imagining what has happened to C. K. continue to be paralleled on the personal level by the final rite of communion he shares with Judith. When he has finished his story, down to the point of hearing the voices of the slaves in the sound of the wind as a sign that they still live, he begins to make another toddy. As he is reaching for the whiskey and sugar, Judith says: "Make me one" (p. 449). Her willingness to hear what she could not before understand is now manifested on a tangible level in her willingness to drink the brew she has identified with the "otherness" in John, with what has separated the two of them. Though not a subtle symbol, the action is nevertheless effective in pointing toward the direction in which the relationship will go.

A footnote to the story widens the reconciliatory implications of John's and Judith's relationship. The twelve slaves and C. K. were buried by the owner of the mill in which the runaways were hiding when C. K. came to their aid. A white man, the mill owner had been among the settlers who had come from Virginia to Pennsylvania with Judith's ancestors. John's admission, then, that a white man has been sympathetic enough to bury C. K. and the group, and his knowledge of that man's particular origins, force him to realize that he can no longer lump all whites other than Judith into a single pile. By connecting the two families, Bradley moves his thesis for reconciliation to a personal level between John and Judith and, we may infer, to a more universal level by implication. After all, he has been careful to minimize race as a motivating factor in their attraction to each other, and he has consistently presented their relationship as one which is more intellectual and spiritual than it is physical, though certainly that level has not been denied.

Because the two families, in spite of their racial animosities and the prevailing attitudes of the times, were brought together in a crucial carrying out of a human and humane act, Bradley implies that it is only fitting and right that these two descendants of that group, though still divided by racial lines, can find similar means for a cooperative relationship. The final signal that John is ready for that cooperative relationship comes when, after sending Judith away from the cabin, he burns up all the tools of his trade which have separated them, "the pens and inks and pencils, the pads and cards" (p. 450) on which for years he has written all the facts and questions surrounding Moses's and C. K.'s lives. The act becomes a different kind of rite of exorcism, for presumably he is exorcising from himself all the hatred, all the blame, all the obstacles to commitment which may have existed in his relationship with Judith, and it is her understanding that he wants when she sees the fire rising from the "far side of the Hill" (p. 450).

With Judith and John, then, a black American writer finally makes a valiant effort to try to resolve the conflicts which exist within and the stereotypes which surround the connections between black men and white women. Though the commitment has not been tried in the fire of the social structure, a major step has been taken in bringing the two parties to the stage of working toward the salvation of their own relationship. If that determination exists within them, then perhaps that in itself will provide the source of strength to combat the rest of the world. By eliminating sexuality as the primary focus of concern between black men and white women, Bradley has negated the reason for violence which has so preoccupied the writers of previous generations. Whether his thesis will work in the real world, or just in the atmosphere of myths and legends which prevades the novel, may be questionable, but the strength of characterization and presentation would suggest that at least one black writer has uncovered a viable method of exploring the complexity of a relationship which usually led to death and ending, rather than to affirmation and beginning.

CHAPTER 7

The Meaning of a Tradition

Authors, Issues, Audiences

Of the works in this discussion which actually depict a lynching or burning, in only half of them is the scene of lynching and burning central to the thematic or structural development of the work *as* literature. Works which fit into this category are those by James Weldon Johnson ("Brothers— American Drama"), Claude McKay, Ralph Ellison, Walter White, Langston Hughes, Paul Laurence Dunbar, James Baldwin, and Richard Wright. With these writers, the presentation of lynching and burning scenes is necessary to the development of the poems, stories, and novels in which they appear. In the works by the other writers, these scenes are asides, attempts to paint group character in a traditional way.

For William Wells Brown and Margaret Walker, with the pre-Emancipation settings for their novels, lynching and burning become incidental to the larger question of slavery. Brown's purpose was clearly to influence public opinion in favor of the abolishing of slavery; thus the horror he presented was yet another evil to be overcome by Emancipation. In *Clotel*, which commentators have criticized for having enough material and subjects inside its covers for twelve novels, the burning joins a long list of catalogued evils and takes up less than two pages in the novel. Similarly, Margaret Walker's illustration of the lynching of two women becomes a part of the background of slavery—what the evils were—and is not thematically central to *Jubilee* as literature. Walker is interested in developing character in a novel which has its context in the antebellum and Reconstruction South; Brown is interested in polemics.

Sutton Griggs's interest in violence is also polemical. He, like Brown, wants to make a plea for the righting of wrongs. His subplot of a black man and woman being killed for protecting their property is designed to strike at the discrepancy in a belief central to American existence. Yet Griggs, like Brown, has too many pieces of stories straining the novel to be able to make one thematic thrust. Chesnutt likewise makes lynching subsidiary to other concerns in *The Marrow of Tradition*, giving the subject even less consideration than does Griggs. Johnson, too, in *The Autobiography of An Ex-Coloured Man*, makes the burning incidental. His narrator just happens to be in the town where the incident occurs, and a decision is made on the basis of that incident. Johnson uses the scene to effect an epiphanic revelation in his narrator, but given the narrator's basically unstable character, a slap in the face from a white person might well have produced a similar reaction.

Toomer's burning scene occurs within a sketch in *Cane*. It is central to that particular sketch, but can only be suggestively connected with the other over two-hundred pages of the book. Yet Toomer, as the writers before and after him, felt a need to include this violent scene in his work. Thus, in addition to their literary purposes, the abundance with which these scenes appear suggests that they occur for other reasons as well.

The scenes put these black writers in a traditional vein of portraiture in black American literature, but were they aware of their position as being traditional? Was Baldwin, writing in 1968, aware of what Sutton Griggs had presented in a ritualized burning in 1905? To answer this latter question affirmatively is to generalize too broadly about the process by which writers learn their craft and acquire their sources. Baldwin may never have read Griggs and may or may not be familiar with his name. To talk about black writers being conscious of bearing a tradition in the presentation of ritualized violence is perhaps, then, to approach the problem at a slant. Baldwin may not have been aware of Griggs, but he *is* aware of black history in this country. Being historically informed about his or her heritage in blood and violence makes each black writer a member of a club from whose membership he or she cannot be severed.

It is interesting, then, that centralized treatment of lynching and burning scenes grew in inverse proportion to the number of Blacks lynched and burned historically, but in direct proportion to the cruelty with which such acts were carried out and to the increased political significance they served. Brown could mention incidentally a burning in 1853. Dunbar, Wright and other writers from the turn of the century on had such bestialities stamped on their minds. If Blacks could be burned in 1933, after Emancipation, those famous amendments, and participation in World War I, then the consequences were infinitely more serious than those resulting from the more widespread suppression of Blacks during slavery. The more centralized treatments of the theme reflect this.

Still, the question can be asked if black writers are being too propagandistic in their treatments of subjects direct from history, of patterns that retain all aspects of their historical counterparts. Obviously this is not the case; literature, we are taught, approximates life, and if the approximation is authentic enough for the fine line between life and literature to become even more indistinct so much the better. Scenes of ritualized violence do not dominate works until after 1920 or so, and few critics, if any, would gainsay the artistic value of works representative of this period, such as those by Wright and Baldwin. In addition, to dismiss such treatments as mere propaganda is to underestimate the significance of the black experience in America; it is as much a part of the present as it is of the past.

These black authors have shown that black heritage, through black history, is a continuing and integral part of black existence in spite of its brutal and dehumanizing aspects, and frequently because of them. Ensuing generations of Blacks are tied to what has gone before them and should not, even if it were possible, sever the bonds of any part of that heritage. The tie to history, by way of a communal memory, strengthens the roots of continuing generations and allows them to grow from a firmer base. Wright articulated this concern for black writers when he wrote: "Theme for Negro writers will emerge when they have begun to feel the meaning of the history of their race as though they in one lifetime had lived it themselves throughout all the long centuries."[1] Wright worked out the same principle artistically in "Between the World and Me." The speaker, who discovers the lynched/burned man, in turn envisions himself being lynched and burned. He is a part of a history he cannot escape, and his awareness of his position makes him stronger. His situation can be generalized to all Blacks —the past influences the present; what happened to the slave is as significant to the contemporary suburban black doctor of philosophy as it is to the pullman porter or to the domestic worker. John Wideman echoes the same idea in a discussion of his character Cecil in *Hurry Home*. He suggests that

> what was specifically Cecil's experience becomes conflated with the whole collective history of his race, that there is a thin line between individual and collective experience which permits one to flow into the other. It has to do with imagination. Cecil can suffer because somebody centuries ago suffered on a slave ship. In the novel this happens through an imaginary voyage, but I feel very strongly that people have this capacity to move over time and space in just such an empathetic way.[2]

The roots of black culture, as Jean Toomer so vividly demonstrates in *Cane*, must be embraced, understood, and accepted in all their varying shades of beauty and ugliness before Blacks can grow into a viable future. The heritage of the fathers strengthens the sons to analyze, confront, and overcome the forces that would destroy them. It is by understanding the psychology of the white destroyer, asserts Purlie Victorious, that one can undermine and triumph over him. By presenting such features of white culture in a medium traditionally open to analysis and criticism, these black authors have provided another key with which black people can unlock the myriad complexities of that portion of the white populace which remains a perennial foe.

Obviously the reading of black American literature is not limited to the black population, as the audiences for Brown's, Dunbar's, Grigg's, and Chesnutt's works reveal, but black writers do, within the medium, exhibit a commitment to the role of artist to their people. Interacting with their audience by presenting and keeping before them material of which they are probably aware, but of which they may need occasionally to be reminded, black writers become active tradition-bearers of the uglier phases of black history. As artists, they also become ritual priests ever keeping in sight of their people those mysteries which affect their lives. This kind of education goes far beyond mere didacticism or propaganda and into an awareness which has survival as its basis. By capturing something traditional in history and traditional in literature, black writers fulfill the double function of artist and priest for their people.[3] Sir James George Frazer maintains that priests officiated at the carrying out of rituals in ancient societies; they were to assist with the ceremonies and to keep the observances in perspective. They, like their followers, *believed* in the rites. Black writers become officiators of a sort in evoking in their literature the rites whites observe in violently dispensing with Blacks. Priesthood here assumes another dimension, however. Not only do black writers evoke the scene and "assist" in carrying it out for their characters, but they reach outside the work in serving a similar function of evocation. If their audience shares their beliefs, as presumably a black audience would, the ritual of presenting the scene of a ritual would serve to reinforce shared beliefs for writer and audience. In spite of the violence they portray, black writers evince a basic belief in racial survival. Their ritual of re-creating a ritual keeps that belief alive. They are artists and priests; neither role can be subordinated to the other.

A Male Tradition

The sexual component of the lynching and burning rituals presented in this discussion brings up an issue relating to gender: only black male writers include scenes of castration as a part of lynchings and burnings. Their concerns with the physical presentation of castrations, and with the fear their characters have of that being a consequence of their interaction with white women, are tied again to the history of black males in the United States. From one perspective, black males have felt more acutely the powerless conditions under which black people have been forced to live in this country. Writers among that group, therefore, have been equally conscious of that shared burden and the symbolic emasculation it represents. Their literary creations are thus in general more reactive to the conditions of black people in America than are those of black female writers.

Black males historically, because they could be physically castrated, had a physical part of themselves identified with their powerlessness. Black women, though equally powerless, and equally dehumanized by rape, did not have a part of their anatomy comparable to a penis physically taken away from them. Though they were raped, that act in itself did not immediately conjure up images of death for them; they could envision a future even after such a brutalizing experience, as Alice Walker's Celie does in *The Color Purple*. After being raped and after twenty years of being beaten by her husband, Celie anticipates the future with peaceful expectation.[4] Black men, on the other hand, knew that castration was almost invariably a prelude to death. Thus black male writers' fascination with that possibility derives from a threat which usually resulted in personal annihilation. It is understandable, therefore, that the male writers are so much more intense in their depictions and so much more unrelenting in their attachments of political significance to the factual history. The personal and communal burden they carried in such depictions highlighted the historical and social condition for Blacks, which, in spite of subtle changes, would continue to be unrelentingly oppressive in its threats of death to black males.

More often than not, when black women were raped, they were psychologically warped, but the violation led to a tainted addition, not to a subtraction from their persons. No matter how perverse we consider such actions today, a black woman in slavery who had several children for her master could feel a degree of pride in her "accomplishments." No matter the father of her children, she still was able to fulfill—in spite of the conditions under which the fulfillment was carried out—her traditional role as woman within the society, that of bearer of children. The black male, on the other hand, could only envision his worth in intangible ways. He may have contributed the sperm which produced the master's children, but the master himself could also, and often did, do that. However, there was no converse situation in which the white woman could be made to bear children who would be sold into slavery. Thus the black male saw his role usurped at will when the white man entered the black woman's bed, and he was powerless to do anything about it. Especially was he forbidden to appropriate the white woman in the way the black woman was appropriated by the white man. Though he may himself have been considered a stud in the breeding of children for sale, he could never really point to any child and be one hundred percent certain that he had indeed fathered it.

If the black man's role could be taken away in these tangible matters of sexuality, and he could be emasculated politically in the symbolic counterpart to the physical emasculation, then he was made to feel in several arenas that he was expendable. How could he assume the role of man when he could not protect his own bed? How could he see himself as a breadwinner when the master provided his food and controlled how much extra money, if any, he could earn by hiring himself out? How, after slavery, could he feel himself a man when he was forced, hat in hand, to go to the white boss and ask for a few more beans and fatback to last his family until harvest? How could he find jobs sufficient to support his family during the Depression, or fight his way into unions for better wages? His condition was such that a large portion of the civil rights activity in this country was designed to enhance his status in the hope that such enhancement would benefit the whole race. Ever confronted with the knowledge that he did not matter, the black man cried out again and again against that diminution of his worth. It is not surprising that his fights through marches and verbal protests were designed to emphasize that black men do indeed matter. And it is equally not surprising that black male writers have taken up that cry of demanding to be noticed by calling attention to the things which have historically so pressed them into the ground. What they write about is both a celebration of survival under circumstances which were not designed for their survival, as well as crying out for the rights of manhood which have never been fully granted to them.

Western civilization has unfortunately long identified manhood with primarily one aspect of maleness—that of sexuality. Black

male writers who focus upon this in their works on lynchings are
reacting to a constraining definition, sometimes simply for the
sake of denial, at other times to expose its limitations, and still at
other times to demand a redefinition of the concept of manhood.
Whenever a black male writer took his pen in hand to depict a
lynching for an accusation of rape, he relived for a moment the
psychological torment that so many of his brothers lived historically. That vicarious identification is most clearly presented in
Richard Wright's "Between the World and Me," but no less is it operating for some of the other writers. James Weldon Johnson, song-
writer, lawyer, and diplomat, felt the absolute uselessness of all of
those designations when he was almost the victim of a mob attack
in Jacksonville, Florida. Whatever separate class distinctions may
have been his as a result of education and training were not enough
to distinguish him from the masses of raping black males when he
was caught alone in a park with a white woman. Johnson's poem,
"Brothers—American Drama," written thirty-four years after he
barely escaped death, may have been inspired by his personal experience as well as by his general knowledge of the lynching atrocities which were carried out in the United States.[5] Vulnerability
defined both Johnson and his black brothers; each experienced
powerlessness against forces which had taken it upon themselves
to determine their fates.

That vulnerability and its accompanying psychological identification served to tie many black male writers to their historically
emasculated brothers. James Baldwin, for example, chronicles in
many of his essays the difficulties he had in trying to arrive at manhood without getting killed in Harlem, for white policemen there
assumed that black males existed for their sadistic pleasure. When
Baldwin tried to escape Harlem by going to work for a short time
in New Jersey, he experienced even more acutely the denial of his
manhood that the whites with whom he worked, especially the
Southerners, considered his due by virtue of his black skin. The
powerlessness he felt, which produced so much rage in him and
contributed to his decision to leave the United States, was equally
as restricting as the space in which black sharecroppers were forced
to operate and that in which many black migrants from the South
had discovered as their lots in Northern ghettos.[6] The accused
black man who is brought before the crowd for "knocking down
old Miss Standish" in Baldwin's "Going to Meet the Man" is as
much the physical plaything of the crowd of whites as Baldwin
was to the policemen in his neighborhood and to the whites who
would not allow him just to *be* on that job in New Jersey. His situa-

tion there can be compared to Richard Wright's in the experience
he describes in working for an optical company in Jackson, Mississippi. His white coworkers, insulted and upset by his presence,
goad him until he is forced to give up the job. He is caught in a
situation in which he must call one white man a liar and run the
risk of losing his job and/or suffering physical violence, or he must
silently walk away from the job that others have now made it impossible for him to keep.[7] Clearly he cannot win; to be a man by
standing up for his rights is to become one more statistic in the racial war. To walk away from the job, as he rather quickly does, is to
suppress whatever he has been taught to identify with maleness
and therefore to be further emasculated, to be made into a sissy
who will not fight back. In life as in literature, then, both Baldwin
and Wright knew the consequences of not living the ethics of Jim
Crow, just as they knew they had to leave the country to salvage
whatever vestiges of manhood they could.

Having his manhood denied at work and being refused the possibility for equal opportunity culminated for Wright in his inability
to protect a black woman with whom he worked, an occurrence
which made it clear how precarious his manhood was. In a vivid
incident in "The Ethics of Living Jim Crow," Wright recounts walking out of the hotel in which he was working with one of the young
black women who worked there as a maid. A white doorman,
whom they passed on the way out, very casually and proprietarily
slapped the black woman on the hip. Wright's objection to the
action put his very life in jeopardy, and the woman was forced to
pull him away for his own safety.[8] Black men could not play Sir
Lancelot to black women in the South, for the white men did not
recognize any claims black men made even to black women, and
certainly not to white women. Black male writers are almost possessed at times in portraying these matters.

Black women writers, on the other hand, are interested in painting on a different part of the canvas of black American life. In their
portrayals of lynchings and of the situations which could possibly
lead to lynching, the two black women writers treated in this study
are more interested in their characters than in the issues surrounding them. Margaret Walker's intention is to show the growth of
Vyry Brown, while Toni Morrison's novel is a study in demyth-
ologizing various characters and the ideas held about them. The
lynching of the two women accused of poisoning their master in
Jubilee is important, but it is one incident confined to a few pages
of an otherwise rather long novel. Morrison uses the contact between the black man and the "white" woman to focus upon charac-

ter as it has been formed by culture and education, rather than upon the potential for explosive violence. Both women writers move inward toward their characters instead of outward toward the environments which have shaped them. I am not suggesting that the women here are not concerned with the larger environments, or that the male writers are not concerned with characters; certainly both are, as, for example, Alice Walker in *The Third Life of Grange Copeland* and Richard Wright in *Native Son*. My focus here is upon the *degree* of emphasis as it varies with the gender of the writer.[9]

There is much more of a tendency among black male writers to use their characters in the thematic illustrations of problems in the society. Such a focus gives to their works an intensity of connection to the world beyond that of their poems, short stories, or novels. The male writers who perpetuate this tradition of ritualized violence are more directly tied to realistic fiction than are the women writers. Certainly Walker is concerned with portraying the slaveholding world, but not to the minutiae of describing in detail the bodies of the two women as they dangle from the ends of their ropes. Morrison, on the other hand, gives us a world in which some incredible events occur; the circumstances under which Son finds his way to Margaret's bedroom, for example, do not have as many parallels in history as does Wright's lynching and burning in "Big Boy Leaves Home." Nor are the interactions of Margaret, Valerian, Jadine, Sydney, and Ondine as realistic in the historical context of American society; they give none of the sense of being commonplace occurrences such as those that pervade the works of Richard Wright and James Baldwin. The women appear to be more selective in their adherence to history than do the men.

The women writers also seem to be less inclined to present graphic details of violence than do black male writers. Sutton Griggs glues the reader's eyeballs to the corkscrew used to bore holes in the flesh of his characters in *The Hindered Hand*, and the pattern of graphic presentation is no less vivid through the works of writers who succeed Griggs and lead up to Baldwin. Action is choreographed in the lynching and burning in "Going to Meet the Man" both to suggest the rising tension of a work of art and to parallel the build-up of tension in the crowd and the ultimate release of that tension. The focus on violence is sustained and unapologetically brutal. It is a rare occasion on which black women writers present violence, either lynchings or otherwise, with the same degree of detail and at the same length. A grisly exception is Alice Walker's depiction of the father cutting off his daughter's breasts in

"The Child Who Favored Daughter."[10] Whether the violence is rape or murder, black women writers seem to be less inclined to dwell upon it.

Consider, too, how male and female writers treat the symbolic castration of black males; for example, Alice Walker in *The Third Life of Grange Copeland* as compared with James Baldwin in *Another Country* and with Chester Himes in *If He Hollers Let Him Go*. Walker presents Grange's reaction to the restrictions that are placed upon him in terms of psychological frustration. We know that Grange is made to feel less than a man because of the mask he is forced to adopt whenever he is in the presence of Shipley, his boss. Grange may swing from the rafters like an animal, but that image is superimposed upon his actions. We do not see that Grange's reactions to his circumstances are ever manifested as fear of a threat to his physical person. He never shows concern that Shipley will slap him, or have him horsewhipped, or otherwise treated violently. The tension he feels is tied to being unable to get his family out of debt and to how that reflects upon his economic abilities as a male.

For Walker, symbolic emasculation is a moral and philosophical issue; she believes that the body may be abused through work, but she does not focus upon the body as the potential recipient of the wrath of the white landowner. Ultimately, Grange blames himself and Brownfield for the dehumanization they have allowed others to impose on them. As a human being, Grange maintains, and especially as a black human being, it was his unique responsibility to hold a part of himself inviolable to the poisons which pervaded the air around him. That philosophy may be more exacting than realistic, but it nonetheless shows the distinction to be made between how black female writers such as Walker perceive of oppression for black males as opposed to how they themselves view it.

For both Himes and Baldwin, economic and social restrictions on black males are centered upon the actual bodies of the characters, and it is that focus which consistently ties them to the executions toward which the bulk of this study has been directed. For Bob Jones in Himes's novel, his bulging biceps and well-developed arms are the measure of his manhood. When those are confined by social restrictions, or when he is attacked physically, his frustration becomes one of *feeling* the physical and psychological damage perpetrated against him. That vicarious emotional tie between author and character is never felt in the works by the female writers, while Himes makes the physical body the center of his metaphorical statements about repression of Blacks in the United States. If Bob Jones cannot win the respect of his fellow workers, either black or white, that is in part a measure of the success of his body in performing the jobs he has chosen for it. If he cannot win the hand of the girl he loves, that is another measure of the attractiveness of the body and the physical ability to caress and make love to the woman. By viewing him as the potential rapist, society thus makes Bob's very body his greatest enemy. His emotions and his constant apprehension are both functions of the flesh, not of philosophy.

The same is true of Rufus Scott. The repulsion he is made to feel is not only tied to the blackness of his skin, but to the form of his body as male. In the Army he was literally beaten by the white officer in rejection of his black body. The pain he felt is therefore in some ways more immediate than the mask-wearing pain Grange Copeland must feel before his sharecropping boss. To Rufus, as to Bob, the body becomes the enemy (even as one prizes it). In that scene on the balcony with Leona, Rufus turns his body into a weapon against her, because that body is what his oppressors have used against him. His feelings of persecution are more intense than are Bob Jones's, for at least Bob can articulate his problem; Rufus is more consistently left in the realm of emotion, and it is those conflicting emotions which eventually lead to his destruction. Again, with Baldwin as with Himes, the author has bridged the gap between his own emotional reaction to oppression and that which he allows his characters to feel. Rufus never reaches the level of introspection that Grange Copeland does, for to do so would be to remove himself from victimization and reaction and to gain control over his life. Both male writers are less optimistic in their beliefs that black males *can* have any control over their lives; consequently, the reactive, feeling stages are viewed as more accurately reflective of their conditions within the society.

The tendency to focus on issues other than the physical, which was identified early in the works of black women writers, seems to have continued into contemporary works. A writer like Alice Walker, for example, has made a conscious effort to move her characters beyond the realm of physical violence and victimization, such as the incident in *The Third Life of Grange Copeland* in which Mem is killed by a shotgun blast in the face, to situations in which they have room to grow introspectively, such as is the case with Celie in *The Color Purple*. Celie may contemplate committing violence against Albert in retaliation for his keeping her sister's letters from her, but she forces herself to react in other ways until she can control the emotional response.[11]

Black women writers have been more willing to let some portions of their history be, and the lynching of black males for sexual crimes against white women is one of those portions. Black men, less able and/or willing to let go of something which was such an integral part of their history, have only in recent years begun to move away from the graphic depictions of lynchings. Yet the subject pervades their work in metaphoric ways, such as providing the emotional touchstone for the characters in John Wideman's *The Lynchers*. The letting go is primarily a function of changing times, or integrationist stances, and of black nationalist emphases which suggest that creation is more rewarding than reaction. For the hundred or more years that reaction did provide a consistent strain of development in black American literature, the male writers depicted violent scenes with a persistency which suggested that they were involved in their own rite of exorcism.

To exorcise fear from racial memory is as formidable a task as is attempting to obtain equality for black people in the United States. Yet that is the task black male writers seem to have set for themselves in that long history of engagement with lynchings and burnings in their works. Each generation took up the task of convincing the next that black males in particular and black people in general could survive, wholly and with psychological health intact, against the desire of whites to exorcise Blacks from personal interactions with them, and to exorcise them from the earth if they could not. Black male writers, heir to those fears and to that possibility for elimination, took up their own rite of exorcism by emphasizing that, though violence was committed and used to generate fear in other black people, that fear could be overcome by constantly identifying the enemy and perpetuating a tradition of unity to combat him. If those whites who committed acts of violence were presented as monsters, and looked like such to the world, would they not be influenced to change their ways? And if black writers kept accumulating cultural records by painting the true characters of those of their enemies, could not that record itself serve as an indication that all black people were not afraid? Each literary depiction of a lynching or a burning, then, became a loud whistle to sustain a people past the graveyard of white suppression and brutality. From Grigg's polemics, to Chesnutt's bid for equality, to Wright's hammerings, to Baldwin's political essays, the concern with ritualized violence became a baton which each male writer handed to the next in a contest for manhood and civil rights which bound them to history and to literature, and which made their works simultaneously artistic creations and cultural documents.

NOTES

Preface

1. The ritual as presented in this paragraph was set forth in my article, "Ceremonial Fagots: Lynching and Burning Rituals in Black Literature," *Southern Humanities Review* 10 (Summer 1976): 235–47.

1. Ritual and Ritual Violence in American Life and Culture

1. Sutton Griggs, *The Hindered Hand: Or, The Reign of the Repressionist* (Nashville: The Orion Publishing Co., 1905), pp. 133–34.

2. John Wideman also uses this quotation as part of the "Matter Prefatory" which sets the tone for *The Lynchers*, his novel about four black men plotting to lynch a white policeman (1973; New York: Laurel, 1974). For another particularly gruesome historical account of torture and the prolonged gathering of souvenirs, see Henry M. Miller, *The Mob's Verdict* (Chatsworth, California: Barclay House, 1974), pp. 130–32.

3. In cases where the bodies were not burned, the lynchers frequently used them for target practice. Many historians and social observers have commented upon the excessive "riddling" of the lynched bodies with bullets. In one case, the bullet-riddling became a substitute for rope; a black man accused of killing a white man in Livermore, Kentucky, "was tied up on stage at the local opera house and his body riddled with over one hundred bullets by mob members who purchased tickets to participate." Robert L. Zangrando, *The NAACP Crusade Against Lynching, 1909–1950* (Philadelphia: Temple University Press, 1980), p. 26. Zangrando refers to the lynching of Blacks as "ritualized murder" (p. 4) and a "sadistic ritual" (p. 210), and to the repeated actions of whites as "ritualized behavior" (p. 11).

4. Jacquelyn Dowd Hall, *Revolt Against Chivalry: Jessie Daniel Ames and the Women's Campaign Against Lynching* (New York: Columbia University Press, 1979), p. 141; and William E. B. DuBois, *Dusk of Dawn* (1940; Millwood, New York: Kraus-Thomson Organization Limited, 1975), p. 251. Newspapers were also attributed with stirring up mob violence, such as in the Atlanta riots of 1906.

5. The phrase "Lynch Law" is said to have derived from the practices of Virginian Charles Lynch, who, during the Revolutionary War, summarily hanged Tories caught in the area. There are also other supposed origins; see James E. Cutler, *Lynch-Law: An Investigation into the History of Lynching in the United States* (New York: Longmans, Green, and Co., 1905), chapter 2.

6. Ibid., p. 85.

7. Ibid., p. 116.

8. Ibid., p. 135.

9. Walter White, *Rope and Faggot: A Biography of Judge Lynch* (New York: Alfred A. Knopf, 1929), p. 229. White's figures are used in this instance for simplicity. He combines the figures from James E. Cutler's *Lynch-Law*, which covered the years between 1882 and 1903 and were based on records kept by *The Chicago Tribune*, with those of the NAACP in *Thirty Years of Lynching in the United States, 1889–1918* (1919; New York: Arno Press and *The New York Times*, 1969). White was himself an NAACP lynching investigator and supplied data through 1927. Other sources which treat lynching and burning are legion. In *White Over Black: American Attitudes Toward the Negro, 1550–1812* (New York: Penguin, 1969), Winthrop D. Jordan traces, over a period of centuries, the psychological attitudes which led to white treatment of Blacks, including the acts of hanging, burning, and castration. John Hope Franklin, in *From Slavery to Freedom: A History of American Negroes* (New York: Alfred A. Knopf, 1967), mentions that, of the 2,500 people lynched between 1884 and 1900, the "great majority" were black, "with Mississippi, Alabama, Georgia, and Louisiana leading the nation" (p. 431). Arthur F. Raper traces the history of lynching to the 1930s in his book, *The Tragedy of Lynching* (Chapel Hill: The University of North Carolina Press, 1933). His discussion of the mob role in such acts is of especial interest (pp. 6–13, 40–54).

For figures after 1927, see records provided by the Association of Southern Women for the Prevention of Lynching, which recorded victims reported between 1931 and 1941. For the Association Report, see Jessie Daniel Ames, *The Changing Character of Lynching, Review of Lynching, 1931–1941* (Atlanta: Commission on Interracial Cooperation, 1942). Beginning in 1882, Tuskegee Institute also kept annual records of lynch victims. For the most recent estimations, see Zangrando, *The NAACP Crusade Against Lynching*, especially pp. 5–8.

10. There is no way to separate which victims were lynched and/or burned. Numbers were kept, not methods. With brutalities being reported throughout the latter part of the nineteenth century, however, it is reasonable to assume that there were many combinations. For the offenses, see Cutler, *Lynch-Law*, p. 175 and the chart following p. 176. Cutler devotes an entire page to listing "minor offenses"; the items listed would be ludicrous if their consequences were not so appalling—see p. 167. Cutler also cites several instances in which Blacks were burned or "roasted alive": see pp. 108, 109, and 127. Statistical data on "lynching by burning alive" can be found on pp. 191–92. In reference to rape, Zangrando points out in *The NAACP Crusade Against Lynching* that, of the total number of estimated lynchings between 1882 and 1968, "less than 26%" involved rape or accusations of rape.

11. Richard Maxwell Brown, "Legal and Behavioral Perspectives on American Vigilantism," *Perspectives in American History* 5 (1971):105.

12. Cutler, *Lynch-Law*, p. 192.

13. Brown, "Legal and Behavioral Perspectives," 110–11. Other cases of summary justice administered on the frontier may be reviewed in John W. Caughey, *Their Majesties the Mob* (Chicago: University of Chicago Press, 1960), pp. 27–109.

14. Cutler, *Lynch-Law*, p. 95.

15. Reprinted in Richard Maxwell Brown, ed., *American Violence* (Englewood Cliffs, New Jersey: Prentice-Hall, Inc., 1970), pp. 107–109.

16. See Nedra Tyre, "You All Are a Bunch of Nigger Lovers," in *Red Wine*

First (New York: Simon and Schuster, 1947), pp. 112–13. The account is related to a social worker.

17. Tyre, *Red Wine First*, p. 116. The following three quotations are also from this source, pp. 119–20, 120–21, and 122, respectively.

18. For a discussion of the relationship between belief (myth) and behavior (ritual), see Clyde Kluckhohn, "Myths and Rituals: A General Theory," *Harvard Theological Review* 35 (1942): 45–79. Note that belief (myth) may apply to religious as well as to secular aspects of behavior. See also Neil J. Smelser, *Theory of Collective Behavior* (New York: The Free Press, 1962). Smelser emphasizes that belief is necessary to mobilize any crowd into collective behavior: ". . . collective behavior is guided by various kinds of beliefs—assessments of the situation, wishes, and expectations. . . . They involve a belief in the existence of extraordinary forces—threats, conspiracies, etc.—which are at work in the universe. . . . The beliefs on which collective behavior is based . . . are thus akin to magical beliefs" (p. 8). The belief that Blacks are threatening the social order, and the specific belief that the suprahuman black male sexuality is a threat, lend a magical quality to the events in which Blacks are lynched.

19. Hall, *Revolt Against Chivalry*, p. 145. Hall also refers to lynching in other places as "communal ritual" (p. 139) and "ritualistic affirmation of white unity" (p. 141); she makes references, too, to the "ritual of rope and faggot" (p. 156) and to the "ritual of lynching" (p. 156).

20. See *The Golden Bough: A Study in Magic and Religion* (New York: Macmillan, 1925), pp. 194–264 and pp. 538–87.

21. John Vickery, "Ritual and Theme in Faulkner's 'Dry September,'" *Arizona Quarterly* 18 (Spring 1962): 7–8.

22. Doris Lorden, "Mob Behavior and Social Attitudes," *Sociology and Social Research* 14 (March 1930): 328.

23. Norman Meier, G. H. Mennenga, and H. J. Stoltz, "An Experimental Approach to the Study of Mob Behavior," *Journal of Abnormal and Social Psychology* 36 (October 1941): 507.

24. Smelser, *Theory of Collective Behavior*, pp. 103–109. See also the chapter entitled "The Hostile Outburst."

25. Walter White was also interested in backgrounds of lynchers in an effort to determine what values, habits, and beliefs formed their destructive tendencies. See *Rope and Faggot*.

26. Lorden, "Mob Behavior and Social Attitudes," 330. Newspapers played a large part in affecting public sentiment. Glaring headlines aroused the populace without reference to innocence or guilt. Meier used such headlines in his controlled experiment with mob behavior; and Ames, *The Changing Character of Lynching*, discusses how Southern newspapers encouraged mob violence by the headlines they chose, pp. 55–58. Zangrando also points out that the movie, *Birth of a Nation*, contributed to mob violence; see *The NAACP Crusade Against Lynching*, pp. 33–34.

27. Frazer, *The Golden Bough*, p. 579.

28. Ibid., p. 580.

29. Even studies which were adamantly pro-Southern and pro-lynching in their bias recognized the special vengeance of lynching when a question of white female honor was involved. Winfield Collins, whose statistics are questionable at best, works out an elaborate formula in which he concludes that, during the years 1885–1907, Blacks were "more than seven times as liable to be lynched in the South for rape than even for murder."

See *The Truth About Lynching and the Negro in the South* (New York: The Neale Publishing Company, 1918), p. 54.

30. "A London Diary: Acquittal of twenty-eight self-confessed lynchers in the South," *New Statesman & Nation* 33 (May 31 1947): 388.

31. David M. Tucker, "Miss Ida B. Wells and Memphis Lynching," *Phylon* 32 (Summer 1971): 120. Miss Wells published three significant pamphlets on lynching—*Southern Horrors: Lynch Law in all Its Phases* (1892); *A Red Record: Tabulated Statistics and Alleged Causes of Lynchings in the United States, 1892–1893–1894* (1895); and *Mob Rule in New Orleans* (1900). These three pamphlets were published as a single volume by Arno Press and *The New York Times* in 1969. The second of these pamphlets, *A Red Record*, is especially interesting for information it provides on lynchings and burnings which resulted from alleged attacks on white women by black men (pp. 58–70).

Miss Wells was so fiery in her antilynching editorials that threats on her life forced her to leave Memphis. She went on a lecture tour abroad in an effort to convince foreigners, especially Britishers, of the atrocities being committed in the United States. A British reporter envisioned her being ritualistically executed if she returned to the U.S. (Tucker, 119–20).

In connection with the comment quoted from Miss Wells, the white woman in Waldo Frank's *Holiday* (New York: Boni and Liveright, 1923) is forced to condone the actions of a white mob, led by her brother, in hunting down and lynching a black man to whom she has been attracted.

32. Jordan, *White Over Black*, pp. 151–52.

33. Gordon W. Allport, *The Nature of Prejudice* (Cambridge, Mass.: Addison-Wesley Publishing Company, Inc., 1954), especially chapter 24, "Projection," but also chapters 15 and 21–23.

34. James P. Comer, *Beyond Black and White* (New York: Quadrangle, 1972), p. 134.

35. Abram Kardiner and Lionel Ovesey, *The Mark of Oppression: A Psychological Study of the American Negro* (New York: Norton, 1951), p. 45.

36. For accounts of the activities of the Association of Southern Women for the Prevention of Lynching, see Henry E. Barber, "The Association of Southern Women for the Prevention of Lynching, 1930–1942," *Phylon* 34 (December 1973): 378–89 and John S. Reed, "Evolution of an Anti-Lynching Organization," *Social Problems* 16 (Fall 1968): 172–82. Reed tried to assess the Association's effectiveness "solely on the basis of the actual prevention of lynching." For more detailed analysis, see Hall's *Revolt Against Chivalry*.

37. Kluckhohn, "Myths and Rituals," 78.

38. Gladys-Marie Fry, *Nightriders in Black Folk History* (Knoxville: The University of Tennessee Press, 1975).

39. Allport offers some interesting commentary on the red herring of intermarriage as far as interracial sexual relations are concerned. He maintains that it is attractive because it "sounds like a legal, and therefore respectable, issue." While it usually dominates discussions of race, "the marriage issue is not rational," but becomes itself "a lesson in rationalization" and is "introduced to protect and justify prejudice"; *The Nature of Prejudice*, pp. 376, 377. See also Charles H. Stember, *Sexual Racism* (New York: Harper Colophon Books, 1976), pp. 11–13, 37–38.

40. Roger Abrahams, *Postively Black* (Chicago: Aldine, 1970), pp. 69–70.

41. Daryl Dance, *Shuckin' and Jivin': Folklore from Contemporary Black Americans* (Bloomington: Indiana University Press, 1978), pp. 102, 104.

42. This discussion is pursued in chapter 3 of this volume with Baldwin's short story, "Going to Meet the Man."

43. In addition to having their homes destroyed, many of the relatives of the accused black men also found themselves victims of mob action. For a discussion of this phenomenon, see Wells-Barnett, *A Red Record*, pp. 33–36; Maude White Katz, "The Negro Woman and the Law," *Freedomways* 2 (Summer 1962): 284; and Ralph Ginzburg, *100 Years of Lynching* (New York: Lancer Books, 1972), pp. 90–91, 102.

44. Lillian Smith, *Killers of the Dream* (New York: Norton, 1949), pp. 158–59.

45. For a version of this rhyme, see Dance, *Shuckin' and Jivin'*, p. 101.

46. A classic study of the sexual politics of interracial relationships is Calvin Hernton's *Sex and Racism in America* (New York: Grove Press, 1965). Hernton is also aware of the scapegoat function imposed on Blacks because of those interactions; see pp. 19, 20, and 27. William H. Grier and Price M. Cobbs also offer some perceptive comments about the black male/white female relationship in *Black Rage* (New York: Basic Books, 1968).

47. Dance, *Shuckin' and Jivin'*, pp. 101–109.

48. Ibid., pp. 107–108.

49. For a discussion of the Southern white male's role in the creation of the myth of white womanhood, see Stember's *Sexual Racism*, especially chapter 2. Stember contends that the pedestalization of the white woman made her more desirable sexually, instead of "desexualizing" her: ". . . it is precisely the white woman's presumed purity that renders her sexually *desirable*. For this reason, it seems the white man sees her as the *eminently desirable sexual object* for all men, blacks especially" (p. 41). For contrasting arguments, see Catherine Clinton's *The Plantation Mistress* (New York: Pantheon, 1982), chapters 5 and 10. Certainly the intense responses to black men "trespassing" with white women would suggest a validity to Stember's contention, but it is also true that some white men viewed white women as sexually sterile, too pure for the sweatiness of sex.

50. For a discussion of this phenomenon, see Wells-Barnett's *Southern Horrors* and *A Red Record*. Calvin Hernton goes so far as to suggest that "*Southern white women are not only sexually attracted by Negroes, but it is they who are the aggressors*"—*Sex and Racism in America*, p. 21.

51. Catherine Clinton spends quite a bit of time in *The Plantation Mistress* arguing against the image portrayed in *Mandingo*. She complains of stereotype and excess, of the free adaption of historical material, and of the creation of a new mythology about the sexual behavior of plantation mistresses. Our positions are different in that one of her primary concerns seems to be to negate the popular imagination, while I maintain that oral tradition was just as central in determining life and death for black males as was factual reality. See chapter 10 in *The Plantation Mistress*, "Foucault Meets *Mandingo*." The film is based on Kyle Onstott's novel of the same title, which was published in 1958.

52. Hernton includes accounts in which black men were forced to perform sexually with white women or be accused of rape; see *Sex and Racism in America*, pp. 13–15, 22–24. Allport also notes that the white woman who may be "fascinated by the taboo against the Negro male" may project

her feelings onto him and imagine that he is the aggressor instead of recognizing the attraction within herself; see *The Nature of Prejudice*, p. 375.

53. Wells-Barnett recounts instances in *A Red Record* in which the tainted reputations of white women did not prevent mobs from lynching and burning black men who were discovered to have been intimate with them.

54. Clinton's *The Plantation Mistress* goes only a very short way in treating the sexual interaction between black males and white females during slavery. She records a couple of instances in which travelers to the South commented upon white women of the planter class being involved with slaves (pp. 209–10). She maintains that most of such liaisons occurred between white women of the lower classes and black men. White women who married Blacks during Reconstruction did so in part because of the shortage of white males, but that trend was "short-lived," Clinton asserts.

55. Lillian Smith, *Killers of the Dream*, and Adrienne Rich, "Disloyal to Civilization: Feminism, Racism, Gynephobia (1978)," in *On Lies, Secrets, and Silence* (New York: Norton, 1979), pp. 275–310. Smith is astutely insightful about Southern mores and attitudes, and she also recognizes the ritualistic characteristics of many of the interactions between Blacks and whites in the South. She refers to "rites of segregation," to "ritualistic" actions, and to "rituals" as a way of life. She further recognizes the nature of the society which has established so many actions as taboo; her references to such taboos appear on pp. 78, 87, 90, 115, 117, 144, 149, 204, and 222. Calvin Hernton, in *Sex and Racism in America*, is likewise aware of the many taboos surrounding the interactions of Blacks and whites, and he uses Smith's *Killers of the Dream* as the source for some of his examples of taboo; such references in his work appear on pp. 20, 26, 28, 37, 40, 58, 60, 64, 68, 72, 73, 94, 97, 100, 109, 129, and 151.

56. Barbara Christian, *Black Women Novelists: The Development of a Tradition, 1892–1976* (Westport, Connecticut: Greenwood Press, 1980).

2. Fear of Castration: A Literary History

1. Sterling Brown, *The Negro in American Fiction* (1937; New York: Kennikat Press, 1968); Sterling Brown, "Negro Character as Seen by White Authors," in *Dark Symphony: Negro Literature in America*, ed. James A. Emanuel and Theodore Gross (New York: The Free Press, 1968), pp. 139–71.

2. William H. Grier and Price M. Cobbs, *Black Rage* (New York: Basic Books, 1968), pp. 60 and 87.

3. Richard Wright, "The Ethics of Living Jim Crow," in *Dark Symphony*, ed. Emanuel and Gross, pp. 238–48.

4. Robert G. O'Meally, *The Craft of Ralph Ellison* (Cambridge: Harvard University Press, 1980), p. 60; Ralph Ellison, *Shadow and Act* (New York: Signet, 1964), p. 40.

5. Paul Laurence Dunbar, "When Malindy Sings," in *When Malindy Sings* (New York: Dodd, Mead, and Company, 1903), pp. 9–14.

6. William Wells Brown, *Clotel; Or, The President's Daughter* (1853; New York: Collier-Macmillan, 1969), p. 99. Further references to this source will be parenthesized in the text.

7. Charles Waddell Chesnutt, *The Marrow of Tradition* (1901; Ann Arbor: University of Michigan Press, 1970).

8. Charles Waddell Chesnutt, *The Colonel's Dream* (1905; New York: Arno Press, 1970).

9. Richard Wright, "Down by the Riverside," in *Uncle Tom's Children* (New York: Harper and Brothers, 1938), pp. 71–166.

10. James Baldwin, *Go Tell It On the Mountain* (1953; New York: Dell, 1974), p. 142.

11. Alice Walker, *The Third Life of Grange Copeland* (New York: Harcourt, Brace, Jovanovich, 1970), p. 207. Further references to this source will be parenthesized in the text.

12. Richard Wright, "Fire and Cloud," in *Uncle Tom's Children*, pp. 219–317.

13. Ralph Ellison, *Invisible Man* (1952; New York: Vintage, 1972), p. 78. Further references to this source will be parenthesized in the text.

14. Richard Wright, *The Long Dream* (New York: Doubleday and Company, 1958). References to this source will be parenthesized in the text.

15. Addison Gayle, *The Way of the New World: The Black Novel in America* (New York: Doubleday, 1976), pp. 211–12.

16. Richard Wright, "The Man Who Killed A Shadow," in *Eight Men* (1961; New York: Pyramid, 1969), p. 159. Further references to this source will be parenthesized in the text.

17. Earle V. Bryant, "The Sexualization of Racism in Richard Wright's 'The Man Who Killed A Shadow'," *Black American Literature Forum* 16 (Fall 1982): 119–21.

18. Ibid., 121.

19. See Ralph Ellison, *Invisible Man*, pp. 121–22, and Charles W. Chesnutt, *The Wife of His Youth and Other Stories of the Color Line* (Ann Arbor: University of Michigan Press, 1972), p. 232. I discuss this phenomenon of ingrained reactions which can lead to fear in *From Mammies to Militants: Domestics in Black American Literature* (Philadelphia: Temple University Press, 1982), chapter 2.

20. I discuss the significance of Bigger Thomas's actions in chapter 4 of this volume.

21. Rufus's inability to escape the judging eyes of whites can be compared to that of a black soldier who finds prejudice against him equally strong for being with a white woman—though he has removed himself completely from the United States and lives in Paris. See Rosa Guy's "Wade," in *Ten Times Black*, ed. Julian Mayfield (New York: Bantam, 1972), pp. 85–99. When a white American captain challenges Wade's right to be with a white woman, the two end up in a brutal fight. Although Wade wins, the captain maintains: "You still . . . ain't nothing but a goddamn nigger" (p. 96), prompting Wade to stomp the man to death. It is Rufus's inability to act in a comparable confrontation which causes at least a part of his frustration. John A. Williams, in *Night Song* (New York: Farrar, Straus and Cudahy, 1961), also treats the relationship between a black man and a white woman. Unfortunately, there are no extended, introspective glimpses of them. It is clear, however, that Keel does have problems with the relationship; in contrast to most other black males in such relationships, Keel finds that his involvement makes him impotent. There is a suggestion near the end of the novel that he has overcome his problem, but the novel does not focus extensively enough upon the relationship for a substantive analysis to be posited.

22. Chester Himes, *If He Hollers Let Him Go* (1945; Chatham, New Jersey: The Chatham Bookseller, 1973), p. 3. Further references to this source will be parenthesized in the text. Himes also treats relationships between black males and white females in *Lonely Crusade* (1947) and in *The Primitive* (1955).

23. Richard Yarborough, "The Quest for the American Dream in Three Afro-American Novels: *If He Hollers Let Him Go, The Street*, and *Invisible Man*," *MELUS* 8 (Winter 1981): 33—59.

24. For a discussion of this ambivalent attraction of black males for white females, see Charles Herbert Stember, *Sexual Racism* (New York: Harper Colophon Books, 1976), chapter 4, "The Sexual Preferences of Minority Males," especially pp. 100—116.

25. Edward Margolies, *Native Sons: A Critical Study of Twentieth-Century Negro American Authors* (New York: Lippincott, 1968), p. 90.

26. James Baldwin, *Another Country* (1962; New York: Dell, 1965), p. 23. Further references to this source will be parenthesized in the text. Calvin Hernton's chapter on "The Negro Male," in which he discusses the interactions of black men and white women in the North, is illuminating for the insights it offers about black men like Rufus Scott. In fact, Hernton makes specific references to *Another Country*. See *Sex and Racism in America* (New York: Grove Press, 1965), pp. 77—78.

27. Ann Petry, in her novel *The Narrows* (1953; New York: Pyramid, 1971), which appeared between the publication of *If He Hollers Let Him Go* and *Another Country*, attempts to develop a romantic relationship between a black man, Link Williams, and a white woman, Camilo Treadway Sheffield, in a Connecticut setting. The lovers carry on a clandestine relationship until Link discovers that Camilo is an heiress. Partly believing that she is using him as a stud, he breaks off the relationship, and, in her grief and helplessness, she makes a half-hearted accusation of rape, which leads her husband and mother to a shooting execution of Link. The progress of the love relationship is hampered by multiple points of view, by long periods during which we do not know what is happening with Camilo and Link, and finally by Camilo's disappearance from the novel at the crucial point of the breakup. She apparently deteriorates psychologically, and it is that deterioration which leads her usually inept husband and her vengeful mother to carry out a plot in which Link is "arrested" by two of the husband's friends, handcuffed, taken to the Treadway mansion, and shot after he presumably confesses to assaulting Camilo. The novel is unusual in the depiction of the romantic relationship, in the genuine affection between the two characters, and in the way in which Link is killed for his "violation."

3. Literary Lynchings and Burnings

1. For representative examples, see Theodore Dreiser's "Nigger Jeff," in *Major Writers of America, II* (New York: Harcourt, Brace & World, Inc., 1962), pp. 472—84; Waldo Frank's *Holiday* (New York: Boni and Liveright, 1923); William Faulkner's "Dry September," in *Collected Stories of William Faulkner* (New York: Random House, 1950), 169—83; and Erskine Caldwell's *Trouble in July* (New York: Duell, Sloan & Pearce, 1940). Frank is especially noteworthy because he and Jean Toomer were contemporaries and shared

writing experiences. Yet the lynching Frank presents in *Holiday* is suggestive, almost surrealistic in comparison to Toomer's graphic and realistic
portrayal in *Cane* (1923).

2. William Wells Brown, *Clotel; Or, The President's Daughter* (1853; New
York: Collier, 1972), p. 55.

3. James Weldon Johnson, *The Autobiography of An Ex-Coloured Man*
(1912; New York: Hill and Wang, 1960), pp. 184–87. Johnson was himself
almost the victim of mob violence. After a particularly devastating fire in
Jacksonville, Florida, Johnson's home town, a white woman reporter from
New York came to write about the effects of the fire upon the black population. She asked Johnson to read her article and provide suggestions, and
he agreed to meet her in a park later that day to read over the material.
The white streetcar conductor who saw him get off the car to greet the
woman reported his rendezvous to the local military authority, who sent
"eight or ten militiamen in khaki with rifles and bayonets" to bring Johnson and the woman back to town. Johnson was beaten and bruised and
cries of "Kill the damned nigger!" were shouted at him. Though the matter
was eventually cleared up, it had a lasting effect upon Johnson: "For weeks
and months the episode with all of its implications preyed on my mind
and disturbed me in my sleep. I would wake often in the night-time, after
living through again those few frightful seconds, exhausted by the nightmare of a struggle with a band of murderous, bloodthirsty men in khaki,
with loaded rifles and fixed bayonets. It was not until twenty years after,
through work I was then engaged in, that I was able to liberate myself
completely from this horror complex." See *Along This Way* (1933; New
York: Viking, 1968), pp. 165–70.

4. James Weldon Johnson, *Saint Peter Relates an Incident: Selected
Poems by James Weldon Johnson* (New York: Viking, 1935), pp. 27–29.

5. Claude McKay, *Selected Poems of Claude McKay* (New York: Harcourt, Brace & World, Inc., 1953), p. 37.

6. Walter White, *Rope and Faggot: A Biography of Judge Lynch* (New
York: Alfred A. Knopf, 1929), p. 3. It should be remembered that White's
task of investigating lynchings for the NAACP was greatly facilitated by
his obvious lack of Negroid features. Robert L. Zangrando reports that
White investigated "forty-one lynchings and eight race riots" during his
thirty-one year career with the NAACP; see *The NAACP Crusade Against
Lynching, 1909–1950* (Philadelphia: Temple University Press, 1980), p. 89.

7. White, *Rope and Faggot*, pp. 4–5. Children sometimes had their pictures taken with adults at the scene of violence. For a representative example from The Schomburg Collection, see Rhoda L. Goldstein, ed., *Black
Life and Culture in the United States* (New York: Apollo, 1971), p. 242b. Another example can be found in Wells, *A Red Record*, p. 55. Other pictures of
lynchings, without the presence of children, can be found in Richard
Wright's *12 Million Black Voices* (1941; New York: Arno Press and *The New
York Times*, 1969), p. 45, and in Henry M. Miller's *The Mob's Verdict: Silence
at the End of the Rope* (Chatsworth, California: Barclay House, 1974),
pp. 49–56 and 121–28.

8. Another poem from this period which contains all the elements of
the ritual is "A Festival in Christendom," by Walter Everette Hawkins. The
part of the poem containing the ritual is published in *The New Negro Renaissance*, ed. Arthur P. Davis and Michael W. Peplow (New York: Holt,

Rinehart and Winston, 1975), pp. 41–42. *Black No More*, a satiric novel written by George Schuyler and published in 1931 also contains elements of the ritual; see pp. 216ff.

9. Gwendolyn Brooks, *Selected Poems* (New York: Harper and Row, 1963), pp. 87–89.

10. See especially Brown's "Legal and Behavioral Perspectives on American Vigilantism," *Perspectives in American History* 5 (1971). White, *Rope and Faggot*, pp. 222–23 includes instances of lynch victims taken from sheriffs from 1925–1927.

11. Ralph Ellison, "The Birthmark," *New Masses* 36 (July 2, 1940): 16–17. Further references to this source will be parenthesized in the text.

12. Alice Walker, *The Third Life of Grange Copeland* (New York: Avon, 1971), pp. 241–42.

13. James E. Cutler, *Lynch-Law: An Investigation into the History of Lynching in the United States* (New York: Longmans, Green, and Co., 1905), pp. 203–204. Also, see Winthrop D. Jordan, *White Over Black: American Attitudes Toward the Negro, 1550–1812* (New York: Penguin, 1969), pp. 112–13 and 116.

14. Cutler, *Lynch-Law*, p. 95.

15. See Cutler, *Lynch-Law*, p. 128. Although Olmsted records this in 1860 and Brown's novel was published in 1853, it is not unreasonable to assume that the practice was not new.

16. Margaret Walker, *Jubilee* (New York: Bantam, 1967), pp. 98–104. Further references to this source will be parenthesized in the text. Walker's account of the two women is significant in that it highlights the fact that black women were indeed lynched, and sometimes their executions were just as brutal as those for men. Maude White Katz comments upon how her research revealed that one black woman was treated by a mob: "One victim was in her eighth month of pregnancy. Members of the mob, suspended her from a tree by her ankles. Gasoline was poured on her clothes and ignited. A chivalrous white man took his knife and split open her abdomen. The unborn child fell to the ground. A member of the mob crushed its head with his heel. They fired bullets into her still body." This woman was killed for protesting the lynching of her husband. Her case, and that of others Katz comments upon, was taken from records kept by the NAACP and *The Crisis*. See Katz's "The Negro Woman and the Law," *Freedomways* 2 (Summer 1962): 284. See also Zangrando, *The NAACP Crusade Against Lynching*, p. 42.

17. The actual incident has been referred to earlier on p. 67. Cutler gives a historical parallel of slaves being thought to instigate a plot of strychnine poisoning against their masters in Texas in 1860; *Lynch-Law*, p. 125.

18. Sutton Griggs, *The Hindered Hand: Or, The Reign of the Repressionist* (Nashville: The Orion Publishing Co., 1905), pp. 133–34. Further references to this source will be parenthesized in the text. A lynching also occurs earlier in the book (pp. 106–107), and when the whites have done their work, another black man cuts the body down and quietly bears it home. Earlier in his career as a novelist, Griggs treated lynching in *Imperium in Imperio* (1899; Miami: Mnemosyne Publishing Inc., 1969), which may best be described as a romantic fantasy. On p. 155 of the novel, Belton Piedmont, one of the two main characters, is hung and shot by a group known as "Nigger Rulers," yet he miraculously recovers from both indignities just as a white doctor is about to dissect him. On p. 225, Griggs

makes mention of the celebrated burning of Henry Smith in Texas, a case mentioned by both Cutler and Wells.

19. For a discussion of initiation rites and the function they serve for youth in guiding them into adult roles, see Arnold van Gennep, *The Rites of Passage* (Chicago: University of Chicago Press, 1960).

20. Griggs, *The Hindered Hand*, p. 299.

21. Jean Toomer, *Cane* (1923; New York: Harper and Row, 1969), pp. 51–67. Later in *Cane*, a pregnant woman is summarily killed because she tried to hide her husband from a mob, and her unborn baby is cut from her stomach and killed; see pp. 177–79. The storyteller calls the brutality a lynching in the sense that the word was used in frontier days. A historical parallel for this can be found in White, *Rope and Faggot*, pp. 28–29. The woman is hanged and burned and the child ripped from her belly and crushed to death. She had dared to cry out against the whites who killed her husband, whose only crime had been acquaintance with the man sought by the mob.

22. Sterling Brown, "Old Lem," in *The Poetry of Black America: Anthology of the 20th Century*, ed. Arnold Adoff (New York: Harper and Row, 1973), pp. 69–71.

23. Walter White, *The Fire in the Flint* (New York: Knopf, 1924), pp. 236–37. Further references to this source will be parenthesized in the text.

24. Langston Hughes, *The Ways of White Folks* (1933; New York: Vintage, 1962), pp. 46–47.

25. Ibid., pp. 47–48. Hughes also deals with lynching in "Father and Son," also in this volume. See also Hughes's *Don't You Want to Be Free?*, in *Black Theater U.S.A.: Forty-Five Plays by Black Americans*, ed. James V. Hatch and Ted Shine (New York: The Free Press, 1974), pp. 262–77.

26. For a review of experiments during the 1920s, see White, *Rope and Faggot*, pp. 114–51.

27. Ibid., p. 148.

28. Charles W. Chesnutt, *The Marrow of Tradition* (1901; Ann Arbor: University of Michigan Press, 1970), p. 182. See White, *Rope and Faggot*, p. 265, for an instance of a black woman lynched by a mob "in search of another."

29. Paul Laurence Dunbar, "The Lynching of Jube Benson," in *American Negro Short Stories*, ed. John Henrik Clarke (New York: Hill and Wang, 1966), p. 6. Dunbar also treats the theme of lynching in "The Tragedy at Three Forks," in *The Strength of Gideon and Other Stories* (New York: Dodd, Mead, 1900), pp. 269–83.

30. Dreiser, "Nigger Jeff," *Major Writers of America*, p. 481.

31. James Baldwin, *Going to Meet the Man* (New York: Dell, 1965), pp. 198–218. Further references to this source will be parenthesized in the text.

32. Peter Freese shares this evaluation of Grace's role. See "James Baldwin: 'Going to Meet the Man' (1965)," in *The Black American Short Story in the 20th Century* (Amsterdam: Grüner, 1977), p. 180.

33. For similar historical burnings from 1921 to 1925, with picnicking crowd participation, see White, *Rope and Faggot*, pp. 23–27. See also James H. Street, *Look Away! A Dixie Notebook* (New York: Viking, 1936), pp. 35–37. In Street's account, the lynchers bring "big six-layer cakes and fried chicken." He records other burnings and/or lynchings, with less of a picnicking air, on pp. 78–79 and 174–75. Street observed these atrocities during the stages of his career as a reporter in Mississippi and other parts of the South.

34. Jordan, *White Over Black*, p. 156.
35. Calvin Hernton, *Sex and Racism in America* (New York: Grove Press, 1965), p. 115.
36. Freese, p. 177.
37. Baldwin seems less secure about the disintegration of portions of that racist structure in *Just Above My Head* (New York: Dell, 1979). The black male characters who go from the North to the South in that novel do so with great fear and trembling which manifest themselves at the level of the specific fear of castration. One of the characters also hallucinates about being chased by a mob of whites and lynched.

4. Ritual Violence and the Formation of an Aesthetic

1. Information on lynching in this paragraph is taken from Arthur F. Raper, *The Tragedy of Lynching* (Chapel Hill: The University of North Carolina Press, 1933). Robert L. Zangrando, in *The NAACP Crusade Against Lynching, 1909–1950* (Philadelphia: Temple University Press, 1980), gives the number of victims for 1930 as twenty-one, with a rise to twenty-eight for 1933, p. 97.
2. Raper, *The Tragedy of Lynching*, p. 2.
3. Ibid., pp. 6–7. This account is discussed extensively on pp. 141–71.
4. For a history of the development of the term lynching from pioneer days to the early twentieth century, see James E. Cutler, *Lynch-Law: An Investigation into the History of Lynching in the United States* (New York: Longmans, Green, and Co., 1905). An infamous lynching, which occurred in Florida in 1934 and with which Wright was probably familiar because of the national attention it received, reiterated at that late date the punishments whites were eager to mete out to Blacks accused of raping and murdering white women. See James R. McGovern, *Anatomy of a Lynching: The Killing of Claude Neal* (Baton Rouge: Louisiana State University Press, 1982).
5. Keneth Kinnamon, *The Emergence of Richard Wright* (Chicago: University of Illinois Press, 1972), pp. 57 and 61.
6. Richard Wright, "Between the World and Me," *The Partisan Review* 2 (July–August 1935): 18–19.
7. Alice Walker, "The Flowers," in *In Love and Trouble: Stories of Black Women* (New York: Harcourt, Brace, Jovanovich, 1973), pp. 119–20.
8. Kinnamon, *The Emergence of Richard Wright*, p. 57.
9. For accounts of white women joining mobs against their black lovers, see Ida B. Wells, *A Red Record* (1895; New York: Arno Press and *The New York Times*, 1969).
10. Cutler, *Lynch-Law*, p. 228. Wells presents a case history of this same incident (she gives the date as February 1, 1893) in *A Red Record*, pp. 25–32. The man lynched was an imbecile. Wells's account is especially worthy of study for the story of the crowd (10,000), the exhibition on a float of "the most inhuman monster known in current history," the absolutely inhuman tortures inflicted before the burning, and the gathering of souvenirs.
11. James H. Street, *Look Away! A Dixie Notebook* (New York: Viking, 1936), p. 35.
12. David Demarest, "Richard Wright: The Meaning of Violence," *Negro American Literature Forum* 8 (Fall 1974): 237.
13. Ibid.

14. Kinnamon, *The Emergence of Richard Wright*, pp. 57–58.

15. Richard Wright, *12 Million Black Voices* (1941; New York: Arno Press and *The New York Times*, 1969), p. 146.

16. Richard Wright, "Blueprint for Negro Writing," in *Richard Wright Reader*, ed. Ellen Wright and Michel Fabre (New York: Harper and Row, 1978), p. 47.

17. Richard Wright, "Big Boy Leaves Home" *Uncle Tom's Children* (1938; New York: Harper and Row, 1965), pp. 46 and 47. Further references to this source will be parenthesized in the text.

18. Noel Schraufnagel, *From Apology to Protest: The Black American Novel* (Deland, Florida: Everett/Edwards 1973), p. 22.

19. Dan McCall, *The Example of Richard Wright* (New York: Harcourt, Brace, 1969), pp. 41, 42.

20. Ibid., p. 42. McCall also refers to the lynching as a "dramatic ceremony" and a "rite" (p. 44).

21. Such accounts may be found in Cutler, *Lynch-Law* and in Raper, *The Tragedy of Lynching*.

22. *Sherwood Anderson's Notebook* (New York: Boni and Liveright, Inc., 1926) includes an incident of a white man showing the "dried ear" of a black man to a friend of Anderson's as "a symbol of the superiority of the whites" (p. 26).

23. See Blyden Jackson, "Richard Wright in a Moment of Truth," in *The Waiting Years: Essays on American Negro Literature* (Baton Rouge: Louisiana State University Press, 1976), pp. 129–45.

24. Ibid., pp. 139–40. Roger Rosenblatt, in *Black Fiction* (Cambridge: Harvard University Press, 1976), also treats the sexual nature of the crowd's burning of Bobo. He suggests that the crowd "rapes" Bobo in addition to murdering him; see pp. 70–76.

25. Jackson, *The Waiting Years*, pp. 140–41.

26. See Doris Lorden, "Mob Behavior and Social Attitudes," *Sociology and Social Research* 14 (March 1930), especially 328 and 330; Norman Meier, G. H. Mennenga, and H. J. Stoltz, "An Experimental Approach to the Study of Mob Behavior," *Journal of Abnormal and Social Psychology* 36 (October 1941), especially 507; and Neil J. Smelser, *Theory of Collective Behavior* (New York: The Free Press, 1962).

27. Richard Wright, "Down by the Riverside," in *Uncle Tom's Children* (New York: Harper and Brothers, 1938), pp. 161–62. Further references to this source will be parenthesized in the text.

28. Richard Wright, "Long Black Song," in *Uncle Tom's Children*, pp. 169–217.

29. Richard Wright, *Native Son* (1940; New York: Perennial, 1966), p. 84. Further references to this source will be parenthesized in the text. For a view of another Wright character who is similarly fearful in the presence of a white women, especially since she is nude, see "Man of All Work," in *Eight Men* (New York: Pyramid, 1969); this story has humorous overtones and eventually ends "happily" for all.

30. Schraufnagel, *From Apology to Protest*, p. 26.

31. Richard Wright, *The Long Dream* (New York: Doubleday and Company, 1958), p. 15. Further references to this source will be parenthesized in the text.

32. For a discussion of this phenomenon, see Trudier Harris, *From Mammies to Militants: Domestics in Black American Literature* (Philadelphia:

Temple University Press, 1982), chapter 2. See the same volume, chapter 4, for a discussion of Carl's discomfort in Richard Wright's "Man of All Work."

33. Calvin Hernton, in *Sex and Racism in America* (New York: Grove Press, 1965), comments upon this phenomenon of the consequences for black men who carry pictures of white women: "I know for a fact that it is dangerous in the South for a Negro to be caught (arrested, for instance) with a photograph of a white female in his possession," p. 59.

34. The policeman's threat is not without its historical basis. Henry M. Miller, in *The Mob's Verdict: Silence at the End of the Rope* (Chatsworth, California: Barclay House, 1974), makes the following comment about the removal of the penis and testes from black lynch victims: "Sometimes the excised organs are rammed into the victim's mouth, to protrude like some grotesque tongue," p. 132. Miller's comment surrounds the torturing, lynching, and burning of a black man accused of raping and killing a white girl. That incident occurred on February 1, 1930, and made news far beyond its Georgia locale. The barbarity of the execution is striking, for it was just that kind of increase in brutality which may have inspired Wright to focus on mob violence in his fiction.

5. An Aborted Attempt at Reversing the Ritual

1. John Wideman, *The Lynchers* (1973; New York: Laurel, 1974), p. 19. Further references to this source will be parenthesized in the text.

2. Sustained critical treatment of Wideman's works is almost nonexistent. One useful article is Kermit Frazier's "The Novels of John Wideman," *Black World* 24 (June 1975): 19–38, which focuses upon the connections between history and imagination in Wideman's fiction.

3. In an interview, Wideman maintained that "the subject of the book is imagination"; it plays a "powerful role" in the relationship between Blacks and whites. Consequently, "it doesn't make any difference whether the conspirators pull their plot off or not," because "people are changed more by their imagination than they are by actual external events," and the conditions under which Blacks and whites live in this country are ones that lend themselves to an imaginative search for some kind of identity on the part of Blacks. See "John Wideman," in *Interviews With Black Writers*, ed. John O'Brien (New York: Liveright, 1973), pp. 217, 218. For a more recent interview with Wideman, see Wilfred J. Samuels, "Going Home: A Conversation with John Edgar Wideman," *Callaloo* 6 (February 1983): 40–59.

6. Beyond the Ritual?

1. Toni Morrison, *Tar Baby* (1981; New York: Plume/New American Library, 1982), p. 79. Further references to this source will be parenthesized in the text.

2. David Bradley, *The Chaneysville Incident* (1981; New York: Avon, 1982), p. 2. Further references to this source will be parenthesized in the text.

7. The Meaning of a Tradition

1. Richard Wright, "Blueprint for Negro Writing," in *Richard Wright Reader*, ed. Ellen Wright and Michel Fabre (New York: Harper and Row, 1978), p. 47.

2. John O'Brien, *Interviews With Black Writers* (New York: Liveright, 1973), p. 219.

3. Ronald Snellings discusses a similar role of priesthood for the black musician. See "We Must Create a National Black Intelligentsia in Order to Survive," in *Black Nationalism in America*, ed. John H. Bracey et al. (New York: Bobbs-Merrill, 1970), pp. 452–62.

4. Alice Walker, *The Color Purple* (New York: Harcourt, Brace, Jovanovich, 1982).

5. James Weldon Johnson, *Along This Way* (1933; New York: Viking, 1968), pp. 165–70. Johnson was poignantly aware of lynching through his work with the NAACP, which kept records on lynchings beginning with the inception of the organization, and which used *The Crisis* to print articles and editorials about lynching.

6. See especially James Baldwin's *Notes of a Native Son* (1955; New York: Bantam, 1968).

7. Richard Wright, "The Ethics of Living Jim Crow," in *Dark Symphony: Negro Literature in America*, ed. James A. Emanuel and Theodore Gross (New York: The Free Press, 1968), pp. 240–42.

8. Ibid., p. 246. For similar incidents, see Calvin Hernton, *Sex and Racism in America* (New York: Grove Press, 1965), pp. 91–92.

9. For contrast provided by another black woman writer, see Angelina W. Grimké's *Rachel* (1920; College Park, Maryland: McGrath Publishing Company, 1969), and "The Closing Door," *The Birth Control Review* (September 1919), pp. 10–14; (October 1919), pp. 8–12.

10. Alice Walker, *In Love and Trouble: Stories of Black Women* (New York: Harcourt, Brace, Jovanovich, 1973), pp. 35–46.

11. Even Walker's story which treats the rape of a white woman by a black man is done so from a distance of years; the incident is not dramatized in the work; see "Advancing Luna—and Ida B. Wells," in *You Can't Keep A Good Woman Down* (New York: Harcourt, Brace, Jovanovich, 1981).

SELECTED BIBLIOGRAPHY

Abrahams, Roger D. *Positively Black*. Chicago: Aldine, 1970.

Allport, Gordon W. *The Nature of Prejudice*. Cambridge, MA: Addison-Wesley Publishing Company, Inc., 1954.

Ames, Jessie Daniel. *The Changing Character of Lynching, Review of Lynching, 1931–1941*. Atlanta: Commission on Interracial Cooperation, 1942.

Anderson, Sherwood. *Sherwood Anderson's Notebook*. New York: Boni and Liveright, Inc., 1926.

Aptheker, Bettina, ed. *Lynching and Rape: An Exchange of Views by Jane Addams and Ida B. Wells*. New York: The American Institute for Marxist Studies, Inc., 1977.

———. *Woman's Legacy: Essays on Race, Sex, and Class in American History*. Amherst: The University of Massachusetts Press, 1982.

Aptheker, Herbert. *A Documentary History of the Negro People in the U.S.* New York: Citadel Press, 1951.

Baldwin, James. *Another Country*. 1962; New York: Dell, 1965.

———. *Go Tell It On the Mountain*. 1953; New York: Dell, 1974.

———. *Going to Meet the Man*. New York: Dell, 1965.

———. *Just Above My Head*. New York: Dell, 1979.

———. *Nobody Knows My Name*. New York: Dial, 1961.

———. *Notes of a Native Son*. 1955; New York: Bantam, 1968.

Baraka, Amiri (LeRoi Jones). *Dutchman*. New York: Morrow, 1964.

Barber, Henry E. "The Association of Southern Women for the Prevention of Lynching, 1930–1942." *Phylon* 34 (December 1973):378–89.

Bradley, David. *The Chaneysville Incident*. 1981; New York: Avon, 1982.

Brooks, Gwendolyn. *The Bean Eaters*. New York: Harper, 1960.

———. *Selected Poems*. New York: Harper and Row, 1963.

Brown, Cecil M. "I Never Raped One Either, But I Don't Let It Bother Me." *Evergreen Review* 16 (May 1972):47–49.

———. *The Life and Loves of Mr. Jiveass Nigger*. New York: Farrar, Straus & Giroux, 1969.

Brown, Richard Maxwell, ed. *American Violence*. Englewood Cliffs, New Jersey: Prentice-Hall, Inc., 1970.

———. "Legal and Behavioral Perspectives on American Vigilantism." *Perspectives in American History* 5 (1971):95–144.

Brown, Sterling. "Negro Character as Seen by White Authors." In *Dark Symphony: Negro Literature in America*, edited by James A. Emanuel and Theodore Gross. New York: The Free Press, 1968.

———. *The Negro in American Fiction*. 1937; Port Washington, New York: Kennikat Press, 1968.

———. "Old Lem." In *The Poetry of Black America: Anthology of the 20th Century*, edited by Arnold Adoff. New York: Harper and Row, 1973.

Brown, William Wells. *Clotel; Or, The President's Daughter*. 1853; New York: Collier, 1972.

213

Brownmiller, Susan. *Against Our Wills: Men, Women and Rape*. New York: Bantam, 1981.

Bryant, Earle V. "The Sexualization of Racism in Richard Wright's 'The Man Who Killed A Shadow.'" *Black American Literature Forum* 16 (Fall 1982):119–21.

Caldwell, Erskine. *Trouble in July*. New York: Duell, Sloan & Pearce, 1940.

Caughey, John W. *Their Majesties the Mob*. Chicago: The University of Chicago Press, 1960.

Chesnutt, Charles Waddell. *The Colonel's Dream*. 1905; New York: Arno Press, 1970.

——. *The Marrow of Tradition*. 1901; Ann Arbor: University of Michigan Press, 1970.

——. "Uncle Wellington's Wives." In *The Wife of His Youth and Other Stories of the Color Line*. 1899; Ann Arbor: University of Michigan Press, 1972, pp. 203–68.

Christian, Barbara. *Black Women Novelists: The Development of a Tradition, 1892–1976*. Westport, Conn.: Greenwood Press, 1980.

Clarke, John Henrik, ed. *American Negro Short Stories*. New York: Hill and Wang, 1966.

Clinton, Catherine. *The Plantation Mistress: Woman's World in the Old South*. New York: Pantheon, 1982.

Collins, Winfield H. *The Truth About Lynching and the Negro in the South*. New York: The Neale Publishing Company, 1918.

Comer, James P. *Beyond Black and White*. New York: Quadrangle Books, 1972.

Coombs, Orde. "Black Men and White Women: 13 Years Later." *Essence* (May 1983):80–82, 137–38, 143–44.

Cutler, James E. *Lynch-Law: An Investigation into the History of Lynching in the United States*. New York: Longmans, Green, and Co., 1905.

Dance, Daryl Cumber. *Shuckin' and Jivin': Folklore from Contemporary Black Americans*. Bloomington: Indiana University Press, 1978.

Demarest, David. "Richard Wright: The Meaning of Violence." *Negro American Literature Forum* 8 (Fall 1974):236–39.

Dollard, John. *Caste and Class in a Southern Town*. Garden City, New York: Doubleday Anchor Books, 1949.

Dreiser, Theodore. "Nigger Jeff." In *Major Writers of America, II*. New York: Harcourt, Brace, and World, Inc., 1962, pp. 472–84.

DuBois, William Edward Burghart. *Dusk of Dawn*. 1940; Millwood, New York: Kraus-Thomson Organization Limited, 1975.

Dunbar, Paul Laurence. *The Strength of Gideon and Other Stories*. New York: Dodd, Mead, 1900.

——. "When Malindy Sings." In *When Malindy Sings*. New York: Dodd, Mead, 1903, pp. 9–14.

Duster, Alfreda M., ed. *Crusade for Justice: The Autobiography of Ida B. Wells*. Chicago: The University of Chicago Press, 1970.

Ellison, Ralph. "The Birthmark." *New Masses* 36 (July 2, 1940):16–17.

——. *Invisible Man*. 1952; New York: Vintage, 1972.

Fanon, Frantz. *Black Skin, White Masks*. New York: Grove Press, 1967.

Faulkner, William. "Dry September." In *Collected Stories of William Faulkner*. New York: Random House, 1950.

Federal Council of the Churches of Christ in America. *Mob Murder in America*. New York: Commission on the Church and Race Relations, 1923.

Fedo, Michael. *'They Was Just Niggers': An Account of one of the Nation's Least Known Racial Tragedies.* Ontario, California: Brasch and Brasch, Inc., 1979.

Foster, Frances Smith. *Witnessing Slavery.* Westport, Conn.: Greenwood Press, 1979.

Frank, Waldo. *Holiday.* New York: Boni and Liveright, 1923.

Franklin, John Hope. *From Slavery to Freedom: A History of American Negroes.* New York: Knopf, 1967.

Frazer, Sir James George and Gaster, Theodor H. *The New Golden Bough.* New York: Criterion Books, 1959.

Frazier, Kermit. "The Novels of John Wideman." *Black World* 24 (June 1975):18–38.

Fredrickson, George M. *The Black Image in the White Mind: The Debate on Afro-American Character and Destiny, 1817–1914.* New York: Harper and Row, 1971.

Freese, Peter. "James Baldwin: 'Going to Meet the Man' (1965)." In *The Black American Short Story in the 20th Century: A Collection of Critical Essays,* edited by Peter Bruck. Amsterdam: Grüner, 1977, pp. 171–85.

Fry, Gladys-Marie. *Nightriders in Black Folk History.* Knoxville: The University of Tennessee Press, 1975.

Gayle, Addison. *The Way of the New World: The Black Novel in America.* Garden City, New York: Doubleday, 1976.

Ginzburg, Ralph. *100 Years of Lynching.* New York: Lancer Books, 1962.

Gloster, Hugh. "Sutton E. Griggs: Novelist of the New Negro." In *The Black Novelist,* edited by Robert Hemenway. Columbus, Ohio: Charles E. Merrill, 1970, pp. 9–22.

Goldstein, Rhoda L. *Black Life and Culture in the United States.* New York: Apollo, 1971.

Grier, William H. and Cobbs, Price M. *Black Rage.* New York: Basic Books, Inc., 1968.

Griggs, Sutton E. *The Hindered Hand.* 1905; Miami, Florida: Mnemosyne, 1969.

———. *Imperium in Imperio.* 1899; Miami, Florida: Mnemosyne, 1969.

Grimké, Angelina Weld. "The Closing Door." *The Birth Control Review* (September 1919):10–14; (October 1919):8–12.

———. *Rachel.* 1920; College Park, Maryland: McGrath Publishing Company, 1969.

Hall, Jacquelyn Dowd. *Revolt Against Chivalry: Jessie Daniel Ames and the Women's Campaign Against Lynching.* New York: Columbia University Press, 1979.

Harris, Middleton. *The Black Book.* New York: Random House, 1974.

Harris, Trudier. "Ceremonial Fagots: Lynching and Burning Rituals in Black Literature." *Southern Humanities Review* 10 (Summer 1976): 235–47.

———. *From Mammies to Militants: Domestics in Black American Literature.* Philadelphia: Temple University Press, 1982.

Hawkins, Walter Everette. "A Festival in Christendom." In *The New Negro Renaissance,* edited by Arthur P. Davis and Michael W. Peplow. New York: Holt, Rinehart and Winston, 1975, pp. 41–42.

Hernton, Calvin C. *Sex and Racism in America.* New York: Grove Press, 1965.

Himes, Chester. *If He Hollers Let Him Go*. 1945; Chatham, New Jersey: The Chatham Bookseller, 1973.

Hughes, Langston. *Don't You Want To Be Free?* In *Black Theater U.S.A.: Forty-Five Plays by Black Americans*, edited by James V. Hatch and Ted Shine. New York: The Free Press, 1974, pp. 262–77.

———. *The Ways of White Folks*. 1933; New York: Vintage, 1962.

Jackson, Blyden. "Richard Wright in a Moment of Truth." In *The Waiting Years: Essays on American Negro Literature*. Baton Rouge: Louisiana State University Press, 1976.

Johnson, James Weldon. *Along This Way*. 1933; New York: Viking, 1968.

———. *The Autobiography of An Ex-Coloured Man*. 1912; New York: Hill and Wang, 1960.

———. *Saint Peter Relates an Incident: Selected Poems by James Weldon Johnson*. New York: Viking, 1935.

Jordan, Winthrop D. *White Over Black: American Attitudes Toward the Negro: 1550–1812*. New York: Penguin, 1969.

Kardiner, Abram and Ovesey, Lionel. *The Mark of Oppression: A Psychological Study of the American Negro*. New York: Norton, 1951.

Katz, Maude White. "The Negro Woman and the Law." *Freedomways* 2 (Summer 1962):278–86.

Kinnamon, Keneth. *The Emergence of Richard Wright*. Chicago: University of Illinois Press, 1972.

Kluckhohn, Clyde. "Myths and Rituals: A General Theory." *Harvard Theological Review* 35 (1942):45–79.

Lee, Robert A., ed. *Black Fiction: New Studies in the Afro-American Novel Since 1945*. New York: Barnes and Noble, 1980.

Lerner, Gerda. *Black Women in White America: A Documentary History*. New York: Pantheon, 1972.

Levine, Lawrence W. *Black Culture and Black Consciousness: Afro-American Folk Thought from Slavery to Freedom*. New York: Oxford University Press, 1977.

"A London Diary: Acquittal of Twenty-eight Self-confessed Lynchers in the South." *New Statesmen & Nation* 33 (May 31, 1947):388–89.

Lorden, Doris. "Mob Behavior and Social Attitudes." *Sociology and Social Research* 14 (March 1930):324–31.

McCall, Dan. *The Example of Richard Wright*. New York: Harcourt, Brace, 1969.

McGovern, James R. *Anatomy of a Lynching: The Killing of Claude Neal*. Baton Rouge: Louisiana State University Press, 1982.

McKay, Claude. *Selected Poems of Claude McKay*. New York: Harcourt, Brace, and World, Inc., 1953.

Margolies, Edward. *Native Sons: A Critical Study of Twentieth-Century Negro American Authors*. New York: Lippincott, 1968.

Martin, Everett. *The Behavior of Crowds: A Psychological Study*. New York: Harper and Brothers, 1920.

Mayfield, Julian, ed. *Ten Times Black*. New York: Bantam, 1972.

Meier, Norman, Mennenga, G. H., and Stoltz, H. J. "An Experimental Approach to the Study of Mob Behavior." *Journal of Abnormal and Social Psychology* 36 (October 1941):506–24.

Meriwether, Louise. "A New Threat to Old Tensions Between the Sexes: Black Man, White Woman." *Essence* 1 (May 1970):15, 62–64, 81.

Miller, Henry M. *The Mob's Verdict: Silence at the End of the Rope.* Chatsworth, California: Barclay House, 1974.

Morrison, Toni. *Tar Baby.* New York: New American Library, 1982.

NAACP, *Thirty Years of Lynching in the United States, 1889–1918.* New York: Arno Press and *The New York Times*, 1969.

O'Brien, John. *Interviews With Black Writers.* New York: Liveright, 1973.

O'Meally, Robert G. *The Craft of Ralph Ellison.* Cambridge: Harvard University Press, 1980.

Petry, Ann. *The Narrows.* 1953; New York: Pyramid, 1971.

Raper, Arthur F. *The Tragedy of Lynching.* Chapel Hill: The University of North Carolina Press, 1933.

Reed, John S. "Evolution of an Anti-Lynching Organization." *Social Problems* 16 (Fall 1968):172–82.

Rich, Adrienne. *On Lies, Secrets and Silence.* New York: Norton, 1979.

Rosenblatt, Roger. *Black Fiction.* Cambridge: Harvard University Press, 1976.

Samuels, Wilfred D. "Going Home: A Conversation with John Edgar Wideman." *Callaloo* 6 (February 1983):40–59.

Schraufnagel, Noel. *From Apology to Protest: The Black American Novel.* Deland, Florida: Everett/Edwards, Inc., 1973.

Schuyler, George. *Black No More.* New York: New American Library, 1969.

Shaughnessy, James D., ed. *The Roots of Ritual.* Grand Rapids, Michigan: William B. Eerdmans Publishing Company, 1973.

Smelser, Neil J. *Theory of Collective Behavior.* New York: The Free Press, 1962.

Smith, Lillian. *Killers of the Dream.* New York: Norton, 1949.

———. *The Winner Names the Age: A Collection of Writings by Lillian Smith,* edited by Michelle Cliff. New York: Norton, 1978.

Snellings, Ronald. "We Must Create a National Black Intelligentsia in Order to Survive." In *Black Nationalism in America,* edited by John H. Bracey, Jr., August Meier, and Elliott Rudwick. New York: Bobbs-Merrill, 1970.

Stember, Charles Herbert. *Sexual Racism: The Emotional Barrier to an Integrated Society.* New York: Harper Colophon Books, 1976.

Street, James H. *Look Away! A Dixie Notebook.* New York: Viking, 1936.

Toomer, Jean. *Cane.* 1923; New York: Harper and Row, 1969.

Torrence, Ridgley. "Granny Maumee: A Play for the Negro Theatre." In *Plays of Negro Life,* edited by Alain Locke and Montgomery Gregory. New York: Harper and Row, 1927, pp. 237–52.

Tucker, David M. "Miss Ida B. Wells and Memphis Lynching." *Phylon* 32 (Summer 1971):112–22.

Tyre, Nedra. *Red Wine First.* New York: Simon and Schuster, 1947.

van Gennep, Arnold. *The Rites of Passage.* Chicago: The University of Chicago Press, 1960.

Vickery, John. "Ritual and Theme in Faulkner's 'Dry September.'" *Arizona Quarterly* 18 (Spring 1962):5–14.

Walker, Alice. *In Love and Trouble: Stories of Black Women.* New York: Harcourt, Brace, Jovanovich, 1973.

———. *The Color Purple.* New York: Harcourt, Brace, Jovanovich, 1982.

———. *The Third Life of Grange Copeland.* Harcourt, Brace, Jovanovich, 1970.

————. *You Can't Keep A Good Woman Down*. New York: Harcourt, Brace, Jovanovich, 1981.

Walker, Margaret. *Jubilee*. New York: Bantam, 1967.

Wells, Ida B. *On Lynchings: Southern Horrors; A Red Record; Mob Rule in New Orleans*. New York: Arno Press and *The New York Times*, 1969.

White, Walter F. *The Fire in the Flint*. New York: Knopf, 1924.

————. *Rope and Faggot: A Biography of Judge Lynch*. New York: Knopf, 1929.

Wideman, John. *The Lynchers*. New York: Laurel, 1974.

Williams, John A. *Night Song*. New York: Farrar, Straus and Cudahy, 1961.

Wright, Ellen and Fabre, Michel, eds. *Richard Wright Reader*. New York: Harper and Row, 1978.

Wright, Richard. *12 Million Black Voices*. 1941; New York: Arno Press and *The New York Times*, 1969.

————. "Between the World and Me." *Partisan Review* 2 (July–August 1935): 18–19.

————. "The Ethics of Living Jim Crow." In *Dark Symphony: Negro Literature in America*, edited by James A. Emanuel and Theodore Gross. New York: The Free Press, 1968, pp. 238–48.

————. *The Long Dream*. New York: Doubleday, 1958.

————. "The Man Who Killed a Shadow." In *Eight Men*. New York: Pyramid, 1961.

————. *Native Son*. 1940; New York: Perennial, 1966.

————. *Uncle Tom's Children*. New York: Harper, 1938.

————. *White Man Listen!* New York: Doubleday, 1957.

Yarborough, Richard. "The Quest for the American Dream in Three Afro-American Novels: *If He Hollers Let Him Go, The Street*, and *Invisible Man*." *MELUS* 8 (Winter 1981):33–59.

Zangrando, Robert L. *The NAACP Crusade Against Lynching, 1909–1950*. Philadelphia: Temple University Press, 1980.

INDEX

Abolition, 6–7
Allport, Gordon W., 17
American Dream, 55
Another Country. See Baldwin, James
Association of Southern Women for the
  Prevention of Lynching, 18, 200*n*36
Autobiography of an Ex-Coloured Man,
  The, 72–73, 185

Baldwin, James, xi, 71, 94, 185; and
  transfer of sin and guilt, 17; and
  myth of black male sexuality, 20; on
  power, 22; themes of, 37, 93; on white
  womanhood, 92; presentation of
  burning, 129; lynching in work of,
  184; Harlem experiences of, 190; political essays of, 195
—*Another Country:* discussed, 54, 62–
  65, 166; symbolic castration in, 193
—*Go Tell It On the Mountain,* 31, 35
—"Going to Meet the Man": and transfer of sin and guilt, 17; compared to
  Clotel, 70; discussed, 86–90, 93, 109,
  175, 190, 192; communal orgasm in,
  92; burning in, 129
"Baptism," 103
"Between the World and Me." *See*
  Wright, Richard
Bible, 29
"Big Boy Leaves Home," 26, 95, 96, 105,
  109, 113, 114
Birth of a Nation, 26
"Birthmark," "The," 31, 77
Black American Literature Forum, win-
  ter 1977, ix
Black men: white attitudes toward, x;
  powerlessness of, xii; and white
  women, 3; sexuality of, 20–21, 22, 89,
  91–92, 171, 189; emasculation of,
  29–30
Black women: as lascivious, 29; degradation of, 142; rape of, 188; lynching
  of, 206*n*16
Black writers: propagandistic tendencies of, 186; male and female compared, 191–93, 194
"Blood-Burning Moon," 80–81

"Boy," use of term, 23–24
Bradley, David, works of discussed, 48,
  162–83
Brooks, Gwendolyn, 76
"Brothers—American Drama," 73–
  74, 76
Brown, Richard Maxwell, 8, 77
Brown, Sterling, 29, 95
Brown, William Wells, 71, 185: sym-
  bolic castration in work of, 35; and
  slavery question, 184; audience for,
  187
—*Clotel; Or, The President's Daughter:*
  discussed, 31, 32–33, 69–71, 184; im-
  plied catechism of, 79
Bryant, Earl V., 52
Burning. *See* Lynching/burning; Rit-
  ual; Violence

Cane, 104, 185, 187
Carolina Regulation, 6
Castration, 30, 67–68; reasons for, 5–6,
  22; fear of, 23–24, 50, 125; symbolic,
  30, 35, 193; in *Long Dream,* 46; Jordan on, 90; Hernton on, 91; and
  white power, 110; as prelude to
  death, 188. *See also* Emasculation
Chaneysville Incident, The, 48, 162–83
Chesnutt, Charles Waddell, xi, 105; kinship in work of, 33; contrasted to
  Wright, 34; symbolic castration in,
  35; makes lynching subsidiary, 184–
  85; audience for, 187; and equality,
  195
—*Colonel's Dream, The,* 34, 83
—*Marrow of Tradition, The,* 33, 83, 85,
  185
—"Uncle Wellington's Wives," 53
"Chicago Defender Sends a Man to Lit-
  tle Rock," "The," 76
"Child Who Favored Daughter," "The,"
  192–93
Chosen Place, The Timeless People, The, 78
Christian, Barbara, 28
Civil War: lynching after, 5–6; absence
  of rapes during, 20
Cleaver, Eldridge, 171

219